THE TEACHING OF GEOGRAPHY

ZOE A. THRALLS

University of Pittsburgh

THE TEACHING
of GEOGRAPHY

New York

APPLETON-CENTURY-CROFTS, INC.

Copyright © 1958 by

APPLETON-CENTURY-CROFTS, INC.

All rights reserved. This book, or parts thereof, must not be reproduced in any form without permission of the publisher.

686–6

Library of Congress Card Number: 58–6701

PRINTED IN THE UNITED STATES OF AMERICA
E–88014

TO

EDITH PUTMAN PARKER

Who has inspired in hundreds of teachers an understanding of and an enthusiasm for geography and the teaching of geography, this book is dedicated.

Preface

THIS BOOK IS DESIGNED for both student teachers and experienced teachers. The author hopes that it will also be useful to the administrator and supervisor who is not well prepared in geography but whose duties involve the direction and supervision of instruction in geography and the social studies.

If the study of geography is to have significance and value to the student the teacher must understand the nature of dynamic, functional geography. He also must know how to develop effectively the skills and abilities involved in reading and interpreting such geographic tools as maps, pictures, the local landscape, graphs, statistics, and reading materials. Only through the mastery of these tools can geographic learning proceed easily and effectively.

The mastery of these tools of learning comes gradually through a careful step by step development of specific skills and abilities as they are used in the acquisition of geographic material. The author attempts to show in a concrete and practical way with numerous illustrations drawn from the classroom how the student may be taught to read and interpret maps, pictures, graphs, and the landscape and use them as sources of geographic information. Even the reading of geographic materials in textbooks and references demands specific reading skills and abilities. If the ability to use these tools of learning are developed effectively, the student will be able to use geography long after specific facts have been forgotten or out-dated. He can continue self-education which is the most worthwhile kind of education.

The book is an outgrowth of a long career in elementary, high school, and college teaching. The author is indebted to hundreds of classroom teachers who have experimented, tested, evaluated, and reported procedures in ordinary classrooms with the usual mixture of children.

Z. A. T.

Contents

PREFACE vii
1. Geography: Its Nature and Function 1
2. Maps and Globes Are Our Business 19
3. Pictures as Geographic Tools 76
4. Graphs and Statistics in Geographic Education 112
5. Reading the Landscape 140
6. Current Events in Geographic Education 161
7. Reading as a Tool in Geographic Education 190
8. Geographic Reading Materials 222
9. Unit Planning and Functional Activities 236
10. A Geographic Readiness Program 275
11. The Teaching of Weather and Climate 305
INDEX 333

THE TEACHING OF GEOGRAPHY

1
Geography: Its Nature and Function

THE DISTINCTIVE CHARACTER OF GEOGRAPHY

GEOGRAPHY IS THE physical-social science which describes, maps, and seeks to explain the interrelations between man and his physical environment. On the one hand, it deals with the natural setting or physical environment in which man lives. Some of the elements of the physical environment are the surface or topography of the earth, soil, rocks and minerals, climate, land and water bodies, native plant and animal life, and location on the earth's surface. On the other hand, geography deals with man's occupation, his religion, art, science, music, literature, types of communities, his means of transportation and communication, and other elements resulting from man's efforts to utilize the materials of his physical environment.

These two sets of elements, the physical and cultural, are interrelated, and the interpretation of that interrelationship gives distinctive character to the study of geography.

This concept of geography may be illustrated by a specific example of how a people have adjusted their ways of living to the kind of country in which they live.

A People of the Fiords. Not all Norwegians live on the fiords but many of them have grown to manhood in the little villages nestled at the foot of the fiords, those long, narrow bays, walled by steep rocky cliffs. The streams rushing down their steep rocky courses from the plateau to the water of the fiord pile up along the foot of the cliffs, stones, gravel, and silt that they carry along, and form fairly level deltas. On these deltas and on a few other level places formed by the sea or by streams, the fiord people of Norway build their little farmsteads, clearing away the rocks for their tiny gardens, orchards, and fields. The level land about their homes is generally so limited in extent that they could not possibly raise upon it enough food for their families, and so they raise cattle, sheep, and goats that pasture all summer long on the steep slopes and high pastures of the plateau back of the fiords. Here they graze almost to the edges of the snow.

A farmstead usually consists of the house, the stable, the milk house, and the boat house. The roomy houses are built of sturdy timbers. The stables are almost as well built as the houses, and are kept almost as clean. The milk houses are generally placed over little streams that flow across the deltas or little patches of home grounds, so that the cold water from the melting snows of the plateau may keep the milk cool and the butter and cheese fresh and sweet. The boat houses are set near the edge of the water, so that the boats may be easily pulled into shelter or dragged into the water.

Every bit of the ground about the farmstead that can be plowed or spaded up is carefully cultivated or kept in grass. A little grain, a patch of potatoes, some carrots, turnips, or other root crops, a few vegetables, and in warm places a few fruits, clover and hay—these are all that can be grown about the home. The cattle are kept in the stable all winter long. As soon as the snow melts along the mountain sides nearly all the cattle, sheep and goats are taken up to the little hillside pastures on the terrace. Here they remain until the snow has melted from the plateau above. The members of the family who act as herdsmen often have little wooden huts in which to stay while they tend the herds on the terrace and along the sides of the valleys. The cows give an abundance of milk, from which the herdsmen make milk and cheese. In some places a strong wire runs from the terrace to the milkhouse below. By means of this the herdsmen can send down to the farmstead the milk and butter from the herds, hay that they cut from the surplus terrace pastures for winter use, and wood that they chop from the trees along the slopes of the terrace. By the wire the herdsmen may also draw up

Norwegian Information Service

Fig. 1. A Norwegian fiord: Nordfiord, West Norway.

mail, some of their food and clothing, and other things they need from the farmstead below.

As late spring and early summer come on, the snow melts away from the plateau above and at once grass and flowers grow on the highland pastures. The cattle and sheep are moved up to the high valleys and plateau meadows, where they fatten upon the rich growth of grass and plants. The days are long, for the sun rises early and sets late. About midsummer the sun sinks so little below the horizon that even at midnight there is no darkness, and sunset and dawn blend together in one short time of shadowless light and quiet peace.

The herdsmen live in little houses called saeters. They milk the cows, make butter and cheese, and carve things from wood. In the autumn when the snow begins to fall they start down the mountainside with their flocks, pasturing as they go.

The fiords are isolated one from the other so that each fiord is a little country almost in itself. Travel from village to village is chiefly by boat as long as the water is open. The people live near the water; they travel over it from place to place. They get much of their food from it—

salmon, herring, cod, and other fish. They learn to handle boats while they are but little children, and feel as much at home on the water as they do on the land. Is it any wonder then that the Norwegians are people of the sea, that they are among the best sailors in the world, and that ships bearing their bright flag are found on all the seas, in all ports?

While this description is typical of Norwegian fiord life, even here a transition is going on. The Norwegians are piping water from the lakes upon the plateaus to run great turbines at the edge of the fiords for the generation of electric power. The power is used in the manufacture of nitrates and paper pulp and for other purposes. People from other parts of the world, attracted by the beauty of the fiords with the forests, waterfalls and glaciers, come in increasing numbers each summer. These visitors like to go up the coast to North Cape to see the midnight sun because for three months in the midsummer the sun does not set, and at midnight it is low in the northern skies. These visitors buy the carvings and embroideries which the people have made while up in the saeters in summer.

The above geographical account of the people of the fiords gives us a very good idea of both the natural and cultural environment of the people who live in the coastal plain of Norway. It tells us about (1) the work of the people and their methods of work; (2) descriptive facts about their homes, food, villages, and means of transportation; (3) the distribution of the people; (4) the reasons in part due to the conditions of the natural environment why the Norwegians live as they do—reasons for the kind of work, and the means of transportation; (5) the reasons why the farmsteads and villages are located where they are.[1]

In viewing this geographical world we must keep in mind that neither man nor the physical environment is supreme. Oftentimes modern man thinks he has conquered nature, only to find that the victory is temporary. The Dutch built great dikes, reclaimed thousands of acres of land from the North Sea. In building dikes and drainage canals, in pumping out water and cultivating and fertilizing the land, the Dutch were modifying the earth about them to their purposes. They were also adjusting their activities to the conditions of their natural environment. Then in February, 1953, a great storm formed over the North Sea—seventy, eighty mile an

---

[1] Zoe A. Thralls, "The Theme of Modern Geography," *N.E.A. Journal*, Vol. 21 (October, 1932), pp. 219–220.

Geography: Its Nature and Function

hour winds whipped up enormous waves which in a few hours broke through the dikes. Thousands of acres were flooded, homes destroyed, herds of valuable cattle were drowned. The sea reclaimed its own. Once again the Dutch began their battle with the sea.

The Dynamic Nature of Geography

Geography is dynamic—never static. Man's adjustments to his physical environment change from time to time because his adjustments are contingent upon his knowledge, techniques and skills, and even his attitudes. Knowledge, techniques, skills, and attitudes are inherited; they are a part of his cultural environment. As Isaiah Bowman has said: "In general, man has done what he thought, and lack of knowledge and the canons of his time have held him back for long periods . . . The physical world changes constantly in its meaning to man because of the constant change in his technology. Earth and man toss the ball back and forth."[2]

Thus the geography of any region changes as man's knowledge of the region increases and as he discovers news ways of using available resources. A new instrument of power such as the airplane, a new chemical, or a new use for a well-known resource may mean a new geography. Consider the change in the geography of northern Canada which man's use of the airplane has made: new towns, mines, oil wells, pipelines, numerous types of human activity where only a few years ago was a wilderness known to the Indian and the fur trapper.

Even the location of a place or region on the earth's surface changes in its significance to man. Most people think of geography in terms of location, and geography does emphasize location or global relations. Location means "knowing where places are in living relations to one another." For instance, the Board of Directors of a steel company, in considering the development of iron ore deposits in Labrador, wanted to know the exact location and

[2] Isaiah Bowman, *Geography in Relation to the Social Sciences* (New York, Charles Scribner's Sons, 1934), pp. 34, 37.

extent of the deposits. But of equal or greater importance, they wanted to know where the deposits were in relation to the St. Lawrence River, the Atlantic Ocean, to the boundaries of Labrador and Quebec. The profitable development of this vast ore body depended on costs of transportation, which involved not only distance but possible means of transportation, the terrain, the climate, and political factors as represented by the policies of the governments of Quebec and Labrador.

Even such a simple act as carrying a plant to another land may change the geography and the history of that land. The introduction of the potato into Europe changed the geography of Germany and Ireland. It was well suited to the damp cool climate and the soil of these two countries, and it supplied the necessary food for the tremendous growth in population. In Germany this population furnished the manpower for industrial development and also for military might. The rest of the story you know. In Ireland the population grew, then a blight struck the potato crop, famine stalked the land, and migration followed.

The introduction of the Hevea rubber tree into Malaya and the East Indies further illustrates the dynamic nature of geography. It resulted in the introduction of the modern plantation system, caused a shifting of people from island to island, developed equatorial forested areas and increased the value of these areas to European nations. It made available a cheap and reliable supply of rubber which was essential to the motor vehicle industry. As Dr. Isaiah Bowman says "Each plant breeding success means the re-appraisal of our climatic boundaries, soil types, and cultivation techniques."

Man lives on the earth. He is subject to the physical conditions of the region in which he lives. However, both he and nature are constantly making changes in the physical environment; and those changes have repercussions, frequently world-wide in scope, both in the present and the future. That is why geography is dynamic and why it contributes to an understanding of the modern world.

THE FUNCTIONAL VALUE OF GEOGRAPHY

Study of the distinctive characteristics of geography contributes to the well-rounded development of the individual. A knowledge of geography and the ability to think geographically aid him in understanding and interpreting the realities of this world. Such knowledge also should aid him in analyzing and selecting values in this rapidly changing world. It contributes to the formation of ideals—the vision of the world as it should be for human welfare. New and desirable realities are brought into existence only through such vision.

Vocational Value

Both in choosing a vocation and later in following a business or professional life, geography has a definite practical value to the individual. Geography contributes to a better understanding of industry and commerce. Manufacturers must know the sources of their raw materials, the conditions, both natural and cultural, under which they are produced, the means and routes of transportation, and the markets for the finished products.

The steel industry offers a striking example of the value of geographical knowledge. Today the American steel industry draws its basic raw material—iron ore—from the Lake Superior Region, Venezuela, Liberia, and Canada as well as small quantities from other areas. A list of the sources of the numerous other minerals needed for alloys and other uses in the industry, such as nickel, vanadium, manganese, chromium, naming only a few, includes every continent and dozens of countries. Iron ore and the other essential minerals are mined under almost all conceivable climatic conditions, from tropical rain forest to Arctic tundra.

The farmer should know about soils, topography, and weather as they are related to his type of farming, and also the possibilities and dangers in the use of irrigation and drainage projects. He also should be concerned with conditions in competing regions, not only in the United States but in other lands.

Many of our tariff problems are the result of our ignorance of world conditions and consequent failure to evaluate the facts and interrelationships of world trade. For instance, in 1955 the United States raised the tariff on fish from Iceland thus reducing greatly the amount sold here. The Soviet Union offered to take the greater part of Iceland's fish. Iceland must sell fish, her one important export, to live. Of course the result was that Iceland turned to the Soviet Union to supply her need of manufacturers.

The American Geographical Society gives some interesting examples of inquiries from corporations when they needed certain geographical information in order to make decisions. The following are some of the inquiries received.

A *steamship company,* limited by its charter to Eastern coastwise operations, was offered a profitable shipment to Vera Cruz. Queried, we advised that Vera Cruz is considered an East Coast Atlantic port. The company took the cargo.

A *mining company,* preparatory to a venture in Saudi Arabia, consulted us on depths of subterranean water tables.

A *Hawaiian pineapple concern,* considering extending its operations to Brazil, was supplied with data on climate, soil, and terrain.

For an oil company, interested in helping the educational system of a South American country, we prepared a three-dimensional map of the country, for free distribution to schools.

An *export company,* in receipt of an order from a small town in Germany asked us to locate the town. We reported it lies in East Germany. The shipment didn't go.

A *business locating service* consulted us on potential industrial sites in the southwestern United States.

A *lumber company,* searching for standing hardwood, came to us for information on Central America.

Engineering companies are frequent visitors. One, preparing to run natural gas pipelines north into Canada, did research in geology and soils. Another needed information on terrain and climate before building telegraph lines in Brazil.

An *airline* sought data on "mushroom cities" of the Middle East.

A *bank,* considering loans in Latin America, got research help on land use and tenure.

For a broadcasting corporation, an island in the Caribbean comparatively free of earthquake tremors was sought and located.

Geography: Its Nature and Function

Oil companies order our "World Geography of Petroleum" by the dozen. A *publishing company* queried us regarding a bit of research for which it lacked qualified personnel. We arranged, for a modest fee.

Even in the selection of a home, a knowledge of geography is worth while. One should consider soil, drainage, bedrock, and wind direction. If the site is on a hillside, there is danger of a slide that may land the house in the valley. In hilly areas of clay or shale, many a home has slipped down into the valley after a long rainy spell. Wind direction and the direction from which heavy rainstorms are likely to come bear on the necessity for insulation and on the cost of heating. Heavy clay soils mean difficulty in maintaining a lawn or a garden. These are only a few of the natural factors affecting a home site.

Intellectual Development

Geography has a place in one's intellectual development. As Pearl Middlebrook has said, "One of the most clearly defined earmarks of a truly cultured person is the judicial mind, questing for truth and withholding judgment until analyzed. Geography offers training in this characteristic from noting reality to a search for reasons for that reality, and the search leads us to the field of natural resources."[3]

In studying geography, children gain the ability to evaluate the earth on which they live; to trace cause and effect, to note relationships. They form the habit of wanting to know the "why" of man's activities and the "why" of natural phenomena such as earthquakes, hurricanes, and soil erosion. They begin to test the accuracy of their own and others' thinking. From the use of maps and pictures, in making field trips, preparing reports, they gain initiative and judgment. As they gain knowledge of other peoples—their ways of living, their products, their culture—they are stimulated and inspired to a broader conception of life, a greater appreciation of man and his problems wherever he lives.

[3] Pearl Middlebrook, "The Place of Geography in American Culture," *Educational Method*, Vol. 17 (March, 1938), p. 274.

Intelligent Citizenship

To survive, a democracy must have an educated, intelligent citizenry. This raises the question, does a knowledge of geography and the ability to think geographically help one to be a responsible intelligent citizen? Let us look at our nation.

The almost constant intermigration of Americans since 1945 has in a sense, educated Americans and has made them aware of the numerous national problems which have arisen or have become intensified. Most of these problems have a geographic base that must be understood in order to deal with them intelligently. Let us consider some of these problems briefly.

Soil conservation has been with us for many decades. It has not been solved completely, although there is a great improvement in many sections as farmers and others have learned the causes of soil erosion and how to check it in its various forms.

In the last decades the problem of water supply has become serious in the humid East as well as in the semi-arid West. Modern industry and the modern home use an enormous amount of water. When considering the location of a new factory or mill, the first questions a company asks are: "How much water is available? What is its source? Is it dependable? Will it need treatment before use?" Many areas can no longer answer such questions satisfactorily. A few years ago the United States Geological Survey spent eight and a half million dollars to investigate water supplies for the TVA, the Bureau of Reclamation, and the Atomic Energy Commission. A few figures help one to realize how vital water is today.

To make a ton of bromine for the manufacture of photographic film takes 2500 tons of fresh water.

Factories use 5 billion gallons of well water in addition to other millions that they draw from city water works.

The average city family uses 250 gallons a day—showers, dish washing, clothes washing, car washing, toilets, air conditioning.

Modern air conditioning of offices, department stores, theaters, restaurants, and factories requires such large quantities of water

Geography: Its Nature and Function

that laws have been passed requiring the return of the water underground in order to replenish the underground water supply.

In the semiarid Southwest, enormous quantities of water, running into billions of gallons, are used for irrigation. In many areas the ground water is so depleted that there is a question of the future habitability of such sections.

Where and how hydro-electric projects shall be developed is another national problem. Because desirable sites are located chiefly in the Northwest, many people may consider that the problem is local. It is not. Some sites are within the national domain and if developed would destroy places of recreational, scientific, or historical value. Then, also, there is the *how*. Shall private companies develop the power or shall the Federal government?

Other problems are land-use planning, flood control, pest control, and development of waterways. These are only a few of the national problems facing the American citizen. All of them involve man's use of his natural environment. The vote of the American citizen determines the answer, whether intelligent or unintelligent.

Citizenship today goes beyond national boundaries. We are world citizens today whether we want to be or not. Since World War I an American citizen has been a world citizen, although a reluctant one. Not until the 1950's, after two world wars, did the average American face the fact that he and his nation had global responsibilities and problems. As a result, too little attention has been given in our educational system to the dynamics and realities of international relations. With the growing importance of international relations and their bearing upon our national welfare as well as on our personal interests, we need to understand other regions, nations, and peoples. There can be no real understanding of a country unless one has a knowledge of its natural features and conditions and the manner in which its people have adjusted themselves to the possibilities and limitations of their natural environment.

Geography is involved in every problem that is presented to our Department of State and to the secretary of foreign affairs in other nations of the world. As Nicholas Spykman says:[4]

> Geography is the most fundamental factor in the foreign policy of states because it is the most permanent. Ministers come and ministers go, even dictators die, but mountain ranges stand unperturbed. . . . Alexander I, Czar of all the Russians, bequeathed to Joseph Stalin, a simple member of the Communist party, not only his power but his endless struggle for access to the sea.
>
> The size of the national domain affects the relative strength of a state in the struggle for power. Natural resources influence population density and economic structure which define vulnerability to blockade. Location with reference to the Equator and to oceans and land masses determines nearness to centers of power, areas of conflict and routes of communication; and location with reference to immediate neighbors defines position in regard to potential enemies and the basic problems of territorial security. Topography affects strength because of its influence on unity and internal coherence. Climate sets limits to agricultural production and conditions transportation and international trade. All descriptions of the power position of a state must, therefore, begin with an analysis of its geography.

Unfortunately there is a pervasive notion among the American people that the United States can make or unmake events at will. Editors, columnists, and news commentators write and speak as if they know the future and can foresee exactly what should be done. Oftentimes they seem to have little regard for the possible consequences of their suggested actions. There is a great need to understand how limited our powers of decision are and how necessary it is for intelligent action to have a greater knowledge of other lands, peoples, and culture. International problems must be seen in other peoples' terms, not just in our own. For example, Asian issues must be seen from the Asian point of view. The United States has been so richly endowed with natural resources that we have difficulty in understanding other nations' limitations.

[4] Nicholas J. Spykman, *America's Strategy in World Politics* (New York, Harcourt, Brace & Co., 1942), pp. 41–42.

Enrichment of Other Subjects

Geography may enrich almost all other fields. One's understanding of them and consequently one's interest increases if the geographic conditions involved are understood. This is true of history, literature, economics, sociology, and science. The music and art of all nations is more meaningful to children and to adults if they know the people and their environment. No doubt, students would recall much better the history of the United States, and also world history, if they knew the geographic setting in which historical events took place. Historical events need to be located, visualized on the globe, and have a setting in order to have real meaning. Without definite, visualized location and setting, they are unreal, merely a story in a vacuum.

Who can understand the struggles of the European colonists in America, unless he knows the climatic and other natural conditions which those settlers faced? The events of the Revolutionary War cannot be understood unless one can visualize the topography of the land and the rivers east of the Appalachians. The rapid penetration and settlement of the interior was made possible by the mountain passes, the Potomac, the Susquehanna, the Hudson rivers, the Mohawk Valley, the Great Lakes, and the Ohio and its upper tributaries. These passes, rivers, and river valleys provided rugged but passable routes for boats, horses, and wagons.

Throughout the ages there have been certain strategic areas and roadways that have influenced history. The Mediterranean—especially the eastern Mediterranean with the adjacent lands of the Middle East—has been a transit zone or strategic bridge from Europe and North Africa to the East. As J. S. Badeau said in 1943:[5]

> The mountains, plains, and river valleys of the Middle [Near] East stand at the crossroads of three continents; they form a portico from which open front, side, and back doors to Europe, Asia, and Africa. Five seas—the Mediterranean, Black, Caspian, Red, and Persian Gulf— meet in the Middle East to furnish easy transportation east, north, and

---
[5] J. S. Badeau, *East and West of Suez,* Headline Series No. 30 (New York, Foreign Policy Association, 1943).

south. The Fertile Crescent opens a well-watered caravan trail to India and the East. Passes through the mountain chains of the north give entry to Russia and Central Asia. The Nile Valley offers the only direct road from the Mediterranean to the heart of Africa. Such a concentration of possibilities will always have world-wide importance.

Today, the automobile and the truck follow those ancient trails and the airplane crosses mountains, deserts, and seas. But none can be used except by permission of the Middle East nations.

The construction of the Suez Canal made the sea route of greater importance than the land routes. With the discovery of enormous oil deposits in Iran, Iraq, Saudi Arabia, and other Arab states along the Persian Gulf, and the construction of pipelines across Arabia, the whole Middle East became of vital world importance. From the dawn of history the Middle East has been a roadway and a battleground for armies and ideas. This was said to Ferdinand de Lesseps when he was welcomed to the French Academy:

> The great sentence, "I came not to bring peace, but a sword," must have often come into your mind. Once the isthmus was cut, it inevitably became a passageway, that is, a field of battle. So far, one Bosphorus has caused quite enough trouble in the world but you have created a second which overshadows it in importance, for it connects not merely two land-locked seas but all the great oceans.... You have set your seal on one of the great battle grounds of the future.[6]

Renan's words came true in World War I, World War II, and again in 1956. Here lies the great test of the United Nations organization as well as the United States. The United States had to face the problem of maintenance of free passage through the Suez Canal and through the seas and straits along the route. Americans dared not safely ignore a region and an international route of such vital importance to western Europe and of great and increasing importance to the Soviet Union.

A knowledge of the geographic background of a people makes the literature of a country more interesting and meaningful. Geography often helps to create an interest in literature by making

[6] André Siegfried, "The Suez: International Roadway," *Foreign Affairs*, Vol. 31 (July, 1953), p. 605.

Geography: Its Nature and Function

pupils aware that many of the scenes and descriptions which they find in novels, poems, and essays are of real places on the earth. Almost all people have a curiosity about the *where* of places they read about.

Enrichment of Travel Experience

A knowledge of geography vitalizes travel. The traveler should have the "seeing eye," the eye that can read the landscape.

The seeing eye enables the traveler to read the symbols written on the face of the earth in cliff, hill, and mountain; in canyon, valley, and river plain; in water worn or wind hewn rock. These symbols have as rich a meaning and tell as wonderful a story as the printed symbols of any book. . . .

If one can analyze the forms and see their life history as revealed in the contours of hill and mountain, valley and plain, these forms acquire greater meaning and beauty. . . . Every region, near or remote, has a story to tell, a beauty to be enjoyed. Even the desert, apparently bare, vast, and monotonous, has a beauty of its own. Nowhere else can such wonderful and mysterious colors be found. Changing, shifting, advancing, retreating, the shades are never the same from moment to moment.[7]

The "seeing eye" also penetrates the cultural or man-made environment. In each landscape one can recognize man's ways of living—his work, his recreation, his religion, and other aspects of his life—from the signs in the landscape, providing one has geographic knowledge and understanding.

Without question, the study of geography makes numerous contribution to a child's education. As a result, it should occupy an important place in the school curriculum. But what children gain from a study of modern functional geography depends in large part on the teacher.

THE TEACHER OF GEOGRAPHY

The teacher of geography should have enthusiasm and the ability to convey this to others. Enthusiasm comes from knowing

[7] Zoe A. Thralls and Edwin Reeder, *Geography in the Elementary School* (Chicago, Rand McNally, Co., 1931), pp. 27–28.

the subject and realizing its values in the development of the individual. The teacher needs to have a creative imagination, that is, the ability to make landscapes and people live before his class. He himself must feel that he has actually seen the region he is presenting to his class. He must have the ability to draw on his own and his pupils' personal everyday experiences to illustrate the new and the unknown. In short, the teacher of geography should have the knowledge and the ability to present the subject in such a way that the class will understand, enjoy, and be eager for more.

Teachers of geography must read newspapers and magazines carefully and critically to select materials which illustrate how people are using their environment, how they are trying to make better use of it, and how they are trying to fit themselves into this changing world. An enthusiastic teacher is never satisfied with his own preparation. He knows that to teach dynamic geography requires constant fresh preparation.

The teacher must have the ability to select and organize geographic materials to fit the child's level of maturity, to arouse his interest, and to develop his ability to think geographically. Furthermore, the teacher must so guide his students that they realize that their study of any people in a specific region is a continuing activity, that they are catching only a glimpse of the people in their present geographic setting. What they are learning today gives them background for understanding a people's actions tomorrow. The teacher should ever keep in mind that *to give reality to anything outside a student's immediate environment necessitates firing his imagination with vivid, dynamic images which have an emotional drive that will cause the student to think and act. Vivid, dynamic images are the means by which men's visions are directed and their loyalties are determined.* Teachers of geography have an unrivaled opportunity to build such images, concepts, and attitudes, but they must select and organize materials to that end. Also they must use techniques which will dramatize and fix the desirable images, concepts, and attitudes. In short, the teacher must teach dynamic geography.

REFERENCES

ATWOOD, W. W., "Geography and the Great Human Drama," *Journal of Geography*, Vol. 39 (December, 1940), pp. 337–343.

———, "The New Meaning of Geography in World Education," *Journal of Geography*, Vol. 46 (January, 1947), pp. 11–15.

BOWMAN, Isaiah, "The New Geography," *Journal of Geography*, Vol. 44 (September, 1945), pp. 213–216.

———, *Geography in Relation to the Social Sciences* (New York, Charles Scribner's Sons, 1934), Ch. I.

BRONSKY, Amy, "Elementary Geography and World Problems," *Journal of Geography*, Vol. 32 (November, 1933), pp. 316–322.

COULTER, John W., "The Significance of Human Geography Today," *Education*, Vol. 77 (September, 1956), pp. 5–10.

EDEL, W., "Geography in World Affairs," *Journal of Geography*, Vol. 51 (September, 1952), pp. 248–252.

FENNEMAN, N. M., "The Circumference of Geography," *Geographical Review*, Vol. 7 (March, 1919), pp. 168–175.

FLEURE, H. J., "Geographical Thought in the Changing World," *Geographical Review*, Vol. 34 (October, 1944), pp. 515–528.

GARRELLS, Agnes F., "Global Geography in the Elementary Grades," *Social Education*, Vol. 7 (May, 1943), pp. 221–223.

GLUCK, H., "Geography Today," *Social Studies*, Vol. 32 (November, 1941), pp. 299–301.

HOFFMAN, Elizabeth, "Is It Essential for the American Student to Be Geographically Informed?" *Journal of Geography*, Vol. 53 (April, 1954), pp. 149–153.

KANDALL, J. L., "Challenge of World Responsibilities," *School and Society*, Vol. 77 (March 21, 1953), pp. 177–180.

KENNAMER, L. G., "The Unique Change in School Geography," *Journal of Geography*, Vol. 54 (January, 1955), pp. 25–31.

LUCAS, W. C., "Making Geography Teaching Click," *Journal of Geography*, Vol. 38 (December, 1939), pp. 349–354.

MILLER, George J., "Geography in Education," *School and Society*, Vol. 43 (April 18, 1936), pp. 1–6.

PEATTIE, Roderick, *The Teaching of Geography* (New York, Appleton-Century-Crofts, Inc., 1950), Chs. 2, 3, and 17.

PETERS, C. P., "Contributions to Civic Education through Geography," *Objectives and Procedures in Civic Education* (New York, Longmans, Green & Company, 1930).

PICKLESIMER, P. W., "Our Changing Geography," *Journal of Geography,* Vol. 42 (October, 1943), pp. 266–271.

RENNER, George T., and MEYER, A. H., "Geography for Tomorrow's Citizens," *Educational Method,* Vol. 22 (February, 1943), pp. 204–209.

Ross, John, "Youth Speaks for Geography," *Journal of Geography,* Vol. 55 (September, 1956), pp. 286–291.

SCARFE, Neville U., "Geographic Education and Teaching Method," *Journal of Geography,* Vol. 55 (February, 1956), pp. 57–66.

SMITH, J. Russell, "How Geography Contributes to the General Ends of Education," *Teaching of Geography,* Thirty-second Yearbook, National Society for the Study of Education (Bloomington, Ill., Public School Publishing Co., 1933), pp. 29–40.

————, "What Shall the Geography Teacher Teach in the Elementary School?" *Journal of Geography,* Vol. 46 (March, 1947), pp. 101–108.

STEVENS, George D., "Geography: The Path to World Understanding," *Journal of Geography,* Vol. 54 (October, 1955), pp. 359–361.

STRONG, Helen M., "The Place of Geography in the Activities of the Government," *Teaching of Geography,* Thirty-second Yearbook, National Society for the Study of Education (Bloomington, Ill., Public School Publishing Co., 1933), Ch. 6.

THRALLS, Zoe A., "The Theme of Modern Geography," *N.E.A. Journal,* Vol. 21 (October, 1932), pp. 219–220.

WARMAN, Henry J., "Environmental Impactors," *Education,* Vol. 77 (September, 1956), pp. 3–4.

WHITAKER, J. Russell, *Geography in School and College* (Nashville, Tenn., George Peabody College for Teachers, 1948).

WRIGHT, J. K., "Geography for War and Peace," *The American Scholar,* Vol. 12 (January, 1943), pp. 118–123.

2

Maps and Globes Are Our Business

MAPS AND GLOBES are our business because they represent man's home, the earth. On maps is recorded the geographic knowledge accumulated through the ages. As a region is discovered, it is named and its location is recorded on maps. Then, as exploration, surveys, and development take place, this knowledge is added.

The word *map* comes from the Latin word *mappa* which means a cover cloth or table cloth; thus a map gives a coverage for the earth or any part of it. Every blank spot or relatively empty space on a map challenges man's curiosity. Furthermore, young and old are fascinated by the variety of symbols on a map. One wonders what all the colors, dots, lines, and shadings represent. As Donald C. Peattie says:[1]

A map is the beginning of adventure. Travel and treasure hunts, wars and explorations, all open with its unrolling. Even in your armchair a map is a magic carpet, taking the mind in a flash just where you want to go.

Road maps are given freely these days, but once maps were closely guarded secrets, men who revealed them might be put to torture or

[1] Donald C. Peattie, "The Romance of Maps," *Reader's Digest,* Vol. 68 (March, 1956), pp. 195–200.

death. To the privateer a captured chart could be booty richer than bullion. For, in the little known world of long ago, it could point the way to fortune. The mariners of Tyre thus had their Mediterranean trade routes to hide, the Arab sailors their sources of ginger, camphor, lacquer, and silk, the Spanish their plundered New World gold, the Dutch their monopoly of East Indian spices.

Maps are the oldest written language. They were made and used by primitive peoples long before any oral language was developed into a written form. The maps made by the primitive peoples of Asia, Africa, and North and South America are correctly oriented and surprisingly accurate. Many of these primitive people used the pole star by night and the sun by day to determine direction. They made sketch maps on sand, stone, bark, slabs of wood, skins of animals, and on clay tablets. Many also made relief maps; for instance, the Peruvians used stone, clay, and straw for such a purpose.[2]

These maps were made to show where hunting and fishing were good and to indicate travel routes and areas inhabited by a tribe. They served somewhat the same function as do modern road maps. These rather simple maps served the needs of primitive peoples, but as a people develop the region in which they live, more permanent and exact maps are needed. Also, there is a need for different kinds of maps.

Uses of Maps Today

"Maps embody some of the most distinctive measurements of geography. A map is a locational guide for both earth features and human distributional elements. It is also a means for putting related things together."[3]

Almost anything may be shown on a map if one has the required statistics—rainfall, temperature, surface features, distribution of people, size, distribution of animals, crops, and even election re-

[2] B. Adler, *Maps of Primitive Peoples* (St. Petersburg [Leningrad], 1910). Abstracted by H. De Hutorowicz in *Bulletin of American Geographical Society*, Vol. 43, pp. 669–679.

[3] Isaiah Bowman, *Geography in Relation to the Social Sciences* (New York, Charles Scribner's Sons, 1934), p. 42.

Maps and Globes Are Our Business

turns. Building highways, engineers and construction men must have maps showing the topography, the kinds of soil and rock along the route, the amount, type, and distribution of rainfall, seasonal temperatures, and snowfall. All of these conditions affect where and how the highway is to be built and the materials to be used.

Maps are needed by public utilities for the establishment of power sites and power lines, water supply, telephone lines, and sewerage. Insurance companies need maps of storm paths, frequency of hail storms and floods, and in some regions earthquake maps. As land values increase because of industrial development, or as a result of the discovery of minerals, accurate maps are essential. Texas and Oklahoma took a boundary dispute to the Supreme Court after the discovery of oil in the Red River Valley. Each state wanted a part in the oil wealth, but the exact boundary had never been mapped.

Adequate basic map data are essential in developing natural resources and in planning economic and social projects. Whether a project involves water conservation and requires reservoirs, aqueducts, filtration plants, or pumping stations, whether it concerns flood control and requires floodwalls, levees, or storage reservoirs, whether it concerns power development and the construction of dams, power plants, and transmission lines, whether it deals with safe navigation, town planning, transportation, the preservation of fish, reforestation, or the development of minerals and fuels—any such study benefits from a sober study of maps.[4]

Thus, as an important means of understanding the world, maps are indispensable today.

Maps are written in a kind of short hand or "map language." As man records his knowledge of a region on a map, he uses a special set of symbols to represent the natural features of the landscape such as rivers, sea coasts, land forms, and topography. He also has certain symbols to indicate the cultural features such as cities, highways, railroads, and the distribution of people and

[4] "Maps and Their Role in World Development," *United Nations Review*, Vol. 1 (October, 1954), pp. 26–29.

crops. The meaning of many of these symbols changes from map to map. For example, on one map yellow may indicate less than five inches of rainfall annually; on another map it may indicate elevation between 1000 feet and 2000 feet. Therefore there must be a legend or key on a map in order that the symbols may be understood. As Isaiah Bowman says: "It [map language] is a language that has to be learned, like any other language. Upon a single map one may find from twenty to fifty signs that 'save an infinitude of words,' to use MacKinder's words."[5]

Distinctive Functions of Maps

Since maps are an essential tool in the modern world, one of the outstanding objectives of geographical education is to teach map reading and interpretation. In order to do this effectively the teacher must know the functions of maps. If one can read and interpret maps one can learn quickly and accurately much descriptive information.

1. The exact and relative location of a place or other feature of a landscape may be found. By means of latitude and longitude one can locate the position of any place on the earth's surface. For example, Seattle, Washington, is at latitude 47° 45′ N., longitude 122° 25′ W. As one locates Seattle on the map, one can note Seattle's relation to Puget Sound, to the Pacific Ocean, to the Cascade Mountains, to the railroad network, to the State of Washington, and to the United States.

2. The size and shape of an area or of a natural or cultural feature may be determined. A map can convey a correct impression of the size and shape of a continent, an island, a state, or a sea.

3. Distances may be read directly, or estimated by the use of latitude and longitude, or by the use of the scale of miles.

4. From physical and topographic maps, the elevation and slope of land may be read at a glance.

5. Various types of distribution maps are of special value, as one can read quickly where and how a population is distributed,

---

[5] Bowman, *op. cit.*, p. 2.

Maps and Globes Are Our Business

the distribution of a given crop, rainfall, mountains, or any other natural or cultural feature.

One important function of a map is as an aid in visualizing large and distant regions. As an ancient Chinese map-maker wrote, "It is as if they were on the palm of your hand." How could one visualize the United States unless he studied a map of the country?

Another function of a map is to provide a basis for noting relationships, by comparing two or more maps. For example, compare a population distribution map with an annual rainfall map of the same area. What relationship between population distribution and annual rainfall do you see? Compare a railroad network map with physical map of the United States. Some striking relationships may be noted.

Another function closely related to the above is that a map may provide a basis for inference if one knows the significance of the facts shown. For example, look at the state of Nevada on a physical map of the United States. Note that only one river, the Humboldt, is shown. It flows into a lake without an outlet, and there are several other lakes without outlets. An area in northwest Nevada is covered with tiny red dots which indicates sand dunes. All of these facts lead one to infer a desert climate. Also the high Sierra Nevada Mountains on the west, the interior location, the latitude ($35°$ N. to $42°$ N.), the lack of cities, and only one railroad crossing the state, all support this inference. From these same facts one can make other inferences concerning population density, natural vegetation, and even the probable occupations of the people.

From the teaching standpoint, maps function in promoting interest. Most maps are attractive and, in a sense, challenging. Nearly anyone looking at a map immediately wants to find a certain place or begins to wonder what this or that symbol means.

Objectives of Map Instruction

Every teacher of geography and social studies should have clearly in mind the major objectives that he is trying to accomplish in teaching map reading. These objectives consist in the development of the following abilities, skills, and understandings.

1. Ability to actually see in one's mind's eye the landscape that the map symbols represent. This ability is the same type of ability necessary to read the printed word. A child reads, "The yellow cat clawed his way up the maple tree." If he reads the sentence—not merely pronounces the words—he must see a yellow cat digging its claws into the bark as it climbs a maple tree. Each word (symbol) is visualized if the sentence has meaning to the child. A child must go through exactly the same process in reading a map. A blue or black line, representing a river, must be translated or seen as a real river flowing between its banks.

This objective is fundamental, because the reading and interpretation of a map depends on this ability to visualize the landscape represented by the map symbols.

2. Ability to understand the distinctive types of information that can best be expressed on maps. A map is a tool, the best source for certain types of information. If one is going to make effective use of a tool he must know what function that tool performs. Just as one goes to a dictionary for the spelling, pronunciation, or definition of a word, so one should go to a map to find the exact and relative location of a place.

3. Ability to draw inferences from the facts revealed on the map. Again we can make a comparison with the development of reading skills. As a child grows in experience and understanding of words, he begins to read, as it were, between the lines. Words begin to have special connotations. So it is with maps. A very wiggly line on a map may indicate to the beginner merely a winding river. He may say, "That is a winding river." To one who has gained experience and background, the winding river is flowing back and forth across an almost flat plain, probably a flood plain with deep rich alluvial soil.

If one compares a cotton distribution map and a rainfall map of the United States, the relation of the facts shown should raise certain questions, and lead one to make inferences. For instance, in the southern states one may note that the leading cotton districts lie within the 20 to 40 inch rainfall areas, therefore the amount of rainfall must be significant. But also one will see certain small cotton-producing districts in the Salt River Valley and in the San Joaquin Valley where the precipitation is less than 10 inches. How can that be? The cotton grown in those two areas must be irrigated.

Map interpretation is seeking out the meaning of the facts shown on the map. Skill comes with study and experience in the use of maps, plus the realization that maps, like great literature, have much to offer to him who seeks.

4. The ability to translate into map language information secured from field work, statistics, and other reading material. Children in the primary grades can make simple maps from information gained on a field trip, or from their own observation around their school. Elizabeth Dudley gives an excellent description of such a map-making activity.[6]

The information gained from statistics or from reading material is more difficult to employ in the construction of maps, but it may be acquired gradually in the upper elementary grades or the junior and senior high school.

Basic Principles for Teaching Map-reading

In developing map abilities and skills, certain basic principles must be applied. Since a map reader must be able to translate map symbols into landscape imagery, the first principle is: *Every map symbol must be visualized* by the child as he learns to read a map. How can this be done? The first symbols introduced to the child should be those which refer to landscape features of which he already has imagery. The teacher must help the child to associate his experiences with the map symbols. It is the same process that takes place in teaching the child to read the printed word. Primary reading teachers are very careful in guiding the child to associate the

[6] Elizabeth Dudley, "An Approach to Map Study," *Journal of Geography,* Vol. 36 (December, 1937), pp. 354–356.

printed words and phrases with the actual object or activity. The teacher of geography must be equally careful in seeing that the child associates the map symbol with the actual landscape feature.

One way of doing this is to make a simple map of the immediate school area. This map should be made on the floor of the school room or on a large sheet of heavy paper laid on the floor. The children should select their own symbols for roads, highways, houses, or other buildings, a railroad, a stream, or other items in the landscape.

In addition, there should be a class discussion of the features of the landscape in order to be sure that the children have observed and know them. At this beginning stage the teacher should take nothing for granted. For instance, in a large city school only a dozen blocks or so from a river, the teacher was positive that all the children had seen a river. She was sure, when she told them the wavy black line represented a river, that all the children visualized a river, the one on which the city was located. Upon investigation, however, she found that 90 per cent of the children had never seen a river. The district was densely populated, and very few of the children had ever been beyond a few blocks from their homes.

The teacher also can help the child to visualize map symbols by the use of pictures. He should collect pictures of rivers, falls, peninsulas, capes, islands, mountain ranges, mountain peaks, and other natural features. Such pictures should be large if possible. Charts with map symbols and accompanying pictures may also be purchased from map companies.[7]

Later, when checking the child's visualization of the map symbols, the teacher may ask the child to sketch an island, a lake, a river with falls in it, and so forth. He may also ask the child to select from a set of pictures the ones which represent certain designated map symbols.

The second teaching principle is: *Map symbols should be introduced as needed.* In most schools, and in textbooks, the conven-

[7] A. J. Nystrom and Co. Also Rand McNally Co. has map symbol charts.

Maps and Globes Are Our Business

tional map is introduced in the fourth grade. At this age level, the child begins to want to use maps for locating places and tracing trips beyond his own local area. As Anderzhon says:[8]

> The interests of nine- and ten-year-olds reach beyond their local neighborhoods. They like to "go places." Maps tell them where places are located, especially with relation to how far it is from where they live. They want to know how to go from "here" to "there" and how long it will take. They are also interested in places on a map with relation to other features such as rivers, lakes, or mountains, especially if they have some familiarity with how the feature looks.

The map symbols introduced should be those needed in developing a specific unit. What units are used at fourth-grade level depend upon the course of study of the particular school. But let us take as an illustration a unit on "Living Along the Congo River." The map symbols needed are river, falls, city, railroad, coastline, tributary river, source of a river, mouth of a river, swamp, and mountains. If there has been a map readiness program in the primary grades, the children will have visual imagery for some of the symbols, others will be new, and the imagery for some will be made clearer or more meaningful. The children may recognize and visualize the river symbol, but with the aid of pictures and discussion they should visualize the Congo River, see its breadth, have a sense of its volume, see the vegetation along its banks, the different kinds of boats on it, the villages, and the cities. Then the wavy black line winding north, then west, then southwest across the map of Africa, and finally ending in the Atlantic Ocean has real meaning to the child, furthermore he is not likely to forget it.

The term *tributary* and how to recognize a tributary stream on a map is explained by pictures and discussion. The terms *source* of a river and *mouth* of a river also need illustration and discussion with pictures and sketches associated with the symbols on the map.

From unit to unit, additional symbols are added to the child's map vocabulary as needed.

[8] Mamie L. Anderzhon, "The Child Looks Upon the Map," *Journal of Geography*, Vol. 53 (September, 1954), p. 239.

The third principle is: *The children should know the cardinal directions.* One of the basic functions of maps is to help us to orient ourselves and to locate places on the earth. Unless a child knows the cardinal directions, he cannot use a map effectively. The teaching of direction should be done in the primary grades by means of sun position. But in almost every grade some reteaching is necessary. Before making or using a map, north should be determined and the children should have practice in finding direction. Next the children should learn to read direction on a specific map and the location of the features shown on the map in relation to one another.

If a teacher follows the three basic principles for teaching map symbols, and gives constant and varied exercises in reading maps, the children will really learn to read maps. Maps will soon be a challenge to them, and from reading descriptive facts from their maps they will move on into the interpretation of such facts.

Gradation of Map Symbols and Ideas

There are two kinds of map symbols—the semipictorial and the nonpictorial. The simplest type is the semipictorial, those symbols which somewhat resemble the landscape item for which they stand, for example, the wavy line for a river, the curved and irregular lines for coast lines. These symbols may be compared to the concrete words in the primers and first readers that can be illustrated by objects or pictures so that the word may be associated with the actual item in the child's mind. As the child recognizes the symbol he visualizes the landscape feature, and thus he begins the translation of the map into landscape imagery. From the simple semipictorial symbols are built the complex semipictorial symbols. These are composed of a combination of several semipictorial symbols, for example, a peninsula which is a certain combination of water, land, and coastline symbols, a strait which is also a specific but different arrangement of the same symbols.

The nonpictorial symbols are those which have no resemblance to the landscape features for which they stand, or perhaps the

Maps and Globes Are Our Business

thing symbolized does not exist on the surface of the earth. Some nonpictorial symbols are color bands representing altitude, or perhaps inches of rainfall. Others are dots or shadings representing distribution of people and crops. Still other nonpictorial symbols are the various *isolines,* lines connecting points of equal value. For example, isotherms are lines drawn on a map connecting all places having the same temperature at a stated time. Similarly, meridians and parallels do not exist on the earth's surface, but they are placed on a map to signify distance from the prime meridian and from the equator. Such symbols present difficulty to the child, for they bear little relation to the thing symbolized, and they may vary in meaning from map to map. Therefore a map key or legend is necessary and the child must be trained to read the key or legend.

Not only are there two kinds of map symbols, one of which is more difficult than the other, but there are also two kinds of facts to be read from maps. There are descriptive facts concerning the landscape represented on the map, and interpretive ideas to be inferred from these facts. The descriptive fact or idea is the simpler, for the child is merely reading the facts represented by the various symbols on a specific map. He observes, recognizes, and names or describes the item symbolized. For example, looking at a map of Africa he recognizes the symbol for the Nile River, he notes that it is a long river, rising in eastern Africa and flowing north into the Mediterranean Sea. It has a large delta; it has many falls or rapids. He recognizes the symbols of certain cities.

Interpretive ideas are more difficult because they are based on the comparison of two or more descriptive facts read from a map or maps. Thus, to interpret a map, the child reads two or more descriptive facts, relates them to each other if possible, and then makes certain inferences. He may read descriptive facts from two or more maps, and noting the location of these items with reference to each other he may infer a certain relationship between them. As an illustration, by comparing a population density map and a rainfall distribution map of the United States one realizes that the amount and distribution of rainfall over the United States has some relation to the distribution of people in the United States. However, before one can make such inferences, he must be able to recognize the various map symbols, and be able to read descriptive facts. Only then will he be able to put two sets of descriptive facts together and reach a tentative conclusion as to their possible relationships. Consequently, teachers must provide much practice for the pupils in identifying the various kinds of symbols, and in relating the descriptive facts to be read from the symbols. Of course, such practice is offered in developing various geography or social studies units. When a child has read all the descriptive facts, training should be given in discovering all of the possible interpretive ideas. For example, the pupil states all the descriptive facts concerning New York City that he can read from a physical-political map of the United States. Some of these descriptive facts would be—size, location in respect to the Hudson River, to Long Island Sound, to the Atlantic Ocean, and to the topography of that part of the United States. Then he may be asked, "Do these facts suggest why New York has become a large city?" In answering this question the pupil begins to relate the size of New York to its geographical location.

TECHNIQUES FOR DEVELOPING MAP SKILLS

Map-reading skills and abilities are developed gradually. Constant practice, frequent reteaching, and review are necessary as in the development of reading and arithmetic skills. The development of map skills should begin in the primary grades, and be carried on consistently throughout the intermediate grades, and the junior and senior high school. Only through such cumulative learning will maps become useful tools "for grasping not only spatial relationships of places on the face of the earth but also for understanding the significance of geography in the development of the various cultures of the world."[9]

[9] Clyde F. Kohn, and others, "Interpreting Maps and Globes," *Skills in the Social Studies*, Twenty-fourth Yearbook (Washington, D.C., National Council for the Social Studies, 1953), p. 177.

The Primary Grades

In the primary grades there should be a geography program that includes map-readiness activities. Such activities are needed to give the child background and experience before the conventional map is introduced.

In the first grade the teaching of the concept of direction is begun. The concept of direction must be developed through a series of planned lessons combined with frequent use so that the children will begin to understand the need of knowing the cardinal directions. The cardinal directions should be taught in relation to sun position through observation and discussion. Ask the children such questions as:

Where is the sun early in the morning?
Where is it at noon?
Where is it late in the afternoon?

Tell them the names of the directions and have them point each time they are discussed.

Discuss the sun and what it does for us, and have them point and give the direction in the sky that we see the sun at different times of the day. Develop a reading lesson on direction and the sun. Later, have them observe and tell the direction that their homes face. If possible, build a model of the school area on a large sand table or on the floor. Put in the school, streets, roads, and as many of the children's homes as practical, and use the model for practice in using the cardinal directions. Have the children tell how they come to school, how they go home, and also have them give directions for visiting other children. They will begin to gain an idea of distance and relative distance by comparing the distances of their homes to the school in terms of city blocks.

The teacher and class should discuss the need for knowing direction when traveling, and for other purposes. For example, on which side of the house in summer is it desirable to have awnings, and where should certain flowers be planted? Such practical applications emphasize the relation of direction to sun position.

By the end of the first grade the children should know and be able to use the cardinal directions. They should have an understanding that:

> The sun is low in the eastern sky in the early morning.
> The sun is high in the southern sky at noon.
> The sun is low in the western sky in the late afternoon.

In the second grade the cardinal directions are reviewed in relation to sun position. The teacher should plan field trips and other experiences in which the children need to use direction. In conversation lessons, when the children tell about their summer trips, they should state in what direction they went from their homes. During this second year they should also learn to use northeast, northwest, southeast, and southwest.

In the second grade the use of shadows to indicate direction may be introduced. The best time to observe shadows is as near noontime as possible. If there is a south-facing window in the schoolroom, the teacher can place an eighteen-inch-square board on the window sill. On the south side of the board drive a nail in allowing it to stick up several inches. Have the children watch the shadow of the nail, noting its length and the direction it is pointing at midday. Mark its length in September and on the same date each following month. The length of the nail's shadow will change as autumn advances and winter comes, reaching its greatest length on December 22, after which date the shadow will begin to shorten.

If the room does not have a south-facing window, select a tree or post in the schoolyard and observe its shadow, marking its length at intervals. Some of the children will raise questions about the changing length of the noonday shadow, and some will observe their own and other shadows during the day. From these observations and discussions the children will begin to realize that direction can be told by the way shadows point during the day.[10]

[10] In the morning, in the northern hemisphere north of the Tropic of Cancer, the shadows point toward a westerly direction. By midday the shadows point north. In the afternoon the shadows gradually shift, pointing in an easterly direction.

Maps and Globes Are Our Business

The children should also use such terms of relative distance as *nearer* and *farther*. They should use number of blocks in stating distances in a city locality. In a farming community even children of the primary grades may have an understanding of what a distance of one mile means. Today distance is so often expressed in terms of time involved that even the use of such terms may begin, depending on the ability of the group.

Early in the third grade the teacher should review direction, for some of the pupils will have forgotten, or there may be new children in the class who have not been taught to use direction. During this third year they should be given additional work in determining direction by the use of shadows. Also they should be given instruction in using direction with their weather observations, telling wind direction, noting the direction from which a storm is coming, and the direction from which the rain is coming. When the teacher feels that they are ready, the class should be guided in the making of a map of the immediate locality.

Developing the First Map. As a result of a trip to a dairy, the post office, or merely from a walk around several blocks near the school to study the landscape, the teacher may find an opportunity to suggest the making of a map. A map growing out of a trip is much more desirable than a map of the schoolroom. In the first place, the children have difficulty in seeing any real value in making a map of the schoolroom, it is a diagram rather than a map. In the second place, a diagram of the schoolroom contains few of the symbols used in a real map.

The day after the trip, the teacher or some of the pupils may suggest that one or more of the children give an account of the trip to a visitor, or to those pupils who were absent. The children may find it difficult to describe the route and what they saw, so the teacher may suggest that a map would help but there is none. "Why not make one? Shall we put it on the floor? No, if we put it on the floor we would erase it in walking on it. Let us use a large sheet of paper, or several sheets, spreading them on the floor." The teacher will have anticipated this and be prepared with paper, crayon, and other materials.

The map should be made on a large scale, if possible large enough so that the children can walk on it. The children should have gained a feeling for distance in the work of the first and second grade, but the teacher will need to explain scale in simple terms.

The paper is spread on the floor and the class gathers around it. First, the cardinal directions are determined and marked. Then, with the help of the class, the teacher draws the map. Many questions come up in rapid succession as the essential features are planned. "What shall we put on the map first? How shall we show the roads or streets, the houses, and other buildings? How shall we show the stream, river, or lake?" The symbols are decided upon as needed, and then used consistently. The question should be asked, "How can someone who did not help in making the map know what the signs or symbols stand for?" This brings the class to realize the necessity for a key or legend. It is worked out and placed in the lower left-hand corner of the map, as in most printed maps, and the children are given the term *key* or *legend* to use in referring to it. If the area being mapped has marked differences of surface, the class may want to indicate the high and low parts. The teacher may suggest, or lead them to suggest, the use of the conventional colors—green for low areas, yellow for higher, the shades of brown for still higher.

After the map is completed, various children may give the story of the trip, or parts of the trip, using their map to explain where they went and what they saw. The children, as they give an account of the trip, should use directions.

When the class has temporarily finished with the map, several questions may come up. "What shall we do with it while we are not using it? Where can we put it so that we can see it from our seats?" The class will probably decide to hang it on the wall unless it is too large. The north wall should be used because in that position the directions remain more nearly correct. If during the first

Maps and Globes Are Our Business

year or so, all large maps used are hung on a north wall, and frequently placed on the floor correctly oriented, the children will have little or no difficulty in knowing directions on a map.

The teacher should also make small mimeographed copies of the map for each child. With this copy, the children can utilize their learning outside the school room.

Drills and games may be invented by the teacher and the children for practice in recognizing the symbols, and the objects or conditions for which the symbols stand. In anticipation of the later use of latitude and longitude for the location of places, the children should be trained to locate things on their map, first in relation to other objects, and then more definitely in relation to roads or streets.

The globe should be introduced in the third grade or even earlier. The teacher should explain that north is toward the North Pole, and south is toward the South Pole, and rotation of the earth on its axis from west to east should be illustrated.

By the end of the third grade, most of the children should know the cardinal and the intermediate directions and be able to use them. They should know that they can use shadows to determine directions. They should know that a map represents by means of symbols the features of the landscape in a certain area. They should understand that a globe represents the earth.

The Intermediate Grades

In the fourth grade, before beginning any textbook work the teacher should check the children's ability to use direction. The teacher should take the children outdoors at midday and check whether they can tell direction by their shadows. The points of the compass should be reviewed, and be oriented in the classroom. If the class has never made a local map as suggested for the third grade, the teacher should provide this instruction.

The teacher should also check their understanding of the use of the globe. In using the globe the teacher should always have the

North Pole pointing north, and in rotating it, rotate it from west to east.

The teacher should also check the children's understanding of distance and relative distance in terms of city blocks or other simple units of measurement within nine- and ten-year-old's comprehension.

In the fourth grade the maps used should be simple, with relatively few symbols. The colors should be clear, blue for water bodies, and gray, yellow, or green for land. If mountains or highlands are needed these should be indicated by shading, or in some cases the color brown with shadings. To give beginners detailed, complicated maps covered with numerous symbols is much the same as giving a first-grade pupil a page from a technical book to read.

By the end of the fourth grade most of the children, if properly instructed, should recognize the following semipictorial symbols: land, river, coastline, falls or rapids, city, mouth of a river, lake, island, peninsula, mountain, glacier, ocean, sea, tributary, delta, and any others that have been taught during the study of the geography units. Symbols should be introduced as *needed*, consequently the number of symbols taught is determined by the nature of the units developed. But the number and difficulty of the map symbols taught to beginners should be determined as carefully as the vocabulary in their readers. Remember that the children are learning a new language—map language.

In aiding the children to visualize map symbols, the teacher should use field trips, pictures, and help them to recall past experiences in order to associate landscape features they have seen with the map symbols. Description and discussion will help so that the river, city, or other symbol becomes more meaningful to the child. For example, pictures of the Congo River showing its width, the vegetation along its banks, the animals, the kind of boats used on the river, and its villages could be used, together with vivid descriptions, to help the child visualize the Congo. Tracing it on the map, noting the direction it flows, finding the

Maps and Globes Are Our Business

falls and rapids, finding its mouth, imagining trips upstream and downstream, are other activities that aid the child's visualization. He must see, smell, and feel the river, which will insure that he not only visualizes the Congo but also remembers its location.

One of the chief reasons why children and adults fail to recall the location of important places is that they do not have sufficient associations with the place. The feature remains merely a dot or a line on a map, not a real thing or place. To be meaningful and to be retained as functional, the concept of a river, city, or any other feature must be built up slowly and carefully. The Nile or any other river studied in connection with a unit must be developed in the same way. Each one has a personality of its own, and the same is true of other landscape features, whether natural or cultural. Of course, not every river, city, mountain, or other natural or cultural feature is so taught, but, certainly, those of world importance or of importance to the American child, should be.

If at any stage the children have difficulty reading direction on the map, the map should be placed on the floor correctly oriented. The finding and use of direction should be reviewed, for such difficulty is not unusual.

By the end of the fourth grade the children should be able to read directions on a map. This involves the ability to recognize the location of the equator, the tropics, and the poles. The children should also be able to locate places in relation to the equator, the tropics, the poles, and to large land and water bodies.

The teacher should explain the equator and the poles when the children begin using the globe. Later when the tropics are needed, they should be located and explained. Some maps and textbooks are now using the easier terms *North Tropic* for the Tropic of Cancer and *South Tropic* for the Tropic of Capricorn. The North Tropic line and the South Tropic line are lines, or circles of latitude, which mark the area on the earth's surface over which the vertical rays of the sun shift during the course of a year. The sun is not always directly overhead at noon on the equator, but shifts north and south. The tilt of the earth's axis determines how far north or south of the geographical equator this "sunshine equator" will shift in the course of a year. The tropic lines mark the extreme limits north and south of the equator which the vertical rays of the sun travel.

The Arctic and Antarctic Circles, which are also sun lines, should be located and explained. The area within each one of these circles is that part of the earth which during certain months of the year the sun does not rise above the horizon and during certain other months does not set or drop below the horizon.

These concepts of the North and South Tropic lines and the Arctic and Antarctic Circles are difficult concepts. They should be taught only if needed in the units specified for the local course of study; and the ability of the class should be considered. The lines or circles may be located on the globe and maps and used to read comparative distance, for example, a certain place is near the equator, is nearer the North Tropic, is north or south of the North Tropic.

The nine- and ten-year-old should learn to associate certain natural conditions with distance from the equator, for instance: Near the equator on lowlands temperatures are always warm; near the equator there is much rain all the year. He also should learn to associate such natural conditions with cultural factors such as: People who live on lowlands near the equator build houses with steeply sloping roofs so that the heavy rains will run off rapidly. Often these houses are built on stilts or poles several feet above the ground because the earth becomes so wet.

Understanding such relationships is developed through the reading of stories and descriptions, studying pictures, making comparisons with local conditions, and class discussion. All of the materials used are descriptive of the landscape and the way people live at different distances from the equator. The map and the globe must be frequently referred to with the reading, with the picture study, and during the class discussion in order to encourage the

Maps and Globes Are Our Business

association of location on the earth, natural conditions with the way people live at various distances from the equator.

At this level the child should know and understand the significance of the terms *upstream* and *downstream*. Upstream means going toward the source of the stream and against the current. Downstream is going toward the mouth of the stream and with the current.

By the end of the fourth grade, most of the children should be able to locate and name all of the oceans and continents, locate the equator, the North Tropic and the South Tropic, the Arctic and Antarctic Circles, and the important places discussed in the various units developed.

Linear or graphic scale may be introduced in the fourth grade if there is a need for estimating long distances and if scale is used in the textbook maps. An understanding of scale should begin with drawing the schoolroom and the schoolyard to scale with measurements in inches, each inch representing so many feet. Later, a large map of the local or immediate neighborhood may be made. These experiences aid the children in gaining an idea of distance as represented on a map.

Some additional understandings and appreciations should be gained during the fourth year. One of these is a beginning understanding and appreciation of a map as a source of information, which grows from the constant use of maps as the child gains in map reading skill. Another is a beginning understanding and appreciation of the importance of location on the earth in relation to the equator, and a third is understanding how the rotation of the earth on its axis causes daylight and darkness.

This discussion of map skills implies the use of a modern geography text. In most of the modern geography textbooks and accompanying teachers' manuals, map skills are developed with care, but every teacher needs additional help, especially an understanding of the need for careful teaching of map language. However, in some schools the social studies program and texts give little or no attention to teaching the reading and interpretation of maps. The above suggested teaching techniques should aid the teachers so handicapped. All the map skills discussed may not be developed under such conditions, but at least a beginning can be made.

Fifth Grade. Because map learning is cumulative, the fifth grade teacher should check the children's map skills before beginning any new work. Their ability to recognize and use direction and the semipictorial symbols taught in the fourth grade should be tested. To do this, place a large physical-political map of the United States on the floor and have the class orient it correctly. Conduct a drill with it for a few minutes by asking them to locate designated places. For example, ask a pupil to find Seattle in the northwestern part of the United States on Puget Sound. Be sure that the child puts his finger or the pointer on the symbol for the city and *not* on the name. Ask one of the pupils to place the pointer on Puget Sound and trace the coastline. If he twists around trying to read the names, he is not recognizing and reading the symbols. Some cities, rivers, or other features should be located and traced.

In most schools the geography of North America, or of the United States and Canada, is taught. For this purpose a large physical-political map of North America, one of the United States, one of the world, and a globe are needed. A physical-political map is the best type because it shows elevation as well as political boundaries. On such a map, increasing elevation may be indicated by color bands—shades of green, yellow, and brown, or varying shades of one color. On some maps shadings for mountain ranges are added to give a sense of height and slope. Political boundaries are shown by solid or broken black or red lines.

Other kinds of maps found in textbooks at this level are distribution maps. Distribution is indicated by dots, shadings, and in some cases, by color. Some of the more common distribution maps introduced at this level are population distribution, various crop distributions, distribution of animal population, and rainfall distribution.

All of these maps are new to the child, consequently a careful

Maps and Globes Are Our Business

introduction is needed. Since these nonpictorial symbols—color, dots, and shadings—have different meanings on different maps, children must be taught to study the map key or legend before attempting to read the map.

A physical map of the United States should be the first taught. Have the children note the colors used and study the key to learn their meaning. Explain and discuss with them what elevation or altitude above sea level means. Also explain how altitude is important to people in the way that they live. Locate their own community, or the region in which their home is, on the map and note its altitude above sea level. Have the class locate some areas at different altitudes. As each one is found, have pictures to show the class the appearance of the landscape in the particular area that they have located. If the teacher has some good descriptions of specific landscapes, he should read these to the class, making comparisons with landscape features of their home area. As each region of the United States is studied, use flat pictures, films, and descriptions to aid the children to see "in the mind's eye" the landscape symbolized on the map.

As the various distribution maps are used, each one should be explained and discussed. A population distribution map is usually the first one introduced. If the children seem to have trouble in understanding it, have them draw a small plan of the school building. Find out how many children are in each classroom, and indicate on the plan how many children are in each room. As one dot for each child will probably crowd some of the rooms, suggest or lead them to suggest that one dot may stand for five children. Place the proper number of dots in each room and make a key for the diagram. Call the children's attention to the fact that anyone looking at the diagram can see at a glance how the children are distributed in the school building. Similarly, a population distribution map of the United States shows one how the people are distributed throughout the country. Have the children locate their home area on the map and note how many people per square mile live there; if the map used does not state the number of people per square

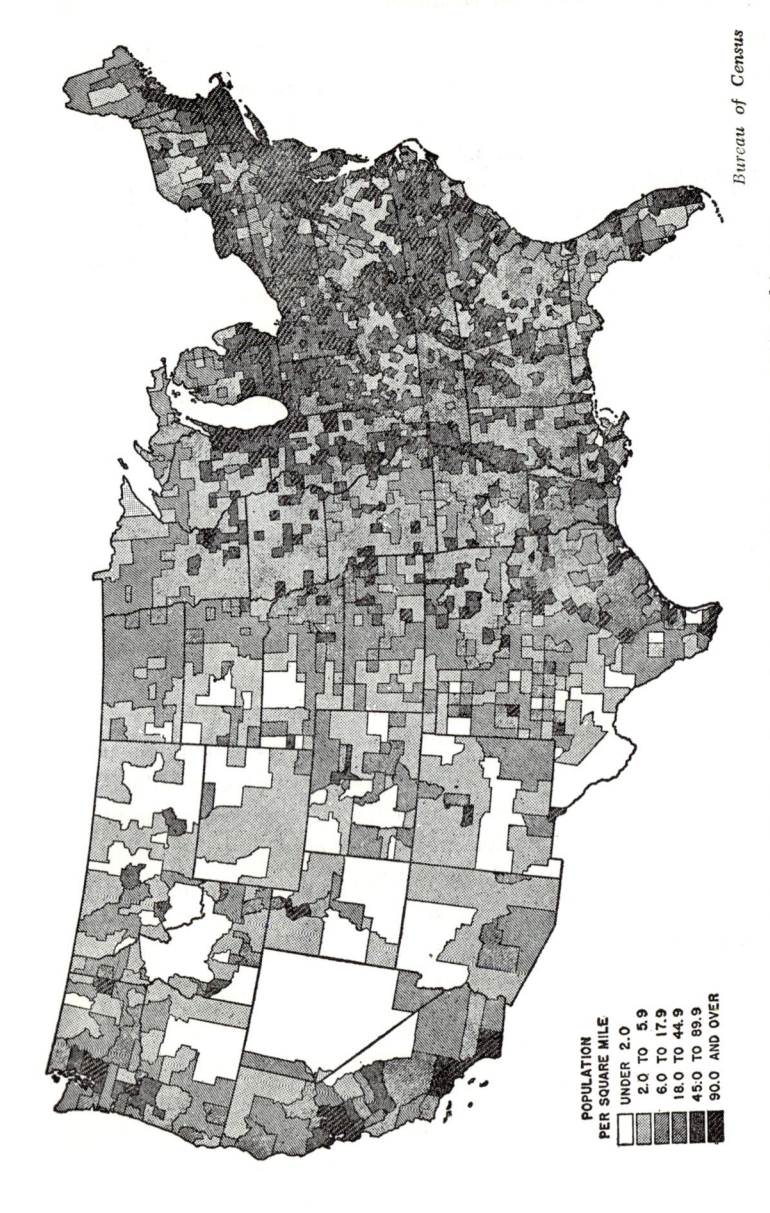

Fig. 2. Distribution of population of the United States, 1950. This map shows the population per square mile by counties.

Maps and Globes Are Our Business

mile, the class can note the relative amount of people living there according to the distribution of the dots.

These maps should be introduced and taught *as needed* so that the children will realize that each one is a source of specific information. Children will not learn to read maps and use them as a source of information unless given specific questions and exercises, any more than they will learn to add or divide without exercises.

The following are examples of simple descriptive facts that may be read from a physical-political map of the United States.

Pittsburgh is in Pennsylvania. It is located at the junction of the Allegheny and Monongahela rivers. It appears to be at an elevation between 500 and 1000 feet.

Denver is in Colorado. It lies at an elevation or altitude between 5000 and 10,000 feet. It seems to be on the South Platte River. There are very high mountains to the west of Denver.

Additional descriptive facts may be read from other maps, such as distribution of population and rainfall, and length of growing season. Before beginning the study of a new region, there should be a class discussion based on readings from maps of the region. These facts may be listed, and as the pupils study the pictures and textual material they can check the accuracy of their exploratory exercises. Children enjoy such exercises because they are active participants.

As the children gain facility in reading descriptive facts from maps, they may be guided into interpretive reading, that is, putting two or more descriptive facts together and drawing an inference. The following are examples.

"On a physical-political map of the United States, note the location of New York City at the mouth of the Hudson on the Atlantic Coast. Trace the Hudson River valley to the Mohawk Valley, and follow it and the Barge Canal to Lake Erie. What is the altitude along this route? Look over the map carefully. Do you see any other place as easy to cross the Appalachian Mountains? Why do you think the Erie Canal and, later, the Barge Canal was built? How would the Hudson River, the Mohawk Valley and the build-

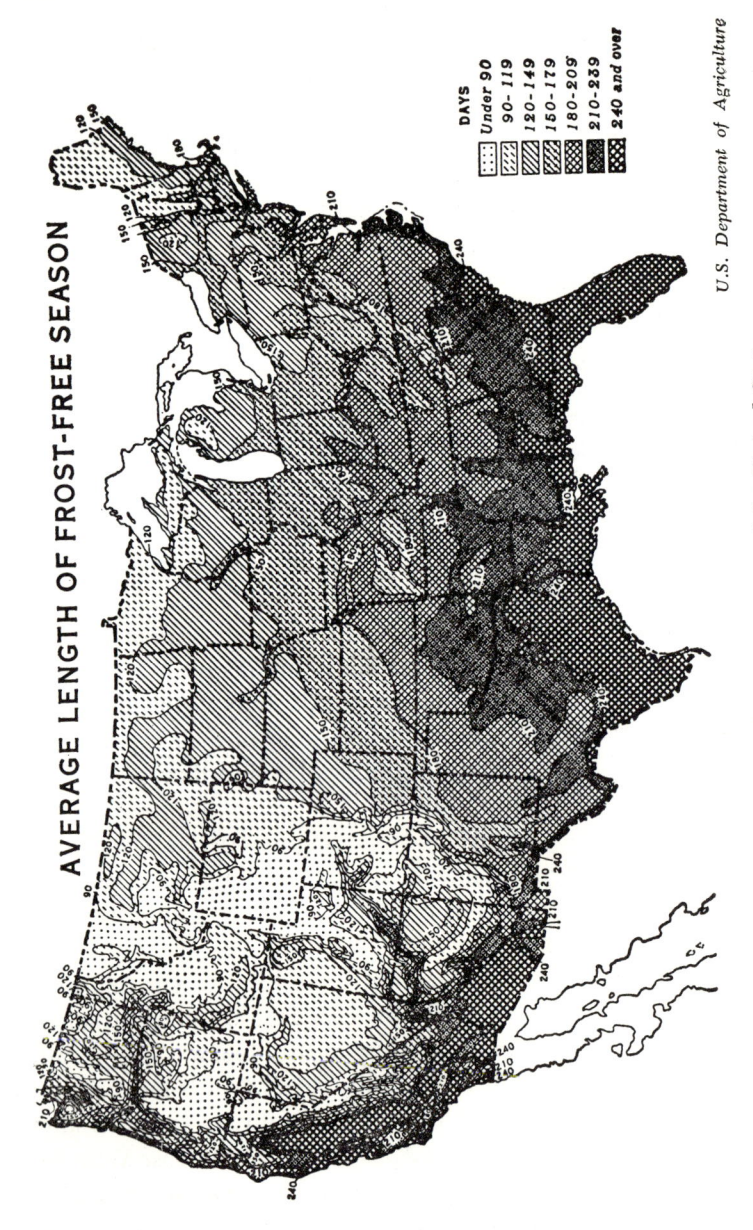

Fig. 3. A growing season map of the United States.

Maps and Globes Are Our Business

ing of the Canal help New York? In addition to the water route, what other type of transportation uses this same route? The New York Central railroad claims that it is the only sea-level railroad in the United States. Is its claim correct?

"Why is New York's location on the Atlantic Coast a help to the growth of the city? How does the map suggest that New York has a large and good harbor? From what you have read from the map, suggest three reasons for the growth of New York."

At the beginning of a study of the southern states, have the class carefully study a map showing either cotton acreage or production. Note the location of the cotton growing areas and consult a rainfall map for the average annual rainfall received in these areas (20 to 60 inches). Consult a growing season map to see how many months or days are without frost. (Some maps give the growing season, that is, the number of days without a killing frost. In the cotton areas this is 200 days or about seven months) Next, compare the cotton distribution map and a physical map of the southern states, and locate on the latter the areas with the greatest acreage in cotton or the highest production, whichever is given. Note that these areas are in the Mississippi Valley in Arkansas, Tennessee, and Mississippi, and that there are also areas in Texas and certain other states. Have the class find the altitude of these areas. After listing these and other descriptive facts from the maps, ask the class to summarize the conditions under which cotton is raised. Some of the children may ask about the small cotton areas in Arizona and California where the rainfall is less than ten inches. Refer the question back to them, that if there is less than ten inches of rain in the California and Arizona areas and cotton seems to need 20 to 60 inches, what could the farmers do?

Not all the children will be able to do such inferential thinking, but the majority can if the teacher guides them with specific directions and questions, and gives them much encouragement. All statements and inferences should be checked against pictures and textual materials or verified in some way.

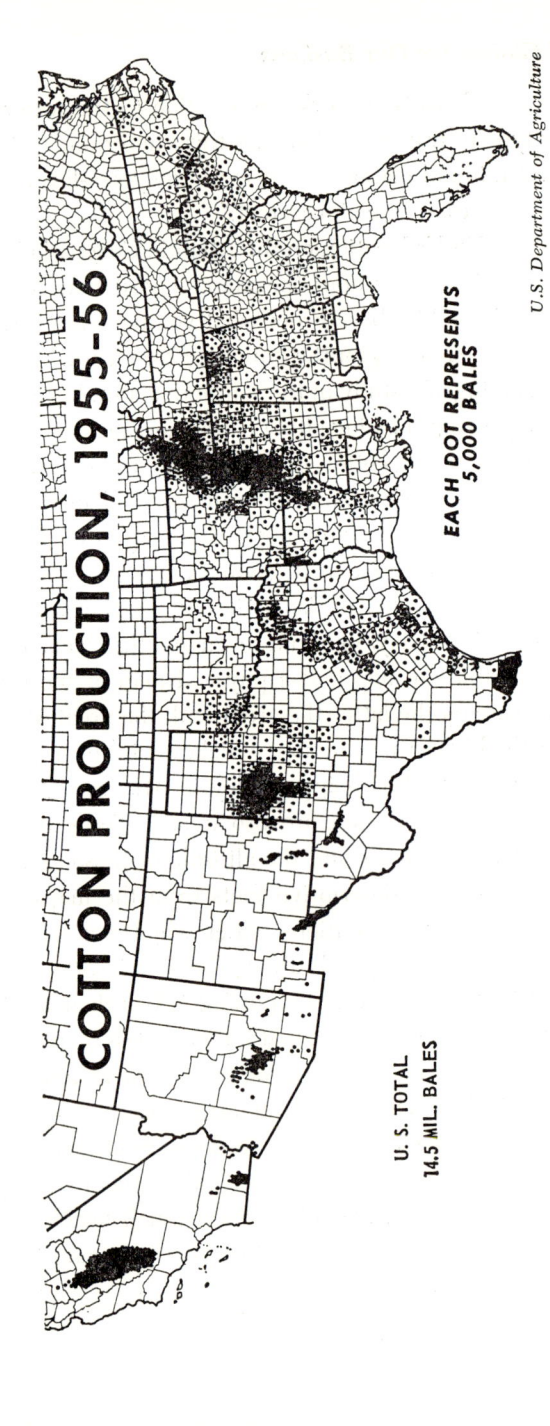

Fig. 4. A cotton distribution map of the United States.

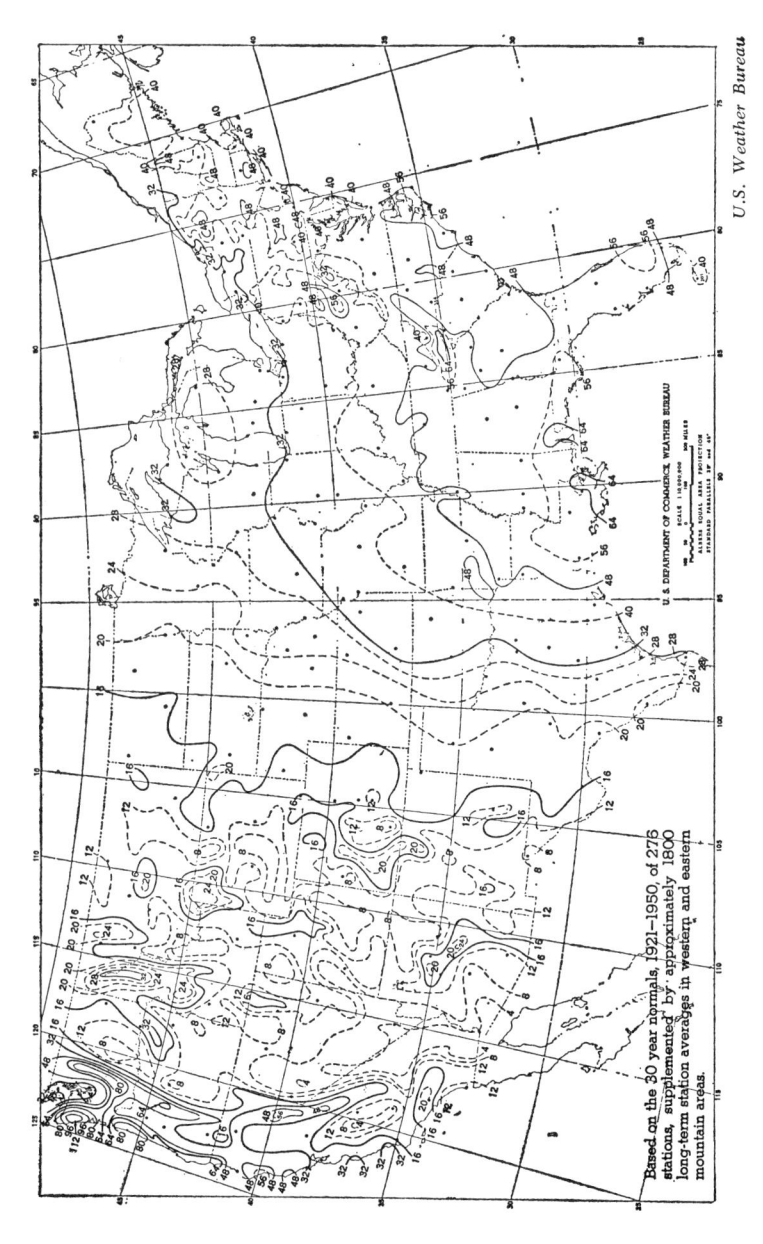

Fig. 5. Normal annual amount of precipitation in inches.

Latitude is introduced in the fifth grade. In the fourth grade the children should have learned something of the significance of distance from the equator. The terms *latitude* and *parallels of latitude* are introduced as a means of finding exact distances from the equator in degrees, and approximate distance in miles. One degree of latitude approximately equals 70 land miles. In explaining parallels of latitude, compare them to streets running east and west parallel to the main street of a town. The east-west streets help one to estimate the number of blocks north or south of the main street someone lives. Parallels of latitude are east-west direction lines. For instance, both Denver and Philadelphia are almost on the 40th degree North latitude, consequently Denver is due west of Philadelphia. The parallel also shows us that both are 40 degrees north of the equator or about 2800 miles north of the equator. After explaining and using latitude by locating places on or near 30°, 35°, 40°, and 45° N., discuss the significance of latitude in respect to length of the seasons, and the length of days during the seasons. In this context review what the class learned in the fourth grade concerning the effects of distance from the equator.

The teacher should give the children specific illustrations of how length of daylight in winter and summer affects their own activities and other human affairs, for instance, comparison of electric light bills in winter and summer, the changing to daylight saving time.

The class should also discuss length of seasons in the southern part of the United States and in the northern tier of states. Why do people in Minnesota go to Florida or southern California in the winter? As the different regions of the United States and Canada are studied, explain how certain crops requiring a long growing season grow in the south but cannot be grown in the north or in Canada.[11]

Scale of miles. In the fourth grade the children have gained a beginning understanding of scale which the teacher should build

[11] Lucia Harrison's *Daylight, Twilight, Darkness and Time,* published by Silver, Burdette, and Co., 1935, gives many illustrations of the part such facts play in human affairs.

Maps and Globes Are Our Business

upon. H. Phillip Bacon describes how the making of a pace map helps children to acquire a basic grasp of the meaning of local distance, and through this activity gain a better understanding of the realities of distance.[12]

In the fifth grade they should be taught to note the scale of miles on every map they use and to compare maps of different scales. They should use the scale of miles to find approximate distances between places, for example, from their home to a large city, or the length of a state's boundary. The easiest way to find approximate distance between two places is to mark off the distance on the straight line edge of a strip of paper, then lay this on the map scale and measure the distance.

If the teacher needs a better understanding of scale, he will find an excellent detailed discussion in the Twenty-fourth Yearbook of the National Council for the Social Studies.[13]

Locational Geography. By the close of the fifth-grade study of the United States and North America, the children should be able to recognize on an outline map the states of the United States, the countries of North America, the most important cities in the United States and in the other countries studied, and the most important rivers and lakes. In order to learn these the class needs practice in locating and visualizing each one. Not only should a river, such as the Mississippi, be located, traced from its source to its mouth, but also many associations suggested—activities along its banks, the cities, the kinds of boats used on it, the vegetation and crops which may be seen as one travels from north to south until "Ole Man River" is a real personality to the child. Other rivers, such as the Hudson, Ohio, Colorado, Columbia, Missouri, and St. Lawrence, should also be taught and comparisons made. These become real friends, quickly recognized and never forgotten. Others such as the Allegheny, the San Joaquin, and the Platte should be taught, but only as "speaking acquaintances" unless any one of them is of

[12] H. Phillip Bacon, "Making a Pace Map—An Activity for the Fifth and Sixth Grades," *Journal of Geography*, Vol. 53 (May, 1954), pp. 203–208.
[13] Clyde F. Kohn, "Interpreting Maps and Globes," *op. cit.*, pp. 146–177.

importance to the local community. The same principle should be applied to the study of lakes, cities, and mountain ranges.

Descriptions, pictures, stories, and poems help greatly in building vivid images and associations. The child will then be able to recall and locate landscape features readily.

Map-making activities. In the fifth grade the teacher may begin training the child to use symbols on outline maps to show significant information of a simple type. Such information may or may not be on the maps in their textbooks. For example, a fifth-grade class used outline maps of the Central States to map important facts as they discussed the area. In doing this the children had to observe carefully the maps in their texts, and also to read their texts. They decided on the various symbols to be used as needed. Some of the facts they mapped were the most important cities, rivers, and lakes. The corn region of the Central States was indicated by the use of yellow and the hog-raising area with horizontal lines. They noted and discussed how these areas overlapped. Even though they had looked at the maps in their text and discussed the relationship between the two areas, many of the children grasped the idea only after putting the two on their own maps. Some texts do not have distribution maps, but in such case the teacher can give the children the needed statistics, help them to determine how to show the statistics by dots, colors, or lines, and help them to map the information. Such map activity may be of little or great value depending upon the teacher's use of it. If he uses it to direct the children's attention to relationships, and to note relative location and its significance, the activity is worthwhile.

Habits. There are three map-using habits that the teacher should continue to check: (1) the habit of consulting maps for information, (2) using the map key or legend, and (3) turning to a map to locate places while reading about a new region. By this time the children should realize that certain types of information can be read from maps better and more quickly than from the printed page.

Understandings. During their fifth-grade experiences the chil-

Maps and Globes Are Our Business   51

dren should have gained a greater understanding and appreciation of the value of maps as a source of information. They should also have gained some understanding of the value of mapping certain types of information from statistical material, reading material, or from local field trips.

Their map vocabulary should be greatly enlarged. They should be able to quickly read the map symbols learned in the fourth grade and should have added the following to their map vocabulary: political boundaries, colors to show elevation, shadings, dots or color to indicate various types of distribution, certain new land and water symbols—cape, isthmus, archipelago, bay, gulf, strait, canal—symbols for different size cities, and parallels of latitude. What new symbols are learned depends on the units studied and the maps used, but a child's map vocabulary should increase each year just as should his reading vocabulary.

Sixth Grade. Map skills to be learned in the sixth grade are built on those already acquired. If a teacher finds that the class lacks some of the basic skills, the map work will necessarily be on a lower level until the class has gained the ability to visualize semi-pictorial symbols and to read descriptive facts. Remedial work is often needed just as it is in reading the printed word.

Kinds of maps and globes. The following maps and globes should be available for use in a sixth grade: physical-political wall maps of the continents studied, a world physical-political map, a large physical-political globe, and such distribution maps as population, rainfall, important crops, and livestock of the continents. Such distribution maps should be in the textbook, which should also contain large-scale maps of important cities and special areas.

Map skills. During the study of other countries or continents the children should gain increased facility in reading and interpreting the physical-political and distribution maps. The teacher should see that the children have continued practice in reading descriptive facts from maps and interpreting such information.

They should gain the ability to see a continent, a country, a city, or any area in relation to other areas, to important physical features, and to the world as a whole. The concept of relative location has been introduced, but in the sixth grade the children have a better background, and relative location should become more meaningful. To illustrate this point examine a series of maps of South America. First study a physical-political map of South America in relation to a world physical-political map. Note that South America lies mainly to the south of the equator, extending from latitude 10°N to 55°S. The largest part of the continent is between 10°N and 20°S. From the fact that most of the continent is within the tropics, it may be inferred that the climate is very warm and moist most, if not all, of the year. It also may be noted that most of the tropical area is a lowland. Noting the Amazon and its numerous tributaries, the inference of heavy rainfall seems likely to be correct. Looking at the world map, it is seen that the continent has the South Atlantic on the east and the vast South Pacific to the west and is distant from the highly developed countries of Europe and the United States.

Examining the map again, it may be noted that all the large cities are either on the coast or very near the coast. Noting the location of the mountain ranges and highlands, the inference may be made that difficulty of transportation is a factor in the location of the cities. From noting that there are relatively few railroad lines and that these start at the coast and extend inland, stopping abruptly at the same interior point, several inferences may be made. Perhaps topography has made railroad building difficult, or perhaps the interior is not developed. The only region with a fairly dense railroad network is in Argentina between 30°S and 40°S. This fact suggests some questions concerning climate and development. This illustration does not exhaust the descriptive facts to be read from the physical-political map of South America or does it exhaust the inferences that may be drawn, for such activity depends upon the background of the class, its training in map reading, and its general ability.

In the sixth grade, large-scale maps of small areas, such as a city or any special area, are introduced. The children should be taught

Maps and Globes Are Our Business 53

how to locate such a city or area on a small map of the country or continent. Such areas should be of sufficient importance as to justify detailed study, for instance the Ruhr district in Europe. The Ruhr district is so small that on a map of Europe, or even on a map of northwestern Europe, one cannot see why it is so important. But a large-scale map of the Ruhr shows better than words why the Ruhr has become an important industrial and political area as one notes the rivers, canals, coal deposits, and cities in relation to each other.

A large-scale map of London and the Thames River used in connection with a physical-political map of Great Britain helps to clarify the location of London in relation to its physical and cultural environment, and aids the child's understanding of the growth and importance of that vast city.

Longitude is introduced in the sixth grade, or in the latter part of the fifth grade depending upon the ability of the class. When introducing longitude the teacher should again bring up the problem of locating places on a globe. Review how parallels of latitude help one to find places north or south of the equator. On a globe find the meridians, or lines of longitude. Note how they extend from pole to pole bisecting the equator and the parallels of latitude. By using both the meridians of longitude and the parallels of latitude one can find places. The question arises, where can we start to number the meridians of longitude? Find the prime meridian and tell the class how the nations decided to use it as the starting line. Note that meridians of longitude are usually placed 15 degrees apart and extend both west and east of the prime meridian. In giving the longitude of a place east or west is used, just as north or south is used in stating latitude.[14]

After longitude has been explained and illustrated, all places should be located according to latitude and longitude. Games may be used to give practice in the use of latitude and longitude. For example the teacher may say, "I am in a beautiful city near 40°N.

[14] Lucia C. Harrison, "The Meaning and Measurement of Longitude," *op. cit.*, Ch. 12.

and 15°E. Where am I?" Whoever finds the city (Naples) first can hide in another city stating the latitude and longitude in order for the class to find it.

The use of outline maps to map information gained from statistics, reading material, or other sources should be continued. Dr. Katheryne T. Whittemore describes such an activity:[15]

> For example, a sixth-grade class studying India worked with an outline map on the blackboard and individual desk outline-maps. Also before them were their textbooks opened to a handsome and accurate map of India. The classwork consisted of locating the river plains of India on the textbook map and then indicating them by the use of colored chalk and crayon, first on the outline map on the blackboard, and then on the outline maps at their seats. Other physical divisions of India were indicated in a similar way. The principal rivers were named, dots were placed for the important cities, and the names of the cities were lettered on the map. The Tropic of Cancer was followed across the map in the book and then drawn on the outline maps.
>
> Proceeding in this way items were added to the outline maps until in the end the map was almost as complex as the map in the textbook. The exercise had, however, enforced careful observation. It provided an opportunity for repetition of facts learned and it made the map of the textbook more meaningful. The children were able to read the map in the textbook more easily.

If a class were doing the above map exercise, the pupils should add to the map new information from newspapers and magazines such as new dams and reservoirs, newly discovered mineral deposits, and other items.

Sketch maps. Simple sketch maps are often an excellent means of illustrating a specific point. The teacher should use them and then encourage the children to sketch their own. For example, a sketch of San Francisco Bay, with the peninsulas and the mountain ranges almost enclosing it, is of help in visualizing the location of the city and its advantages and disadvantages. In a sketch the salient features stand out because the details are left out.

[15] Katheryne T. Whittemore, "Maps," *Geographic Approaches to Social Education,* Nineteenth Yearbook (Washington, D.C., National Council for the Social Studies, 1948).

Maps and Globes Are Our Business

Outcomes of sixth-grade program. What are some of the habits, understandings, and appreciations that the sixth-grade teacher should check? The teacher should note whether the children consult maps for information without specific direction; whether they consult maps when reading newspapers, magazines, or other references about a region; whether they use maps when planning a trip; whether they consult the map legend and scale of miles; and whether they use latitude and longitude in finding places.

Their understanding and appreciation of the value of maps as a learning tool should have greatly increased and be revealed in their attitude toward maps. Also, their map vocabulary should have increased.

Junior High School (7-8-9)

During the junior high school years the children should show considerable facility in map-reading. They should now have a large map vocabulary and have had enough practice in reading descriptive facts, visualizing the landscape, and making inferences that they should be able to use maps with less dependence on the teacher. No doubt, some reteaching will be necessary and practice in certain skills should be continued. Consequently, map skills and abilities gained in the first six grades should be checked and any weaknesses eliminated as far as possible. Weak points usually are found in the use of latitude and longitude, scale, the reading of slope of land, and interpreting the legend.

Kinds of Maps. In addition to the maps already mentioned, a few new maps are introduced and others already introduced are used more intensively. The United States weather map is a new map which should be introduced. World pattern maps may have been introduced, but in the junior high school they are used more extensively and intensively. These are maps which indicate world climate, population density, vegetation, world distribution of crops, livestock, and minerals. Also, maps of world ocean routes, railroads and air routes, ocean currents, and wind belts should be available

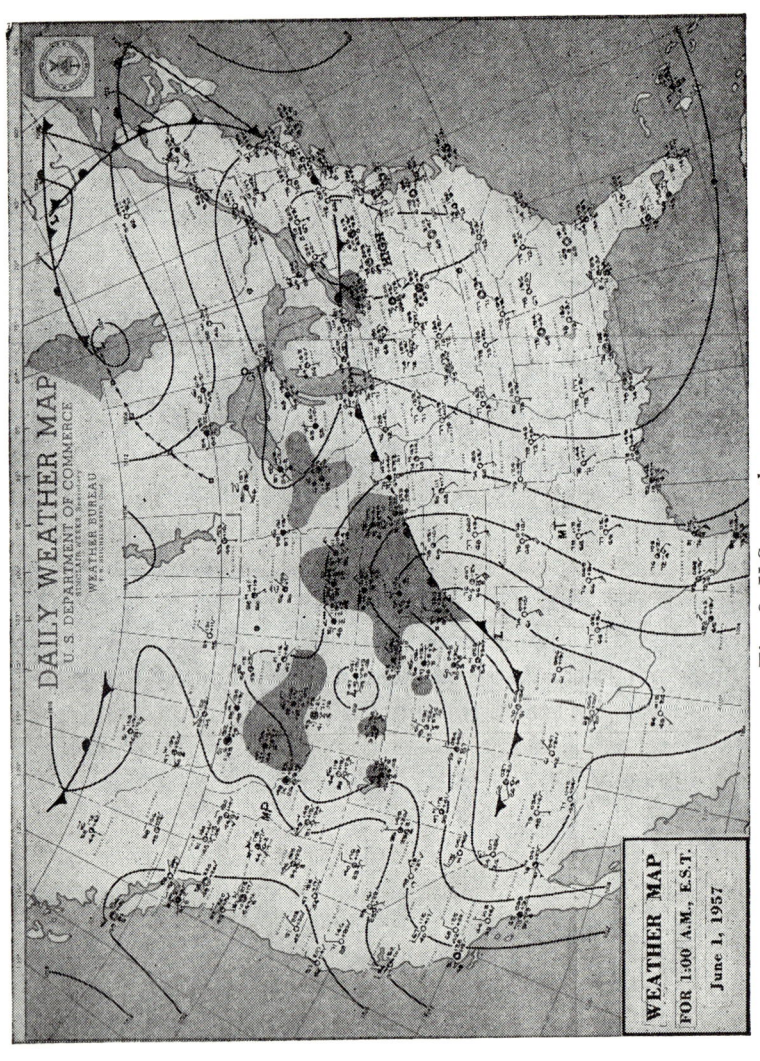

Fig. 6. U.S. weather map.

FRONTS AND AIR MASSES

The boundary between two different air masses is called a "front." Important changes in weather and temperature often occur with the passage of a front. Half circle and/or triangular symbols are placed on the lines representing fronts to indicate the kind of front. The side on which the symbols are placed indicates the direction of movement. The boundary of relatively cold air of polar origin advancing into an area occupied by warmer air, often of tropical origin, is called a "cold front." The boundary of relatively warm air advancing into an area occupied by colder air is called a "warm front." The line along which a cold front has overtaken a warm front at the ground is called an "occluded front." A boundary between two air masses, which shows little tendency at the time of observation to advance into either the warm or the cold areas, is called a "stationary front." Air mass boundaries are known as "surface fronts" when they intersect the ground, and as "upper air fronts" when they do not. Surface fronts are drawn in solid black, fronts aloft are drawn in outline only.

Front symbols are given below:

▲▲▲▲ Warm front (surface)   ◠◠◠◠ Warm front (aloft)

▲▲▲▲ Cold front (surface)   △△△△ Cold front (aloft)

▲▲▲▲ Occluded front (surface)   ▽▲▽▲ Stationary front (surface)

A front which is disappearing or is weak and decreasing in intensity is labeled "Frontolysis."

A front which is forming or increasing in intensity is labeled "Frontogenesis."

A "squall line" is a line of thunderstorms or squalls usually accompanied by shifting winds and heavy showers, and is indicated as ⎯⎯ · ⎯⎯ · ⎯⎯ .

The paths followed by individual disturbances are called storm tracks and are shown as ⎯→. The symbols ⊠ indicate past positions of the low pressure centers at 6-hour intervals.

Masses of air are classified to indicate their origin and basic characteristics. For example, the letter P (Polar) denotes relatively cold air from northern regions and the letter T (Tropical) denotes relatively warm air from southerly regions. Letters placed before P and T indicate air of maritime characteristics (m) or continental characteristics (c). Letters placed after P and T show that the air mass is colder (k) or warmer (w) than the surface over which it is moving. A plus sign (+) between two air-mass symbols indicates mixed air masses, and an arrow ⎯→ between two symbols indicates a transitional air mass changing from one type to the other. Two air mass symbols, one above the other and separated by a line, indicate one air mass aloft and another at lower levels. Air mass symbols are formed from the following letters:

m = Maritime;   c = Continental;   A = Arctic;   P = Polar;   T = Tropical;
E = Equatorial;   S = Superior (a warm, dry air mass having its origin aloft);
k = colder, and w = warmer than the surface over which the air mass is moving.

Areas where precipitation is occurring at the time of observation are shaded.

Fig. 7. Explanation of weather map.

and used. A large globe is a definite need as are also a number of small globes for individual use.

The introduction of the U.S. weather maps involves the ability to read isotherms, isobars, the symbols for cold front, warm front, and other weather symbols. The prefix *iso* denotes equality, thus an *isoline* is a line connecting all points of equal value. An isotherm is a line connecting all points of the same temperature, and an isobar is a line connecting all points of equal air pressure. A simplified form of the weather map is published daily in many newspapers and also shown on television. These should be studied, but a daily weather map from the U.S. Weather Bureau, which may be subscribed for, should be the one introduced and taught. This large map should be posted daily so that the class can follow the changing weather pattern.

In some school systems, weather and weather maps are taught in the science course. In such cases, the teacher of geography can use the information and the skills that his pupils have learned in the science course as he develops the idea of the relation of weather to man's activities. Many people think that the farmer is the only one interested in weather, but actually almost every modern industry has to take weather conditions into account. Many industries pay a large sum annually to private weather-forecasting companies for special forecasts for their specific industry. Furthermore, weather forecasting is a relatively new career with which junior high school students should become acquainted.[16]

In the junior high school, the ability to compare two or more world pattern maps, and to draw conclusions as to the reasons for certain distributions, should be stressed. For example, compare a world population distribution map with a world physical map and a world average yearly rainfall map. Note possible relationships between density of population in various areas, the type of topography, and amount of rainfall. Of course there are other factors

---

[16] H. H. Newberger and F. B. Stephens, *Weather and Man* (Englewood Cliffs, N.J., Prentice-Hall, Inc., 1948). An interesting book for both teacher and pupil.

Maps and Globes Are Our Business

beside land surface and rainfall that affect density of population, but nevertheless these two maps suggest two important reasons why men live where they do.

In the junior high school the student should become aware that all maps of the earth are distorted either in the size or in the shape of the earth features. By comparing different maps with the globe they may note such distortions, especially in the high latitudes. From comparing the grid lines on maps and on a globe they should reach the conclusion that scale, projection, and true relationship of areas are best shown on a globe. Only by using a globe can the many erroneous ideas gained from flat maps be corrected.

In connection with the above the student should be able to read direction on a map even though the parallels and meridians may be curved lines.

In addition to the habits which should have been formed in the intermediate grades, junior high school students should acquire the habit of looking at the daily weather map and forecasting weather from the information gained from this map. They should also check their tentative forecasts with the official forecasts and the actual weather of the following day.

During the junior high school period the student should develop the following understandings and appreciations:

1. An understanding of weather maps and of their value to the individual and to industry.

2. An understanding that world pattern maps are generalized, but that they help us to visualize different types of world distribution and thus aid us to think in global terms.

3. An understanding that on some maps parallels and meridians may be curved lines.

4. An understanding that the choice of scale for a map depends upon what one wants to show on a map.

Some additions to the student's map vocabulary are the following: world pattern, isoline, isotherm, isobar, cold front, warm front, wind direction, wind velocity, ocean current, warm ocean current, and cold ocean current.

Senior High School (10-11-12)

A high school student should be trained in the basic map-reading skills which will enable him to interpret world affairs more intelligently. He also needs such skills in order to use maps intelligently in his business or personal affairs. By the time he has reached the senior high school he should have acquired most of the necessary map-reading skills. However there are always some who have never been taught to read maps, and others who have not mastered the necessary skills. Again, reteaching or even the introduction to maps is necessary. If this is necessary, several weeks should be devoted to a map-reading unit in which the great value and many

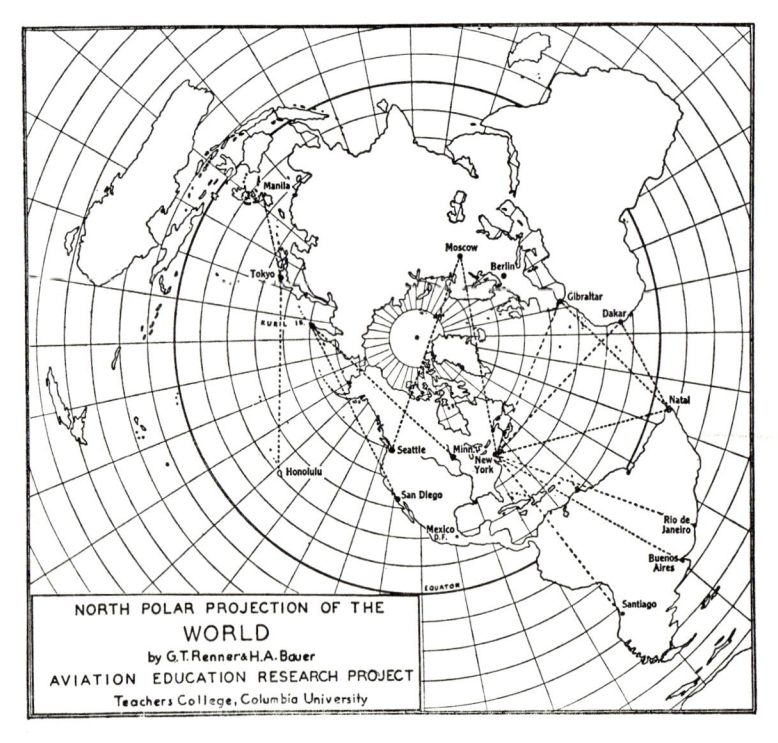

Fig. 8. A polar projection map.

Maps and Globes Are Our Business 61

uses of maps in the modern world are discussed and illustrated not only by the teacher but also by student activities. For example, the students collect maps from newspapers, advertisements, and business and note how each map is used. Students interview private individuals and those in industry to discover the need for, and use of maps. Then an intensive map-reading development program should be followed. The teacher may develop the exercises for such a program or use a map-reading workbook or text.[17]

Two new maps are introduced in the high school, one being the polar projection map. This map was introduced in the schools during World War II, then, following the war, it was neglected until 1956 when numerous expeditions were sent to Antarctica. At that time the United States and Canada were building radar installations in northern Canada and Greenland, and the Scandinavian airlines began regular commercial flights across the Arctic. These events resulted in a revival of interest in the polar projection map.

The topographic map made and published by the United States Geological Survey should be introduced and used in connection with local community studies. The introduction of the topographic map requires the teaching of new map symbols, including contour lines that indicate elevation and slope.

In the high school the concept of great circle routes should be developed. An understanding of these is necessary in studying ocean and air routes. The use of air transportation involves changes in relative location. Places formerly isolated are now important as air transportation routes girdle the globe. Much practice in tracing great circle routes on a globe from one point to another is necessary if the student is to gain an understanding of them.

Much functional map-making should be done in the high school. A study of the local community or an important local industry should include the making of a number of maps based on field work. High school teachers of geography and social studies have

---

[17] Mamie Anderzhon, *Steps in Map Reading* (Chicago, Rand McNally and Co., 1949).

found that the mapping of the home town is a valuable learning activity.[18]

The high school student should be encouraged to use sketch maps to illustrate points not only in geography but in history classes, science, and even in literature classes. Many students who have difficulty in expressing their ideas or explaining a point in words can do so with a sketch map.

In summary, the basic map skills to be learned by high school students are:

1. Ability to read all the commonly used map symbols representing both physical and cultural features.

2. Ability to read descriptive facts from regional maps and world distribution maps.

3. Ability to draw inferences or raise questions from a comparison of two or more maps or from two or more descriptive facts on a map.

4. Ability to use latitude and longitude for location.

5. Ability to use the latitude of a region or a country and its location in relation to land and water bodies to make inferences concerning its climatic conditions.

6. Ability to read large-scale sectional maps of cities, harbors, and special areas, and to locate such a large scale map on a small scale map of a country or continent. (Such large scale sectional maps are used frequently in newspapers to spot important places.)

7. A sufficient understanding of projection as to be able to understand the advantages and disadvantages of those more commonly used.

8. An understanding that maps may be distorted deliberately and used for propaganda purposes. A cartographer, making a map to create a wrong impression, uses special symbols. He uses lines and arrows to focus attention on a minor point, thus giving it false importance. He may use large-scale pictorial symbols or exaggerate the size of areas by the use of color. He may omit scale, direc-

[18] Margaret Stowell, "A High School Class Surveys Its Town," *Journal of Geography*, Vol. 41 (May, 1942), pp. 179–185.

tion, lines, roads, or other details so that one has no basis for comparison.

9. An understanding that many current events or situations cannot be correctly assessed unless the scene is located on a map and studied in its relationships to other areas of the world.

10. An understanding of a polar map and its usefulness under specific circumstances.

CONTRIBUTIONS MAPS CAN MAKE IN DEVELOPING A UNIT

In developing a unit in geography the teacher can use maps effectively at every stage. In fact, if the geographic region, area, or topic is to become meaningful to the child maps are essential. In the final analysis a person's geographic knowledge will consist in the ability to relate facts and places. Such relationships can be developed only by the use of maps and globes.

Introducing a Unit

Beginning in the fifth grade, physical-political maps and distribution maps may be used to introduce a unit. For example, a unit on Canada may be introduced with a study of the physical-political map of Canada or a population map. Ask the pupils where most of the people in Canada live. They can read the population distribution easily from the population map but they can also read such facts from the physical-political maps by the location and distribution of the cities. After noting how the Canadian population is concentrated in the southeastern and southern parts of Canada, the question arises as to why this is true, and why such large areas of Canada have so few people living in them. The pupils may also note that the railroad pattern is related to the population distribution, but the reason for the population distribution is still unanswered. Call attention to the latitude of Canada and ask what this suggests as to a possible reason for the population distribution. At this point, a growing season map may be examined to check their probable suggestion that temperature and the length of winter may be factors explaining in part the population distribution. As the class studies the map other points will be noted, such as the relation of the population distribution to the St. Lawrence River and to the lower Great Lakes.

The maps suggest only a few reasons for the population distribution, but the textbook should supply other related factors, all of which should be verified.

A map study of the northeastern states may be used with such questions and directions as follows:

> On the outline map on which you have colored other parts of the United States, color the eight northeastern states. As you look at the map of the United States what differences do you notice between the northeastern states and the other groups of states? What does the large number of cities suggest to you? Look at the population map and the map showing the distribution of cities. Do these maps verify your suggestions? Count the number of cities in the northeastern states that have a population of more than 100,000. Compare this number with the number of cities of that size in each of the other groups of states which we have studied. Now, what definite statement can you make about the population of the northeastern states. What question does this suggest? (Why are there more large cities and more people in this section?)

Beginning in the sixth grade and on through junior and senior high school a map or a series of maps may be used in a unit introduction. There are three steps in finding the story a map tells.

The first step is to guide the students in reading the descriptive facts from the map. As the class gives these, they should be listed on the board. These are descriptive facts concerning location, surface features, water bodies, cities indicating population distribution, transportation, and so forth.

The second step is making inferences from these facts. For instance, opposite the latitude state inferences concerning climate which may suggest possible crops. For example, use the area of southeastern Asia—Siam, Indo China, and Malaya—defined by latitude 0° to 20°N. The inference to be drawn regarding climate is a high temperature all year and probably much rain. Reading the descriptive facts concerning topography, noting the large river

Maps and Globes Are Our Business

valleys, and associating these with probable climate suggests that rice is probably an important crop. Continue until the class has listed all the information possible from the map, and have them suggest as many inferences as they can.

The third step is to verify information and inferences by reading the textbook, references, and also by consulting additional maps. This third step completes the development of the unit. Such a map study gives a reason for reading the textbook.

In introducing a study of Argentina, maps of Argentina and the United States may be compared including physical-political maps, rainfall, growing season, crop, and livestock distribution maps.

In high school a study of the world production and commerce in wheat, for instance, may be introduced by a study of a world map showing distribution of wheat production. Then compare this map with world seasonal rainfall maps, a growing season map, a physical map, and finally a map of the trade in wheat. Some interesting facts may be noted and inferences made.

Map-reading and map-making can be used at every stage in the development of a unit. Catherine Cox taught Africa by guiding a junior high school class through a series of map-making and map-reading activities.[19] Alvin V. Burgess tells how a high school class studied Australia by reading and interpreting a series of maps.[20] Other teachers have used the same technique in the study of Australia in the sixth and seventh grades.

Assimilation or Problem-Solving

In the assimilation or problem-solving stage in the development of a unit, the map is used chiefly as a source of information. The teacher should give the class specific map questions to guide them as they study. During class discussions the teacher should use the map and see that the students use the appropriate maps whenever they are needed. During the discussion of a city, an area, a river,

---

[19] Catherine E. Cox, "Teaching Africa by Regional Map Making," *Journal of Geography*, Vol. 39 (December, 1940), pp. 362-364.
[20] Alvin V. Burgess, "The Use of Maps in Developing Geographic Personalities," *Journal of Geography*, Vol. 40 (February, 1941), pp. 57-64.

or other important landscape feature, see that the students recognize the symbol and can locate it specifically and in relation to other important features.

Summary and Application

At this stage in the development of a unit, the making of maps is of great value for individual or group work. For example, three boys in an eighth grade summarized on a map their learning concerning the production of cotton in the southern states. The teacher supplied them with a large outline wall map of the United States.[21] On this map the boys drew the 200-day growing season line, the 20-inch isohyet, or rainfall line, and the 50-inch isohyet because along the Gulf Coast where the annual rainfall is more than 50 inches little or no cotton is raised. They indicated by means of a light color the whole cotton raising region, then by a deeper shade indicated the three most productive areas. They used special symbols to represent interior cotton collecting cities, exporting ports, textile centers, and the railroads that transport cotton. On small outline maps placed below the large map they made a rainfall distribution map, a soil distribution map, and a population distribution map. In making these maps, the boys reviewed maps in their textbook and in an atlas, and found statistics on the movement of cotton in the collecting and exporting cities.

Another activity is having the class find three maps which can be used to bring out the relationship between the raising of sheep and the location of irrigated areas in the western United States. Another is asking the class what maps may be used in developing the relationship between the raising of hogs and the raising of corn in the United States.

Following the study of a country or region, another map activity suitable for either individual or group work is making a large sketch map of a river or some special area of importance. For example, a student selects the Rhine River, and draws a large sketch map to show the course of the river, its main tributaries, cities,

[21] Such maps on heavy paper may be purchased from any map company for thirty-five to fifty cents.

and other important landscape features. Around the margin of the sketch map the pupil places sketches or pictures of scenes illustrating man's activities on the river or along the river valley.

The development of a current-event map during the study of a unit is worthwhile. For example, a class which was studying Mexico watched the newspapers for interesting and worthwhile items about Mexico. As these were clipped and brought in, they were discussed and then placed on the margin of a large outline map of Mexico which the teacher had placed on the bulletin board. The place where the event took place was located and marked on the map and a line drawn from the account of the event to the place where it occurred. The class gained a feeling that Mexico was a real place and learned the names and locations of many places not mentioned in their text. Whenever the pupils had any free time a group would be at the map rereading the items or discussing some items of particular interest.

Testing

There are a number of ways of using maps to test map-reading skills. Emily V. Baker gives a method of testing children's ability to use maps by constructing a series of questions on the textbook maps of Europe and Asia.[22] Grace Jessop describes another method in which a hypothetical map (see Fig. 9) is used to test the children's ability.[23]

In testing for location the teacher should use outline maps, numbering the city symbols and lettering rivers and other water bodies. The pupils are given the outline maps with a mimeographed sheet containing the numbers and letters and then asked to make the identifications. Such a test tests recognition of location and is quickly graded.

The recognition of the distribution of crops, livestock, and other items may be tested by the use of uncaptioned maps. If more than one kind of distribution is shown, the different ones may be lettered. If a child, for instance, mixes corn distribution with sugar

After a number of the semipictorial map symbols have been taught and used for some time, the teacher should check the class' mastery of the symbols. Draw on the board or mimeograph a map of an imaginary land somewhat like the one adjoining.

Make a test similar to the following:
Directions: If the sentence is true, write YES for the answer. If the sentence is not true, write NO.

1. A is an island.
2. C is a lake.
3. A railroad connects 8 and 5.
4. You would travel west in going from 3 to 11.
5. A traveler landing at 3 would be going down stream to reach 2.
6. It is farther from 9 to 8 than it is from 5 to 6.
7. The city 9 is on a river.
8. City 8 is near a delta.
9. The figure 12 is near a peninsula.
10. The letter G is near a desert.
11. River L is a tributary.

Directions: In each of the following sentences you have three answers suggested. Only one in each question is correct. Underline the correct answer.

12. The place 11 is connected to 3 by:
    a. A river
    b. A road
    c. A railroad

13. City 2 is
    a. on the seacoast
    b. on a river at falls
    c. on a peninsula

14. 10 is near:
    a. A delta
    b. A cape
    c. An island

15. F is placed west of:
    a. A fiord coast
    b. A river
    c. A bay

16. You would be on water at:
    a. K
    b. 10
    c. E

17. C is:
    a. An island
    b. A lake
    c. A river

18. A boat going from 9 to 8 would be going
    a. downstream
    b. upstream
    c. north

Pictures and the numbered or lettered map symbols could be matched in order to check their visualization of the map symbols. Other map symbols familiar to the class could be added.

A. J. *Nystrom* Co.

Fig. 9. An example of a hypothetical map.

cane or rice on a map of the United States, the teacher knows that the child does not know the climatic conditions required by each, or else cannot read latitude.

Special Problems

The use of maps in teaching the blind is a problem seldom touched on. John C. Sherman is doing research on this problem.[24]

Training slow learners how to read maps is another challenge to teachers. Jessie Asa describes the four steps in introducing a slow learning group to the map, and also how she met the problem of teaching direction. The chronological ages of the group ranged

[22] Emily V. Baker, "Diagnosing Children's Ability to Use Maps," *Journal of Geography*, Vol. 37 (September, 1938), pp. 227–231.
[23] Grace Jessop, "A Map for Diagnostic Purposes," *Journal of Geography*, Vol. 37 (March, 1938), pp. 112–114.
[24] John C. Sherman, "Maps the Blind Can See," *Journal of Geography*, Vol. 54 (September, 1955), pp. 289–295.

from eight to thirteen; their mental ages varied from five to nine years. As she says, "The making and reading of maps by an immature group can be developed through working out an introductory unit on where we live in relation to our school, and the things we see along our way to school."[25]

THE USE OF THE GLOBE

At one time a globe was to be found in every schoolroom. What fun children had playing with it—finding places about which they had read or heard, noting unusual names, tracing the outlines of land masses! In a sense they were exploring the world, learning even though they thought they were playing. Then, for some reason, the globe disappeared from our classrooms. Maps were used in its place, but they never had the same fascination as the globe. Children began to have wrong ideas concerning the relative position of countries, continents, islands, and even cities, for only the globe gives a true conception of relative position and direction. They held many other erroneous concepts of world relations because they were unfamiliar with the globe.

If a correct conception of world relationships is to be gained, one must have a globe. The globe is the best representation of the earth that we have. On it the meridians and parallels are in correct relation, the scale of distance is the same in all directions, and areas are represented correctly in their relation to each other. Consequently, the globe is an essential tool of instruction in the social studies, especially in geography and history.

The Primary Grades

Every schoolroom, even in the primary grades, should have a globe. The globe for the primary groups should be relatively simple to enable the children to become familiar with the water bodies and land masses. No formal teaching should be done, but the children's questions should be answered.

In the fourth grade the children should be taught to use the

[25] Jessie Asa, "Maps and Slow Learners," *Journal of Geography,* Vol. 50 (April, 1951), pp. 145–149.

globe just as they are taught to use a textbook and other tools. They should locate on the globe the areas which they study in the various units. Their attention should be directed to the size of the region in relation to the world as a whole, its relative position, and its location in respect to the equator. Direction on the globe should be taught. Rotation and some of the results of rotation should be illustrated with a light and the globe. Direction and length of noonday shadow can be illustrated by using a flashlight and fastening a series of thumbtacks on the globe at different distances from the equator, for instance at the tropics, at 40° north, at 40° south, and at the circles. The thumbtacks should be fastened heads down with masking tape at each of the above points along one meridian on the globe. By pointing the ray of the flashlight directly on the thumbtacks that marks the place where the equator crosses the meridian, the teacher can show that when it is midday there, the length of the shadow increases at the other points to the north and to the south of the equator.

By the end of the fourth grade the children should have: (1) the ability to recognize the equator, the tropics, the arctic and antarctic circles, the continents, and the oceans; (2) the ability to read directions; and (3) the ability to read comparative location in respect to the equator, to either of the tropics, and to the circles or the poles. They should be able to read the same symbols they have learned to read on maps. Also by the end of the fourth grade, from the facts which they read from a globe, the children should be able to make certain inferences such as: (1) the approximate length of the day, the sun position, and the noonday shadow at any given place; (2) the possible climatic conditions that may be expected from the location of a given place; and (3) the human activities which are related to length of day, temperature conditions, and seasonal changes.

The Intermediate Grades

In most schools, North America is studied in the fourth grade. At this point, teachers are likely to neglect the globe and concen-

Maps and Globes Are Our Business 71

trate on the map of North America with the result that the children think of North America as an isolated land mass. At the beginning of the fifth-grade work, the globe should be used in the study of North America. The size and shape of the continent should be noted and compared with other continents. North America's location in respect to the other continents, to the adjoining water bodies, to the equator, the tropics, and the Arctic Circle should be noted and the significance of these facts discussed. In brief, these introductory lessons with the globe should help the children see North America in its world locational relations.

Similarly, as the class studies the various regions of the United States, Canada, Mexico, and Central America, the globe should be used in the introductory discussion. By this time the children should be able to point out significant facts concerning the location of South America and make many inferences without much help from the teacher. Children enjoy such exploratory work because they feel that they are making discoveries for themselves. Later they should verify their inferences through reading and the study of a variety of maps.

In the sixth grade as Europe, Asia, Africa, and other lands are studied, the same general procedure should be followed. When the children have completed the sixth grade, they will be able to visualize the earth with the continents in their relative locations to each other and the large water bodies. They will also understand something of the significance of location—what a specific location suggests in respect to climate and accessibility to the world's developed regions.

Junior and Senior High School

The globe is essential in the junior and senior high schools, where world patterns are developed. Correct concepts of world climate, trade, transportation, and production patterns can be developed only through constant use of globes—a physical globe, a political globe, and a slated or project globe. On the slated or project globe, the children can build their own world patterns. In junior high school, rotation and revolution should be demonstrated with explanation and discussion. Great-circle routes can best be explained by demonstration with a globe.

Not all possible uses of the globe have been touched on, but space does not permit further discussion. Do not leave the globe on a shelf to gather dust while the children garner a mass of erroneous ideas concerning world relationships. If the teacher depends entirely upon maps the world will not be One World to them but a flat patchwork of isolated land masses separated by large water bodies. Even their ideas of direction and size may be distorted; for example, it might appear to them from a map that South America is south of North America, rather than southeast; North America is far larger than Africa; Europe is not a peninsula of Asia but a land mass almost as large as North America; the Arctic Ocean is not a sea surrounded by land bodies but a long narrow body of water touching North America on one side and dropping off into space on the opposite side.

William S. Miller sums up the need for maps and the necessity of teaching map-reading and interpretation as follows:[26]

> Man found it necessary to use maps because words alone were failing to provide the images required for clear understanding. The key to the successful *use* of maps and globes is through the development of a mental image of such strength that it remains fixed in the minds of the students—something which provides a logical, meaningful background for the written and spoken word. . . . There must be something concrete on which the whole structure rests, not something that is transitory in appearance, but something that is present before the class all of the time. One cannot have good mental image maps without having made frequent use of actual maps. The mental map is the framework on which much valuable subsequent knowledge can be organized or oriented. . . . We must remember that everything which is or happens involves a real place and has a relationship to other real places, finds its best, its *natural* expression in the map or globe. These indispensable, though silent, visual teaching aids ask only that the teacher bring to them the same imaginative qualities, the same drama, the same willingness to use

[26] William S. Miller, "The How of Map and Globe Use," *Audio-Visual Guide*, Vol. 15 (October, 1948), pp. 26–29.

Maps and Globes Are Our Business

them for class experiences and activities, the same dignity, that the rest of the group learning processes provide. When full abilities in learning to read maps and globes have been acquired, and an appetite created to read more and more, reading maps to learn will indeed become a highly profitable experience. Let's look at the map. See what it tells us.

REFERENCES

AHNER, B., "Our Own Globe," *School Arts*, Vol. 52 (May, 1953), pp. 320–321.

ANDERZHON, Mamie L., *Steps in Map Reading* (Chicago, Rand McNally & Co., 1955).

———, "The Child Looks Upon the Map," *Journal of Geography*, Vol. 53 (September, 1954). pp. 238–242.

———, "Writing Our Own Map Language," *Journal of Geography*, Vol. 45 (January, 1946), pp. 35–38.

———, "What Is in the Mile Behind an Inch on a Globe or Map?" *Journal of Geography*, Vol. 44 (October, 1945), pp. 288–294.

ASA, Jessie, "Maps and Slow Learners," *Journal of Geography*, Vol. 50 (April, 1951), pp. 145–149.

BACON, H. P., "Making a Pace Map—An Activity for the 5th and 6th Grades," *Journal of Geography*, Vol. 53 (May, 1954), pp. 203–207.

BAKER, E. F., "Diagnosing Childrens' Ability to Read Maps," *Journal of Geography*, Vol. 37 (September, 1938), pp. 227–231.

BARTON, Thomas F., "Teaching Geography with Globes," *Education*, Vol. 45 (January, 1945), pp. 312–315.

BOLGE, G. R., "Flannel Maps: An Activity in Fifth Grade," *Journal of Geography*, Vol. 51 (September, 1952), pp. 236–237.

BOSTICK, M. L., "Best World Map—The Globe," *School Science and Mathematics*, Vol. 40 (April, 1940), pp. 324–325.

BOWMAN, I., *Geography in Relation to the Social Sciences* (New York, Charles Scribner's Sons, 1934), Ch. II, "Measurement in Geography."

BURGESS, Alvin V., "The Use of Maps in Developing Geographic Personalities," *Journal of Geography*, Vol. 40 (February, 1941), pp. 57–64.

COLESON, E., "Teaching Locational Geography on the Elementary Level," *Journal of Geography*, Vol. 51 (April, 1952), pp. 147–151.

COX, Catherine E., "Teaching Africa by Regional Map-Making," *Journal of Geography*, Vol. 39 (December, 1940), pp. 362–364.

DAY, P., "Making Geographic Symbols for Rivers Signify Reality," *Journal of Geography*, Vol. 42 (April 1943), pp. 145–148.

EISEN, E. E., "Maps and Graphs as Tools in Teaching Geography,"

School Science and Mathematics, Vol. 32 (March, 1932), pp. 302–313.

FULLER, K. A., "Developing Map Reading Skills for Global Emphasis," *Journal of Geography,* Vol. 42 (September, 1943), pp. 216–220.

GARLAND, John H., "The Superior School Giant Globe: An Elementary School Activity Project," *Journal of Geography,* Vol. 41 (December, 1924), p. 328.

GREGORY, W. M., "Maps in Community Studies," in W. H. Hartley, ed., *Audio-Visual Materials and Methods in the Social Studies,* Eighteenth Yearbook (Washington, D.C., National Council for Social Studies, 1947), p. 131.

HANSON, R. M., "Locating Places is a Skill," *School Science and Mathematics* Vol. 53 (April 1953), pp. 309–312.

HOWE, George F., "The Teaching of Directions in Space," *Journal of Geography,* Vol. 31 (May, 1932), pp. 207–210.

ILLINGWORTH, Audrey, "An Approach to Map Reading," *Geography,* Vol. 31 (June, 1946), pp. 53–58.

JAMES, Linnie B., "The Teaching of Hypothetical Maps," *Journal of Geography,* Vol. 50 (December, 1951), pp. 361–366.

JESSOP, Grace, "A Map for Diagnostic Purposes," *Journal of Geography,* Vol. 37 (March, 1938), pp. 112–114.

JONES, E. L., "Relation of Mapping to Modern Civilization," *Science,* N.S. Vol. 63 (May, 1928), pp. 535–538.

KOHN, Clyde, and Associates, "Interpreting Maps and Globes," Ch. VIII, *Skills in Social Studies,* Twenty-fourth Yearbook (Washington, D.C., National Council for the Social Studies, 1953).

KOHN, Clyde, "Maps as Instructional Aids in the Social Studies," in W. H. Hartley, ed., *Audio-Visual Materials and Methods in the Social Studies,* Eighteenth Yearbook (Washington, D.C., National Council for Social Studies, 1947).

McDAVITT, N., "Map Pre-tests: Devices To Discover the Ability of Pupils To Interpret Maps," *Journal of Geography,* Vol. 44 (May, 1945), pp. 207–209.

MIKESELL, Ruth Weaver, "Geographical Activities Involving the Use of Maps and Graphs," *Journal of Geography,* Vol. 33 (March, 1934), pp. 105–113.

MOYER, Josephine, and Taylor, Frances E., "Introduction of the Map to Fourth Grade Children," *Journal of Geography,* Vol. 34 (September, 1935), pp. 249–252.

Maps and Globes Are Our Business 75

PICKLESIMER, P. W., "Map Needs for a Modern World," *Journal of Geography*, Vol. 53 (October, 1954), pp. 301–306.

QUAM, Louis O., "The Use of Maps in Propaganda," *Journal of Geography*, Vol. 42 (January, 1943), 21–32.

RENNER, George T., "Globe and Map," *Teachers College Record*, Vol. 47 (April, 1946), pp. 446–458.

———,"The Map as an Educational Instrument," *Social Education*, Vol. IV, No. 7, pp. 477–482.

SHERMAN, John C., "Maps the Blind Can See," *Journal of Geography*, Vol. 54 (September, 1955), pp. 289–294.

SHYROCK, Clara, "Gradations in Map Learning," *Journal of Geography*, Vol. 38 (May, 1939), pp. 181–187.

———, "Maps and Mapping in the Grades," *Journal of Geography*, Vol. 22 (October, 1923), pp. 265–274.

SORENSON, Frank, "The Influence of Specific Instruction on Map Interpretation," *Journal of Geography*, Vol. 35 (November, 1936), pp. 300–307.

STEPHENSON, O. W., "Drawing and Evaluating Maps," *Social Studies*, Vol. 25 (March, 1934), pp. 124–127.

STRATTON, C. G., "Fifth Grade Experiment in Mapping," *Journal of Geography*, Vol. 21 (November, 1922), pp. 302–305.

THRALLS, Zoe A., "Use of Maps in Geographical Instruction," *N.E.A. Journal*, Vol. 21 (December, 1932), pp. 301–302.

WADDLE, Thelma, "In One Inch on the Map," *School Science and Mathematics*, Vol. 40 (May, 1940), pp. 401–402.

WALKER, C. Lester, "How the War Maps Are Made" and "War Maps: Techniques and Secrets," *Harpers*, Vol. 189 (August and September, 1944), pp. 371–378.

WHIPPLE, Gertrude, and James, Preston E., "Instructing Pupils in Map Reading," *Social Education*, Vol. 11 (May, 1947), pp. 205–208.

WHITAKER, J. R., "Flat Maps Are Not Enough," *Nation's Schools*, Vol. 32 (October, 1943), p. 32.

WHITE, Helen M., "Diagramatic Map Making," *Journal of Geography*, Vol. 32 (September, 1933), pp. 242–244.

WIDER, Stella E., "Map Making," *Journal of Geography*, Vol. 31 (November, 1932), pp. 345–347.

WRIGHT, J. K., "Map Makers Are Human," *Geographical Review*, Vol. 32 (October, 1942), pp. 527–542.

———, "A list of Articles on Maps and Their Use in Geographic Education," *Journal of Geography*, Vol. 49 (October, 1950), pp. 288–300.

3

Pictures as Geographic Tools

ALL GEOGRAPHIC KNOWLEDGE of the world is the result of a study of the landscape. As Isaiah Bowman says: ... "it [geography] is also and chiefly a study of the living conditions of mankind as affected by regional combinations of specific soil types, climatic averages and extremes, vegetational resources and potentialities, and other environmental conditions, and landscape effects that give every area its characteristic stamp."[1]

Thus the actual landscape is the geographer's laboratory. If time and cost permitted, the ideal way to study a region would be for the class and teacher to go to a region to live in it and study it. Since such procedure is impossible, pictures may be used as a substitute. Of course pictures must be authentic and carefully selected, and the teacher must train and guide the pupils in reading and interpreting the pictures.

VALUE OF PICTURES

One of the chief values of pictures is to give meaning to language symbols and thus build a meaningful vocabulary. To vis-

[1] Isaiah Bowman, *Geography and the Social Sciences* (New York, Charles Scribner's Sons, 1934), p. 13.

Pictures as Geographic Tools

ualize and understand how people live in a region and why they live as they do, a student needs a large number of accurate ideas of the natural and cultural features characteristic of a particular region. Too often the teacher takes for granted that the child has these concepts, and then is dismayed by the errors made. Every teacher can cite numerous examples of such errors. The absolute necessity of developing accurate concepts is the basic reason for the use of pictures in teaching geography.

The proper use of pictures economizes both time and effort; it "can short-cut the learning process." As one reads, words must be translated into mental images. Each child's mental image is built from his own experience, consequently each child's mental image will differ. Furthermore, his mental image of the idea may be entirely erroneous. For instance if you ask a class to describe what they see when the word *cat* is mentioned, each one will describe the cat that he knows, and no two may be alike. If the word *rhea* is mentioned, no image results unless someone has seen such a bird or a picture of it. If you try to describe it, each child will build a mental image only partially correct, depending upon his background and his ability. An authentic and clear picture quickly gives the correct image which will be common to the class, thus saving time.

Another value of pictures is to stimulate thinking by providing a basis for thought and arousing questions. Often a child wants more information than the picture offers or some item or action in the picture arouses his curiosity.

Pictures stimulate interest in a topic. Such interest is aroused oftentimes because the picture gives reality and meaning to some concept that before had no meaning to the child. Neville V. Scarfe found that a child's emotional reaction to the geographic subject matter of a picture played a considerable part in stimulating interest through the use of pictures.[2]

[2] Neville V. Scarfe, "Testing Geographical Interest by a Visual Method," *Journal of Geography*, Vol. 54 (November, 1955), pp. 377–387.

Fig. 10. Isolated natural feature.

Fig. 11. View of natural landscape.

CRITERIA FOR THE SELECTION AND EVALUATION OF GEOGRAPHIC PICTURES

To be worthwhile in geographic education, pictures must be carefully selected for their value in developing vocabulary, geographic concepts, and understandings of geographic relationships. Using this general principle as a basis for evaluation, pictures useful for geographic instruction may be divided into three main groups: pictures of natural features and landscapes, pictures of cultural features and landscapes, and finally those of a natural-cultural landscape. All are of value, but the third group are the most worthwhile.

Natural Features and Landscapes

Such pictures may show only isolated natural features such as a mountain peak or a native plant. These pictures have limited teaching value but they aid in developing vocabulary and standardizing a needed specific concept. Others may show a natural landscape, but without any indication of man's activities or use of the land. If given guidance, from such a picture the student can gain knowledge of the topography, the climate, the plant and animal life, and the rock and soil of an area. He can draw inferences concerning relationships between the plant life and the topography and climate, and perhaps gain an idea of the relationship between certain land forms and the climate. These pictures may arouse a discussion as to why the land appears as it does or how man might use the land.

Cultural Features and Landscapes

These pictures may show isolated cultural features such as a temple, church, office building, or a machine. Such pictures have limited value but are useful in building vocabulary. For instance, the picture of a mosque makes the characteristic architecture of a mosque clear to the child thus giving visual imagery for the language symbol. It also suggests the Moslem religion. A view of a

Fig. 12. An aerial view of Buenos Aires showing the Casa Rosada (Pink Palace), where the President resides, in the center foreground, with the Plaza de Mayo immediately in back of it. In the foreground in front of the Palace is the monument to Christopher Columbus.

Panagra

Pictures as Geographic Tools 81

specific city not only helps the child to visualize that city but may suggest certain characteristics of the people, their activities, and stage of development. Such pictures also have value in making comparisons of cultures and raising questions as to why differences exist.

Views of the interiors of factories have almost no value unless they show processes. Exterior views are of some value for the factory or mill may have certain external characteristics which are a key to the industry. Then if such a building is seen in a landscape it suggests at least one activity of the people in a region.

Fig. 13. An exterior view of Masjid-I-Shah (Mosque of Shah) in Iran, showing the entrance, minarets, and part of the dome.

Fig. 14. A view of a natural-cultural landscape: a farmer plowing in Oregon.

Natural-Cultural Landscape

These pictures are of the highest geographic value. In such a picture either man's activity or signs of his activity are shown in the natural setting. Imagine a view of the Connecticut River Valley with the river and its wooded banks, forest-covered mountains in the distance, farmhouses, fields of tobacco covered with white cloth to shade the precious plants, one or more long tobacco sheds near each farmhouse, and also carefully cultivated fields of other crops. In such a view one instantly recognizes intensive agriculture, evidently profitable judging from the farmhouses and other buildings. The green of the fields, the crops, and the forest suggest an abundance of moisture and fertile soil. Such a picture presents a landscape in which man's relation to his natural environment can be observed and analyzed. Furthermore, it gives meaning to language symbols descriptive of the valley and also helps to give reality to the map symbols for the river and valley.

Pictures as Geographic Tools

In addition to the geographic qualities of pictures the teacher should consider their physical qualities. They should be large if possible, clear and distinct, and correct in every detail. If the picture is artistic in composition, that is fine, but artistic composition must not be a substitute for authenticity or geographic quality. A picture may be beautiful but be of little use to the teacher of geography. A picture should also contain some objects by which comparisons of size may be made.

TECHNIQUES IN THE USE OF PICTURES

If pictures are to serve their purposes in geographic education, the teacher must train children to read pictures for geographic concepts. The teacher must select and use the picture or pictures for a definite purpose and at the proper time. He must employ specific techniques to guide the student.

The first step is to direct the child to the significant features or activity in the picture and ask him to name or enumerate them. If the significant feature or activity is new to him he is asked to compare it with something similar in his own environment. At this stage he is acquiring mental images from which concepts may be formed. For instance, at this stage a palm tree is merely a kind of tree, different in many ways from the trees with which he is familiar.

In the second step, the teacher has the child describe and explain what he sees. He begins to differentiate and to associate certain items. For instance, a palm tree is a certain kind of palm—a date palm or perhaps a coconut palm. The kind of palm tree suggests certain other facts. A date palm suggests an oasis, and the teacher directs his attention to or he notices other items in the picture that confirm or contradict this inference. He begins to think also in terms of the possible temperature and rainfall, and where the scene is.

The third step is interpretation. In this step the teacher guides the child in the interpretation of the significant items in the pictures, noting relationships between certain geographic facts. The teacher may use such questions as: "What items in this picture suggest much or little rainfall? Why? What is the kind of work shown in this picture? (Logging) How do you know? What items in the landscape suggest a reason for logging?" The questions should be as specific as possible to eliminate guessing.

The teacher should require the student to verify the information gained by the use of other pictures, maps, textbooks, and references. He should encourage questions from the children, especially "why" questions. In all cases the child must be the active agent in picture study.

The following general questions may assist the teacher in guiding students in the interpretation of pictures. A teacher should modify the question or questions to suit the particular picture and the child's level of ability. Because children enjoy a puzzle element and often like to play detective, the word *clue* is used instead of the word *item*.

> What clues in a picture will tell you about the rainfall? the temperature? the season of the year?
> What clues suggest the fertility of the land?
> What clues in a picture give you an idea of the economic development of the country?
> What clues suggest whether a farm is prosperous or not?
> What clues may tell you in what country a picture is taken?
> What clues suggest the standard of living of the people?
> What reasons are suggested by this picture as to why people are doing this particular type of work here?
> Do you think this region is densely, moderately, or sparsely populated? Why? What appears to be the major economic activity or activities? Why?

USING PICTURES IN THE DEVELOPMENT OF A UNIT

Pictures may be used (*a*) for introducing or motivating a unit, (*b*) for detailed study in the assimilation or problem-solving stage, (*c*) in the summarizing and reviewing step, (*d*) in the application step, and (*e*) in testing.

Pictures as Geographic Tools

Introducing a Unit

In introducing or motivating a unit, pictures may serve as a means of orienting the class in the new region and in developing a concept that is needed immediately. For instance, in a study of Norway the idea of a fiord and a fiord farm and the map symbol for a fiord are needed. Three pictures can be used effectively to develop the idea and the map symbol: (1) a view of the entrance of a fiord showing the very high, steep sides; (2) a scene inside the fiord showing a small farm, farm house, and other buildings clinging to a narrow shelf of land, perhaps a tiny field; (3) another fiord view similar to the second but with more cultivated land. Through questions and discussion the idea of a fiord can be developed. At the same time, the pictures should be related to the way a fiord is represented on a map. Then the class will be able to visualize what those deep irregular indentations of the Norwegian coast represent. Also as they read about the fiords, fiord farms, and life on a fiord farm, they can visualize the scenes and the words will become more meaningful.

Another method of using pictures is comparing a new region with one previously studied. For this ten or twelve pictures may be needed. The pictures should be selected to show the outstanding characteristics and activities of the region. An example of this use is the following. The class has studied the Congo region and is now ready to study the Nile Valley. The teacher selects the following scenes, (1) a view of Cairo, (2) a village, (3) a farm house, (4) a man raising water from the river to irrigate a field, (5) a river scene with boats, (6) plowing with oxen, (7) making clay bricks, (8) a date garden, (9) herding sheep, (10) tents of the nomads, and (11) a camel caravan. If the teacher has slides, the class may work together. The class is asked to make two lists as they look at the pictures. One list is of the items that they have seen along the Congo, the other list is of new items. After the pictures are shown, the lists are discussed, and the differences noted. Many questions are bound to come up. "Why are the houses so different?

What is the man doing?" There may be a good many "what" questions as well as some "why" questions. Some of the "what" questions should be answered at once. The "why" questions should motivate the reading of the text and the study of other pictures.

If the teacher does not have slides but has a good set of flat pictures, he can place them around the walls of the room at a height suited to the children. Number each picture. Divide the class into eleven groups and have group number one go to Picture 1, and so on, allowing two or three minutes for each group to study its picture and make its list, then at a signal pass to the next picture. Because this plan requires more time, the discussion probably will be left for the following day.

The "why" questions of the class should be listed so that they may be available to guide the study. In addition the teacher may wish to add or suggest some questions. During the discussion of the picture the teacher has the opportunity to develop new terms and check the pupils' understanding of words which they should know. Through such a picture study and discussion, the pupils are prepared to attack the reading material and have a motive for reading.

Another method of using pictures to introduce a unit is illustrated in the following lesson on the Pacific Coast States—California, Oregon, and Washington. Either slides or a set of flat pictures may be used. If flat pictures are used the teacher should place them around the room about three feet apart. In addition to the general suggestions he gives to the class, he attaches any special questions or suggestions to the individual pictures. The teacher divides the class into groups and has them take their textbooks with them in order to use the map. If slides are used the textbook is kept open at the map.

The pictures used were: (1) A logging scene in Washington; (2) seining for salmon on the lower Columbia; (3) irrigating an orange grove in southern California; (4) canning peaches; (5) a petroleum field; (6) the High Sierras from Yosemite Park; (7) a waterfront scene at Seattle.

Pictures as Geographic Tools

DIRECTIONS TO THE CLASS: Draw three columns on a blank sheet of paper. At the top of the first column write, "Kind of Work"; at the top of the second column write, "Possible Reasons"; at the top of the third column write, "Notes or Questions." As you study each picture, note and follow any map directions or other questions. (If slides or textbook pictures are used, the teacher can give the questions and directions orally.)

PROCEDURE:

Picture 1. This scene was taken in Washington. Fill in the first and second column. In the third column answer this question: "What does the picture suggest to you concerning the rainfall in this part of Washington?"

Picture 2. On the map of the Pacific Coast States, find the Columbia River. Where is its source? Across what state does it flow? Between what two states does it form the boundary? This picture was taken on the lower Columbia. Fill in the first and second columns. In the third column answer these questions: "What do you see in this picture that you also saw in number one? What is suggested concerning the amount of rainfall?"

Picture 3. In Southern California, locate Los Angeles. Using the scale of miles, measure 50 miles east. Here is the city of Redlands. Your map may have it. If it does not, you have the approximate location. This picture was taken near Redlands. Fill in your first and second columns. Now, in the third column, answer these questions: "What does the picture suggest concerning the rainfall in southern California? Why do you think so? What does it suggest concerning the temperatures during the year? Why?"

Picture 4. On your map find the large valley in central California. What is the name of the valley? In the southern half of the valley, find the city of Fresno. Have you ever heard of Fresno in connection with any other product? (Some of the class may have heard or seen the name in connection with raisins or other fruit. If they haven't, do not tell them, but ask them to keep the question in mind.) This picture was taken in a little town about 40 miles south of Fresno. Fill in the first two columns. In the third column answer these questions: "Upon what other kind of work is the industry shown here dependent? What, then, must be one kind of work carried on in the Great Valley of California?"

Picture 5. This picture may be a puzzle to some of you, although I suspect that most of you will recognize this kind of work. This scene could have been taken near Los Angeles or in the southern part of the Great Valley. Fill in the first two columns.

Picture 6. What is in this picture? This picture was taken in Yosemite National Park, looking toward the High Sierras. On your map find the Sierra Nevada Mountains. Find Yosemite National Park. Scenes different from this, but as beautiful, may be seen in many places in California, Oregon, and Washington. Now, write in your first and second columns what this scene suggests to you. In your third column, answer this question: "Are the Sierra Nevada Mountains very high?" State a reason for your answer.

Picture 7. Fill in the first and second columns. This picture was taken on the waterfront at Seattle, Washington. Find Seattle on your map. On what body of water is Seattle? With what ocean is it connected? Study your map to see if there are other cities in these states in which you might see similar water front scenes?

Now, we shall discuss our lists. How many kinds of work have you listed? What reasons are suggested by the pictures for each kind of work?

The teacher and class may continue the discussion, noting what they have learned from the pictures and the map concerning the work of the people, the land, and the climate, and also listing questions that should be followed up.

A general or reconnaisance survey is somewhat similar to the lesson on the Pacific Coast states, except that a larger number of pictures, perhaps as many as fifteen or twenty, are used. This is one of the few instances when it is legitimate to introduce a fairly large number of pictures, at one time. However, these pictures must be chosen with care to emphasize the most important natural and cultural characteristics of the region. There should be a number of pictures to illustrate the leading occupations and containing enough of the natural environment to suggest reasons for these activities. The location of the scene of the picture should be given in order to help the child associate the various activities with specific parts of the country or region. A map of the region should be referred to frequently.

During the discussion in an upper grade the teacher should raise the question, "What impression did the picture or pictures give you concerning the density and distribution of the population? Why?" Check the answers with a population map.

In such a survey a film may be used effectively if it contains the necessary geographical material. However, before the film is shown, the teacher should prepare the class. He should trace the route or the places to be seen on a map with the class, and discuss what the map suggests concerning the topography and the places. He should suggest factors that the class should look for as they watch the film such as topography, work activities, methods of farming or other work, crops, products, the people, the appearance of villages, houses, roads, means of transportation, and the like.

Assimilation or Problem-Solving

The motivation or introduction of a unit should move so smoothly into the assimilation or problem-solving stage that the two merge. After the problem has been raised as to why the people are carrying on specific types of activities in a region, have the students use the picture during their study to discover some of the probable reasons and to secure specific information. At this point they should be reading the picture for definite information just as they read textual material to solve a problem. As Hile states,[3]

It is during the study period that pictures other than those found in books can also be used effectively. If such pictures are to further learning, however, children must be given something definite to do with them. Every teacher, with a little practice, can write her own legends for these pictures. These captions might be written with the purpose of leading children to find relationships in the picture, developing new concepts, or checking relationships by means of a short objective test consisting of only two or three questions. Such as:

Fig. 1 (Developing Relationships). Can you find the land in the background where there is very little vegetation? This barren land is part of the desert of Palestine near the Dead Sea. Find the part of the picture where crops are growing. What must there be here that enables plants to grow? The trees in the foreground are banana trees. What do

[3] Martha Jane Hile, "The Use of Photographic Material in the Teaching of Geography," *Journal of Geography*, Vol. 37 (February, 1938), pp. 56-57.

these trees tell you about the temperatures found here all year round? Can you find the home near the banana trees? Why are the roofs flat?

Fig. 2 (Developing Concepts). This picture shows olive trees growing on *terraces* outside the city wall of Jerusalem, Palestine. Terraces are level patches of land built by man on mountain slopes and hillsides. By building terraces, slopes can be farmed without danger of the soil washing away. Can you see what holds the soil of the terraces in place? What do the terraced slopes suggest about the amount of level land suitable for farming?

Fig. 3 (Checking Relationship Ideas). Draw a line around the correct answer. 1. The growing of olive trees tells you that: *a.* The winds are strong; *b.* the land is mountainous; *c.* the winters are cold; *d.* the rainfall is scarce.

Riley[4] describes how she uses a picture library during the assimilation stage. For a unit on Switzerland she selected about thirty good geographic pictures, mounted them, numbered each picture, and made a set of questions to be answered from the pictures and the captions. The questions were put on a sheet and together with the thirty pictures placed in a manila envelope. The following is a sample of her directions and questions which she used with a fifth grade:

SWITZERLAND

The best way to do this lesson is to look first at *all* the pictures and read over *all* the questions in order to get a general view of the lesson. For some questions you need give only the number of the correct picture. For the others you must give your answer and also the number of the picture where you found that answer. In some cases you may have to decide which of several pictures is the *best* to choose.

1. How do the mountains provide a means by which the Swiss can make a living?
2. Which of the mountain scenes interests you most?
3. List five types of transportation provided for the convenience and pleasure of travelers in Switzerland. For each give the number of a picture that is a good example of that type.
4. What feature of the train on the scenic mountain line is especially designed for sightseers?

[4] Norma Riley, "A Picture Library and Its Use," *Journal of Geography,* Vol. 37 (May, 1938), pp. 202–205.

Pictures as Geographic Tools

5. What is an advantage of electrified railroads in the long and numerous tunnels?
6. What country is most easily reached from Switzerland? What language would you expect to be spoken by most of the Swiss? What language second? Third? Trace a main railroad line of Europe that passes through Switzerland. What is it called? (Pictures included a transportation map bringing out the communications of Switzerland with the rest of Europe.)
7. How do the Swiss get along with no coal of their own?
8. You have learned that Swiss industries produce valuable products from small amounts of raw material. Complete the following table, giving the number of a suitable picture to illustrate each industry.
    a. Cotton + Swiss skill =
    b. Silk + Swiss skill =
    c. Wood + Swiss skill =
    d. Fine metals + Swiss skill =
9. Choose a picture to illustrate this statement from your textbook: "It is customary for the men and older boys to drive the cattle to the higher pastures and remain there for the summer."
10. Choose a picture to illustrate this statement: "Even the smallest areas of grass are carefully mowed and the hay gathered and stored for use in winter."
11. Give the numbers of the pictures that illustrate these steps in the cheese industry.
    a. Making the cheese high in the mountains
    b. The finished product
    c. Exportation to foreign countries
12. Examine the picture of the little chalet and tell which of the following statements are true:
    a. It is probably used only during the summer season.
    b. There are stones on its roof as a protection from winds, and to hold the snow for warmth.
    c. Most of the material for its construction was brought up the mountain from the valley below.
13. Find the picture that might be the interior of such a chalet.
14. Is it true or false that electrical power is available for even very small villages?
15. Is it true or false that Switzerland has a program of forest conservation?

16. In what part of Switzerland do most of the people live? (Pictures included a population map.)
17. What is the only waterway by which Swiss products can be shipped to the sea?
18. Find the picture that best illustrates each of the following:
    a. Timber line
    b. Alp
    c. Rhone Glacier
    d. Crevasse
    e. Matterhorn
    f. St. Bernard Hospice
    g. Simplon Tunnel
19. Name the city for each of the following:
    a. City of the League of Nations
    b. Fashionable winter sports center
    c. Well located on the Rhine
    d. Leading silk manufacturing center
    e. The capital
20. After looking at all the pictures which four of the following do you think would be the busiest in Switzerland?
    a. Superintendent of a steel mill
    b. Manager of a hotel
    c. Manufacturer of tractors and reapers
    d. Manufacturer of oil derricks
    e. Manufacturer of electrical equipment
    f. Manufacturer of arms and munitions
    g. Leader in international affairs
    h. Exporter of grain
    i. Importer of cacao

Summarization and Review

There are a number of ways of using pictures in summarizing and reviewing a unit. The following are some suggestions.

1. Select a set of pictures that illustrate what one would see traveling from the mouth of the Mississippi to its source. Number the pictures but not in the correct order. Have the students arrange the pictures in the correct order. This same idea may be used in following a certain route in a country.

2. Another method is to have a student, from a large number of

Pictures as Geographic Tools

pictures, select five or more that illustrate the outstanding work activities or characteristics of a region or country and explain his selection.

3. Individual reports using a slide or large picture will provide a starting point or center of interest. The class also should ask questions of the reporter and add worthwhile comments. If such pictures are well selected, the reports will constitute an excellent summary and review of the unit.

4. Another exercise is having individual students or the class compare pictures of the same activity taken in different regions and give reasons for likenesses or differences, for instance, a set of pictures showing dairying in Wisconsin, in the Netherlands, in Italy, in Switzerland, in Norway, or in New Zealand. The scenes should be characteristic of each country with features in the picture suggesting dairying and showing enough of the landscape. The student should recognize the country, and be able to explain his answer and discuss why dairying is important.

5. Each child is given an outline map of a continent or country. On the map are ten numbers which he is to match with ten pictures that illustrate the landscape features of the region.

All of the above exercises require large numbers of pictures, but excellent pictures from magazines, calendars, and advertisements are so abundant that any teacher should be able to accumulate a large and worthwhile file in a few years.

Application

The teacher should train the students to use the knowledge and skills which they have acquired in new situations. To plan worthwhile application exercises requires creative imagination and skill. Some of the activities suggested under summarization and review may be adapted by the use of new pictures.

Testing

The teacher can use pictures very effectively to test student's understanding of landscape features. Brockmeyer[5] tells how she used pictures in a test on the southern states. She used thirty-two pictures under each of which was printed three words or groups of words. Each child was given a sheet on which the thirty-two groups of words appeared. As he looked at each picture he checked his choice of the correct words. For example, one picture showed the winding course of a river, and under it were the words *delta–meandering–source*. Another picture tested their understanding of the steps in "growing cotton—seeding—chopping out—picking." Another tested the recognition of crops, and still another tested the time or season of a certain activity.

A true and false test can be made based on a set of pictures, with three to five statements for each picture. Another test is to have the students associate pictures with specific places or districts numbered on an outline map.

Understanding may be tested by making explanatory statements concerning a certain feature in the picture from which the student selects the best answers. For instance, a view in China showing a low thatched roof, mud house, a wooden plow drawn by oxen and a donkey, level land, and no trees paired with this statement, "A low standard of living is suggested by (1) the level land, (2) the wooden plow and mud house, (3) the absence of trees, and (4) the growing of crops.

Picture tests have four testing possibilities—(1) the ability to identify specific activities, (2) the ability to identify specific natural items, (3) the ability to recognize suggested relationships, and (4) the ability to associate specific regions on the map with typical scenes. As Brockmeyer says, "A picture appeals to the pupil. [For the teacher] It is easy to work, rapid to check, and gives him an opportunity to correct wrong impressions quickly. . . . If a class doesn't know something, pictures almost always tell you with rather embarrassing frankness. There are gratifying results, too,

[5] Irene Brockmeyer, "Testing With Pictures," *Journal of Geography*, Vol. 50 (February, 1951), pp. 54–57.

which are equally plain and which make the construction of a picture test well worth the effort."

SLIDES AND FILMS

Most of the discussion in this chapter has been on the use of flat pictures, either black and white or color reproductions, because such pictures are available to every teacher in such variety and abundance. Furthermore there are almost unlimited possibilities for their use by an ingenious teacher. Slides may be used in almost all the ways as the flat picture.

The film is limited in its usefulness. Some are suitable for introducing a unit and some may be used to present supplementary information. A film may add more meaning in some cases, especially if movement is desirable for understanding. The film probably is most useful to summarize and review a topic of study. For example, Loya and Newhouse[6] describe how they used a film on the banana industry to summarize facts already learned. The students were expected to watch for certain details. Mimeographed sheets of instructions and questions were given to the students for study in preparation for the film showing. After the film showing there was a discussion with many questions asked by the students.

In using a film, a discussion should always precede the film showing and also follow it. Before showing the film there should also be a map study so that the class knows *where* the scenes are taking place and has some ideas concerning the terrain. Any new words or concepts should be listed and called to the attention of the class. In some situations specific questions and directions should be given preceding the showing of the film so that the students will be looking for certain facts and ideas. Often it is worthwhile to show a film twice, first to introduce the unit and then later for review. At the second showing the teacher will find it in-

---

[6] Julia M. Loya and Lucille A. Newhouse, "The Use of Visual Aids in the Classroom," *Journal of Geography*, Vol. 48 (September, 1949), pp. 257–259.

teresting to ask the class how much more they learned from the film after their study of the country or region.

The following "Ten Commandments For Use of Films in the Classroom" should be observed by every teacher using films.[7]

TEN COMMANDMENTS FOR USE OF FILMS IN THE CLASSROOM

Note: These ideas are the author's; any similarity to already existent ideas is purely accidental, and any offense to others' opinion is regrettable.

FIRST COMMANDMENT:

Thou shalt not use any film not previewed by you.

SECOND COMMANDMENT:

Thou shalt always make and present a list of new vocabulary words to be explained before showing a film.

THIRD COMMANDMENT:

Thou shalt present all films as if they were reading lessons with objectives to be reached.

FOURTH COMMANDMENT:

Thou shalt not use a film in vain. Always follow a film with a discussion of the outline or points to be covered (as presented previously to the showing).

FIFTH COMMANDMENT:

Thou shalt not take the acquisition of vocabulary for granted. Vocabulary words should be used after each showing—either by discussion of the words as they were used in the film, or as a written exercise in summarizing points covered in the movie.

SIXTH COMMANDMENT:

Thou shalt not use the sound track if your own explanations are better or more simplified. Many commentaries of sound films are too technical or contain too high a level of vocabulary for average or below average classes. Yet these films are too good to be omitted.

[7] Permission for the use of these "Ten Commandments" given by Miss Mabel McGirr, North Bethesda Junior High, Montgomery County, Md.

Pictures as Geographic Tools

Previewing more than once may make it possible for you to pick out relationships, conditions, or facts that can point out geographical studies that the editor of the film did not choose to mention after all, many films were not meant specifically for geography. There are many examples of this.

SEVENTH COMMANDMENT:

Thou shalt not conclude that one showing of an excellent film is sufficient for maximum learning. In many cases, one showing is only enough to get the general gist of the ideas presented. A second showing insures finding points overlooked or only noticed in the first showing. In rare cases of a film packed with good information, a third showing is not amiss, for example, "Gift of Green."

EIGHTH COMMANDMENT:

Thou shalt not show an entire movie when only part of it is valuable. In previewing a film you may find that only one or two parts serve your purposes. In such a case, mark the outside reel with chalk or some other device and wind until that part is reached. If sections in the middle are to be omitted, discussion of the part shown can be held while the projector runs the film through to the next section shown. Turning off the lamp will eliminate the students' watching the screen instead of participating in discussion. Many times this is a way of getting past undesirable material.

NINTH COMMANDMENT:

Thou shalt not use class time to show any film unless it pertains to the subjects being studied at that time. In other words, give to Caesar what is his, and your classes only what they can use. Using a film that is not correlated with the work at hand, no matter how excellent it is, leads to the Saturday afternoon matinee idea of movies to the children. They should be guided into the idea that classroom movies are for educational not recreational purposes.

TENTH COMMANDMENT:

Thou shalt not use thy neighbor's time on a film. In using free films this is extremely important. Carelessness in returning a film may throw someone's else's schedule into confusion. It may also put you in the distributor's doghouse—no more films. The S.D.S.S. Approach for showing long pictures—or for use in below average classes:
1. Go through the procedure of vocabulary, presenting the outline or list of questions to be answered.

2. Show film through once—to get an over-all view of it as a unit.
3. Second showing—interrupt at propitious points in film.
   a. stop at intervals
   b. discuss vocabulary and relevant questions
   c. start again—stop—discuss—start—stop

In short:
STOP—DISCUSS—START—STOP

until film is ended. It is not different than the approach to a long involved reading or literature lesson, is it?

The following lesson, using the film "Green Harvest," is one used by Miss Mabel McGirr.

EXAMPLES OF PICTURE STUDY LESSONS
A Lesson for Use of the Film "Green Harvest."

FORESTRY

GREEN HARVEST (29 minutes)

Type: 16 mm color
Source: M.T.P.S.
Sponsor: Wilding Picture Production, Inc., for Weyerhauser Sales Co.

STUDY SHEET (EIGHTH GRADE)

Vocabulary words to be explained:

1. virgin forest
2. renewable resource
3. tree farming
4. increment borer
5. tallywacker
6. jammer
7. selective logging
8. seed block
9. green harvest
10. second-growth
11. reforestation
12. cambium layer
13. white pine blister
14. beetle
15. hemlock looper
16. tussock moth
17. annual rings
18. ponderosa pine
19. seedlings
20. entomologist
21. maturity
22. tree nursery
23. cultural practices
24. combat
25. mobile equipment
26. summit
27. alidade
28. strategically spaced
29. spores
30. eradicated
31. sustained timber production
32. skidder
33. "tree farmers deal in lifetimes"
34. flume

Pictures as Geographic Tools

(Omit the first part of the picture, for Junior High School students are not receptive to the honeymoon idea, although they would enjoy the bear scene.) Introduce the film by telling what occurs in the first part. Explain Uncle Ray's title of "entomologist."
What to look for:

1. What is an entomologist and what is his part in saving the forests?
2. We consider corn, apples, and other such plants as crops. Why do we consider timber a crop? What is the chief difference?
3. What is meant by tree farming?
4. Notice the differences in structure of the species of the trees in our Northwest.
5. In what two ways does reforestation take place?
6. What are the two chief causes of forest destruction?
7. How does climate make harvest methods differ?
8. A tree farmer practices "selective logging." What does this mean?
9. How does the forester decide which trees are to be cut? (maturity, increment borer, and tallywacker).
10. Notice the many kinds of machinery used in logging in this Northwestern region. (Point out that this wide use of machinery is not the case in all American regions.)
11. How does an entomologist help the tree farmer? (tussock moth, hemlock looper, beetle colonies of western pine, white pine blister).
12. Why is it necessary at times to cut all the trees in one area, leaving only a "seed block strategically spaced"? (To insure growth of only the Douglas Fir which is not as prolific as the hemlock but of more value.)
13. Can a tree suffer from "old age"? How can the forester decide which trees have reached maturity?
14. How can you as a student help save our forests?

TEST: GREEN HARVEST

Fill in with answers that you have learned from the film:

1. The chief difference between apples as a crop, corn as a crop, and timber as a crop is _____.
2. Cutting all of a Douglas Fir tract except for a seed block is done for what reason? _____.
3. Cutting only trees that are mature, to allow younger ones to mature, from year to year insures sustained timber production.

This is known as _____ logging.
4. A man who studies insects' habits is an _____.
5. An increment borer is not an insect. What is it? _____
_____.
6. Annual rings set closely together indicate _____
_____.
7. Three of the chief species of trees found in the Northwest are:
   a. _____
   b. _____
   c. _____
8. The man in the look-out tower uses an _____ to locate the exact position of a fire.
9. The fire tower is located on the _____ of the mountain.
10. The machinery rolled to the site of the fire is called _____ _____ equipment.
11. The ranger counts the trees to be cut on a _____.
12. Several insects which cause damage to trees are:
    a.   b.
13. What is meant by "the tree farmer deals in lifetimes"? _____
_____.
14. The beetle paths are found under the _____ layer of the tree.
15. White pine blister, or rust, is carried from tree to tree by the winds blowing the _____ of the rust.
16. Rust goes from trees to currant bushes, so that the forest ranger is _____ currant bushes to combat the disease.
17. Cutting trees, or deforestation, leads to the problem of _____ _____. (From discussion in class. No study of forests would be complete without mention of deforestation and conservation.)
18. There is little undergrowth in these dense forests. Why? _____ _____. (Discussion again, should bring out the point that foliage keeps sunshine at a minimum on the forest floor.)
19. Does the size of the trees reflect climatic conditions? _____ (Refer to windward slopes of our Northwest, and the mild marine climate on lower slopes)
20. How does selective logging benefit you? _____.
You may use your vocabulary lists for the words

Pictures as Geographic Tools 101

NOTES FOR THE TEACHER

1. This movie is a much better summarization than an introduction to a unit.
2. This is a film which deserves more than one showing. The S.D.S.S. approach is also suitable because of the length of the movie.
3. You may find with lower grades that the film can best be explained by you, but you must be thoroughly familiar with it first.
4. Every film naturally needs your help to make it thoroughly understood. The points in parenthesis contained in the test are examples of such help.
5. There is an excellent booklet sent with the film.

ILLUSTRATIVE UNITS

Introducing a Unit on Florida

The pictures used in this unit on Florida were mounted on separate pieces of paper and each picture was given a number. They then were placed around the room on a level with the children's eyes, with sufficient space between each picture to permit several children to gather in front of it. In this way the pictures were available to all at one time, with the least possible amount of confusion. Each child was given a number to correspond with the number on one of the pictures, and asked to number his paper for as many numbers as there were pictures. The children were told that when the signal was given they were to go to the picture bearing the number they possessed and examine the picture carefully, noting the important activity shown and any indications that helped explain why the activity was carried on. The name of the activity and any suggested reasons for the activity were written on their paper after the number corresponding with the number of his picture. After each child finished with the picture bearing his number, he moved to the right until all the pictures had been examined. When the children had finished they found it very interesting to interpret their findings. Some of the inferences they made as a result of the investigation were as follows:

1. Truck farming seems to be an outstanding activity of the people. Such things as tomatoes, potatoes, celery, and strawberries are grown.
2. Other agricultural scenes show that citrus fruits, tobacco, and sugar cane are grown.
3. There are some good natural pastures for the raising of cows.
4. Florida has many recreation centers near the ocean where people may rest and play.
5. Shipping is an important industry in Key West and Tampa.
6. Forests suggest the gathering of turpentine as well as logging and lumbering.
7. Some men make a living by gathering sponges.
8. Fishing is important near the coast.

If the child was sufficiently trained to ascertain why these activities are carried on, he was able to list a great number of natural features included in the pictures, such as:

1. Level land.
2. Forests suggesting abundance of rain.
3. Palm trees suggesting a very long growing season.

With the foregoing introduction, the children were led to raise some very worthwhile problems, the solution of which they found through a study of their textual materials, maps, graphs, and other pictures. Some of the problems raised by the children were the following:

1. Why do so many people in Florida engage in truck farming even though the state is many miles from the densely populated portion of the United States?
2. Why do many northerners spend their vacations in Florida?
3. Does Florida raise as much citrus fruit as California?

A Study of Norway

In introducing a unit on Norway the teacher used five slides showing the following scenes:

1. A fiord farm.
2. The harbor of Bergen, Norway showing the wharves.
3. Forested mountain slopes and lumber rafts on a lake in Norway.

Pictures as Geographic Tools

4. A fiord scene showing waterfalls.
5. Milking time at a saeter, Norway.

He directed the picture study with the following questions:

Figure 1 suggests an important kind of work done in Norway. What is it? Does your map help you understand why these farms are located on the mountain slopes? Can you find two things in the picture that help explain whether this region has sufficient rainfall for agriculture? Would you expect to find as much land that is good for farming in Norway as you found in France? Give some reasons that help explain your answer.

Figures 2 and 3 show two important kinds of work. What are they? In what part of Norway might Figure 2 have been taken? Why? What kind of work do the boats in the background suggest? What do you imagine will be done with the numerous boxes on the wharf? Does Figure 3 suggest any reasons that help explain why lumbering is being carried on in this region?

Figure 4 does not clearly show, but suggests, another industry that might be carried on in Norway. What do you notice on the mountainside in the background of the picture? How might the power of this waterfall be utilized? What industry, then, is suggested by a natural feature shown in this picture?

Figure 5 shows summer homes of the Norwegian herders. Can you suggest any reasons why the homes were built here? Does the picture tell you anything about the climate of Norway? What can you learn about the rainfall by examining the roofs of the houses? Do you think the two men are Norwegians? Can you suggest any reason why they are talking to the Norwegian girl? Do these visitors help you suggest another way in which some of the people make a living? As you glance over the five pictures make a list of places visitors might want to see.

As you read about Norway, see if you can find any other industries not shown in these pictures.

1. Make a list of all the ways in which man makes a living in Norway.
2. See if you are able to find reasons that help explain why man makes a living as he does in Norway.

A Study of the North Central States

Today we are going to see how much we can learn about the North Central States. It would be nice if we could take a trip through this section of our United States, but as that is impossible, let us see how much we can see in pictures. What are some of the things we may learn about the North Central States from pictures?

A picture is like a book, sometimes you cannot understand everything in a picture without help. Questions may help you see the important things in a picture and remember them. The following suggestions are to help you study the pictures.

Take a sheet of paper and place the numbers from one to sixteen along the margin, leaving space between each number for answers.

Read all the questions carefully. As you look at each picture, think which question it helps you answer. Some pictures will help you to answer several questions. Some pictures you may want to look at several times.

1. List the different kinds of manufacturing shown in the pictures.
2. List all the products raised on the farms of the North Central States.
3. What animals are raised on the farms?
4. What minerals are found in the North Central States?
5. What other industries besides manufacturing, farming, and mining are suggested by the pictures?
6. What machines do the farmers in the North Central States use?
7. What large river is shown in the pictures? Locate this river on your map.
8. In manufacturing, power is necessary to run the engines and machinery. What two sources of power are shown?
9. Scenes from what three large cities are shown? Locate each one on your map.
10. What cities are on the Great Lakes?
11. Which one is on the Mississippi?
12. What cities seem to be important for the automobile industry?
13. What city seems to be an important flour milling center?
14. What city is important for meat packing?
15. From the scenes in the pictures, is most of the surface of the North Central States mountainous, hilly, rolling, or flat?
16. What industry seems to be the most important? Why?

We have learned all that we can from the pictures but they have only given us a bird's-eye view of what we might see if we were to go to the North Central States.

A Study of the Northern States

On the outline map on which you have colored other parts of the United States, color the nine northeastern states (Maine, New Hamp-

Pictures as Geographic Tools

shire, Vermont, Massachusetts, Rhode Island, Connecticut, New York, New Jersey, and Pennsylvania).

As you look at the map of the United States what differences do you notice on this map between this group of states and the other group of states? (Smaller size and a larger number of cities.) If there is a large number of cities what does that suggest to you? Look at your population map showing the distribution of cities. Do these maps verify your suggestion? Count the number of cities in the northeastern states which have a population of more than 100,000. Compare this number with the number of cities of this size in each of the other states which we have studied. Now, what statement can you definitely make about the population in the northeastern states? What question does this suggest? (Why are there more large cities and more people in this section?) Before trying to find an answer to this question, look again at your map showing the distribution of cities. What is another thing the map shows you about these cities? (Concentration in specific spots.) What states have very few cities and much less dense population? (Maine, New Hampshire, and Vermont.) What two questions do these facts suggest to you? (Why are the cities concentrated in these specific spots? Why do Maine, Vermont, and New Hampshire have few people in comparison with the other states?)

To see why people are distributed as our maps indicate, one looks of course to see how the people are earning their living. Look at the pictures of these people and list the ways they appear to be making a living. Opposite each way of making a living you find put down anything which you see in the picture which suggests to you a reason for the people doing that particular thing. For instance, what do you see in this picture which suggests a way of making a living? (A picture of a large hotel on the shore of a lake, boats on the lake, and a mountain background.) What in the picture suggests why people like to come to this section during vacation time? (The children suggest the lake, the mountains, and because of the mountains the summer climate may be cooler than in other places nearby.) Look on your map and see if you can find anything that verifies what you have said. (They find some lakes and mountains, and one child suggests that perhaps the ocean is a factor.)

Now look at each of the pictures, and as you finish with each, put it back where others can get it for exchange with someone. If you cannot find anything in a picture which explains what the people seem to be doing, leave a blank space.

The pictures given to the children, mounted but with no captions, were as follows:

1. Pictures like the above with several others showing winter and summer sports in these states.
2. Agricultural pictures showing a dairy farm, a potato farm, a tobacco farm, and crops on other types of farms.
3. A picture to show a New England type of farmhouse, and another characteristic of Pennsylvania and New York.
4. A factory located on falls of a river, and also one showing the factory section of a city.
5. A lumbering scene.
6. A paper pulp mill.
7. A picture of a quarry, and one of a coal mine.
8. Two or three fishing pictures—a fishing vessel, drying fish.
9. Several pictures showing docks, wharves, and vessels coming into harbors.

Others may be added to this list, but each of these pictures was selected to show a specific outstanding type of human activity in its natural setting. An hour or more was given to this activity, then the class was called together for a discussion and comparison of what they had found. At this stage the map was again used to find, if possible, on the map any sign of either the specific activity or the natural features which the children thought helped to explain the specific activity. At this time some of the children said that they were surprised to find tobacco grown in this region because they didn't think that the growing season would be long enough, as it is in the southern states. The teacher told them that there was another crop raised which was unusual, and showed them a picture of a cranberry bog, having them locate the cranberry section, Cape Cod, on their maps. This picture had not been included in the original set given to the children because the teacher knew that the children would not recognize the activity or many of the features shown.

From this picture study, the class saw that in the less densely settled areas, taking care of the visitors, fishing, lumbering, quarrying, and farming were the chief ways of making a living, whereas

Pictures as Geographic Tools

in the more densely settled places, there were numerous signs of mining, manufacturing, and trade.

The class then turned to their texts and reference books to find out more definitely where these kinds of activities were carried on, and to find all the reasons that they could which would help to explain each activity. They also were to note any new ones. Another exercise was to make a list of the articles manufactured in these states which they found advertised in magazines.

As the study continued, some of the questions to which the class sought answers were:

How manufacturing started in the New England section.
How the rivers, the ocean, and the forests helped man.
What special types of manufacturing began in certain localities. Why textile manufacturing is so important in Massachusetts and Rhode Island. What other section of the United States these factories depend upon for raw cotton. Why the manufacture of shoes is important in Massachusetts. What other section supplies some of the hides and skins for leather. Why silk manufacturing is located chiefly in New Jersey and Pennsylvania. Why the Pittsburgh district has become famous for its iron and steel goods. Why metal products are manufactured in Connecticut and jewelry in Rhode Island.
How the people in the city depend upon the people in other sections of these states, and also on people in other regions of the United States.
Why the types of farming are changing.
Why dairying and the raising of fruits and vegetables are important.
Why fishing has been and still is an important industry.

Because this group of states is a decidedly urban group, special attention should be given to the cities. There are three groups of cities to be noted, the coastal group from Boston to Philadelphia, the group from Albany to Buffalo on the inland route, and the group in western Pennsylvania. Each of these groups has characteristics peculiar to itself as a result of the types of work carried on.

Outstanding cities in each group should be studied so that the individuality of the city becomes apparent, then comparisons made so that the children are also aware that each group of cities has certain common characteristics.

Summary and Application Exercises. Following the study of the pictures, the following questions were given to the class:

1. List facts to explain each of the three groups of cities.
2. How are the activities carried on in these cities related to activities in other parts of the U. S.?
3. A ranchman in the west reads in the paper that the price of leather in Boston has dropped. Why would he be concerned?
4. All the coal miners in Pennsylvania and West Virginia go on a strike. In a few months many of the textile mills and other factories in New England close, and the price of raw cotton drops. What connection is there between these events?
5. Explain the reasons for the less densely populated areas in some sections.
6. List all the ways in which the ocean is connected with work or play in these states.
7. Explain each one of the following: (1) Stone fences in New England; (2) Long rambling houses in New England with sheds connecting the house and barn; (3) In New England the chief grain crop is oats, and much land is used for hay and pasture; (4) Raising of corn for silage; (5) Raising of tobacco in the Connecticut Valley and in eastern Pennsylvania; (6) The cranberry industry; (7) Lumbering for wood pulp; (8) The importance of textile manufacturing, and other human activities.
8. Plan a summer vacation trip and explain why you selected the route and the place where the vacation is to be spent. Do the same for a winter vacation.
9. Be able to identify the city plan or map of Boston, Buffalo, Pittsburgh, and Philadelphia, and be able to tell how you make the identification.
10. Be able to pick out the pictures which are characteristic of this section from a set containing pictures from various parts of the U. S.

SUMMARY

Pictures are valuable geographic tools. They may be used as a source of facts, to give meaning to symbols, and to build geographic concepts and understanding. But they must be selected for their geographic value and used with discrimination. The teacher must know how to guide children and train them in picture interpretation. The student must be trained in interpreting size, distance, and relief of the land from a comparison of the features in the pictures with their own experience with features in their local landscape. The picture should always be correlated with the map and the textbook. The teacher should plan exercises that stimulate thinking and action on the part of the student.

REFERENCES

BARTON, T. F., "Are We Adequately Utilizing the Geographic Film Strip," *Journal of Geography,* Vol. 53 (April, 1954), pp. 171–178.

BLOOD, B. R., and KOOSA, E. J., "Teaching Geography through Pictures," *National Elementary Principals,* Vol. 13 (June, 1934), pp. 204–208. Very good suggestions on using pictures for testing.

BROCKMEYER, Irene, "Testing with Pictures," *Journal of Geography,* Vol. 50 (February, 1951), pp. 54–58.

CRAWFORD, E. W., "Pictures in the Teaching of Geography," *Education,* Vol. 64 (March, 1944), pp. 438–441.

DALE, Edgar, "Teaching with Pictures," *Social Education,* Vol. 12 (March, 1948), pp. 102–104.

DEXHEIMER, Lora A., "Picture Study in Geography," *Journal of Geography,* Vol. 28 (November, 1929), pp. 334–340.

———, "Systematizing the Use of Pictures in Sixth Grade Geography," *Teaching of Geography,* Thirty-second Yearbook, National Society for the Study of Education (Public School Publishing Co., Bloomington, Ill., 1933) pp. 507–519.

EISEN, Edna E., "Aerial Views—Aids to Geography Study," *Educational Method,* Vol. 17 (March, 1938), pp. 285–287.

FLICKINGER, Alice, "A Filmstrip Lesson on the U.S.S.R.," *Audio-Visual Methods in the Social Studies,* Eighteenth Yearbook (Washington, D.C., National Council for the Social Studies, 1947), pp. 94–97.

GOEBEL, A. M., "Use of Pictures in Teaching Geography," *School Science and Mathematics,* Vol. 33 (May, 1933), pp. 473–478.

GREGOR, Howard F., "Slide Projection Techniques in the Geography Class," *Journal of Geography,* Vol. 55 (September, 1956), pp. 298–303.

GREGORY, W. M., "Motion Pictures as an Aid in Geographical Instruction," *School Science and Mathematics,* Vol. 45 (March, 1945), pp. 223–229.

——, "Materials for Visual Instruction in Geography," *Teaching of Geography*, Thirty-second Yearbook, National Society for the Study of Education (Bloomington, Ill., Public School Publishing Co., 1932), pp. 385–394.

HALVERSON, L. H., "Pictures in Teaching Geography," *Journal of Geography*, Vol. 28 (December, 1929), pp. 357–368.

HILE, Martha J., "The Use of Photographic Material in Teaching Geography," *Journal of Geography*, Vol. 37 (February, 1938), pp. 55–63.

KENNY, Lucille, "Demonstration Lesson Using the Film—The Corn Farmer," *School Science and Mathematics*, Vol. 45 (May, 1945), pp. 447–452. An excellent illustration of questions and activities for using a film.

LOGAN, Marguerite, "Pictures as Geographic Tools," *N.E.A. Journal*, Vol. 39 (January, 1950), pp. 44–47.

LOYA, Julia M., and NEWHOUSE, Lucille A., "The Use of Visual Aids in the Classroom," *Journal of Geography*, Vol. 48 (September, 1949), pp. 257–259.

MACE, F. Borden, and DOHRS, Fred E., "Motion Pictures," *Geographic Approaches to Social Education*, Nineteenth Yearbook (Washington D.C., National Council for Social Studies, 1948), pp. 140–145.

MARCH, Leland S., "Social Learnings Through Pictures," *Audio-Visual Methods in the Social Studies*, Eighteenth Yearbook (Washington, D.C., National Council for the Social Studies, 1947), pp. 83–87.

MEADER, M., "Are Pictures an Effective Aid in the Teaching of Geography," *Educational Method*, Vol. 11 (November, 1931), pp. 97–103. An analytical study of the value of pictures as seen by results of experiments in Cincinnati, Ohio, schools.

MORTIMER, Dorothy B., "Our Class Uses Lantern Slides," *Audio-Visual Methods in the Social Studies*, Eighteenth Yearbook (Washington, D.C., National Council for the Social Studies, 1947), pp. 98–108.

PARKER, Edith, "Pictures as Laboratory Material in Geography," *Education*, Vol. 64 (March, 1944), pp. 434–437.

PROUDFOOT, M. J., "Use of Photographic Material in Teaching Elementary Geography," *Journal of Geography*, Vol. 31 (December, 1932), pp. 381–390.

——, "Use of Photographs in Teaching Geography at Four Primary Levels," *Journal of Geography*, Vol. 34 (February, 1935), pp. 61–67.

RILEY, Norma, "A Picture Library and Its Uses," *Journal of Geography*, Vol. 37 (May, 1938), pp. 202–205.

SCARFE, Neville V., "Testing Geographical Interest by a Visual Method," *Journal of Geography*, Vol. 54 (November, 1955), pp. 377–386.

SVEC, Melvina M., "Better Captions for Picture Study," *Journal of Geography,* Vol. 43 (October, 1944), pp. 266–270.

―――, "Still Pictures," *Geographic Approaches to Social Education,* Nineteenth Yearbook (Washington, D.C., National Council for the Social Studies, 1948), pp. 130–139.

THRALLS, Z. A., "Selection and Use of Pictures," *N.E.A. Journal,* Vol. 21 (November, 1932), pp. 247–248.

VAYETTE, Kenneth E., "A Study of Children's Responses to Geography Pictures," *Journal of Geography,* Vol. 40 (October, 1941), pp. 262–263.

VEGETER, Dorothy O., "Using Still Pictures in Geography," *Journal of Geography,* Vol. 48 (November, 1949), pp. 334–336.

4

Graphs and Statistics in Geographic Education

GRAPHS AND STATISTICS have a definite value in geographic education because they serve a variety of purposes. The chief function of graphs is to present statistical materials in a simple and interesting form. Graphs facilitate comparisons of quantities, areas, distances, values, and other quantitative facts. People tend to shy away from tables of statistics, but when such statistics are put into graphic form they become concrete and vivid. Graphs often clarify important facts, relationships, and generalizations that are not easily grasped from statistical tables. In graphic form a person can grasp the facts presented at a glance. As Henry D. Hubbard of the National Bureau of Standards has said, "There is a magic in graphs. The profile of a curve reveals in a flash the whole situation —the life history of an epidemic, a panic, or an era of prosperity. . . . Wherever there are data to record, inferences to draw, or facts to tell graphs furnish unrivalled means whose power we are just beginning to realize and apply."

The business world has long realized the power of graphs. Nearly all corporations use numerous graphs in presenting their financial and production reports. The graphs make the statistics readily comprehensible to their stockholders and to the public. Newspapers and magazines use graphs to present statistical material to their readers in a vivid, readable, and interesting form. Graphs are used by local, state, and federal government agencies to make clear government facts and figures. Even the local school boards use graphs in their annual reports.

Because graphs are so widely used, the average person needs to be able to read and interpret them if he is to be an intelligent and responsible citizen. He should be sufficiently familiar with statistical tables as not to be frightened by them and skip them as he reads. Instead, he should regard them as a valuable source of information.

Statistical tables and graphs help both teachers and pupils to keep up-to-date on many important facts, because neither textbooks nor general reference books can be corrected every year in this rapidly changing world. For instance, since World War II, world trade has undergone remarkable changes. Nations formerly primarily agricultural have become industrialized with a consequent change in their exports and imports.

OBJECTIVES OF INSTRUCTION IN GRAPHS AND STATISTICAL MATERIALS

The reading and interpretation of statistical tables and graphs requires special skills. These skills, involving the selection of pertinent information and the drawing of conclusions, are important factors in the development of critical thinking. The acquisition of these abilities by the student of geography must not be left to chance or incidental teaching. They are to be developed gradually and cumulatively.

These skills are:
1. The ability to read from graphs and statistical tables the distinctive facts shown.
2. Ability to select desired information for a given purpose and draw conclusions.

3. Ability to recognize and state geographical problems suggested by the information contained in the graph or statistical table.
4. Ability to locate the facts in a graph or statistical table that aid in the solution of a specific problem.
5. Ability to use statistical information to explain human activities in a region.
6. Ability to construct a simple graph.
7. Ability to locate authoritative sources of statistical material.

The extent to which pupils gain these abilities depends upon their mental aptitude, their interests, the type and complexity of the graph and statistical table, and finally the teacher's skill in arousing interest and presenting the materials. Apparently nearly all pupils above the primary level can learn to read the pictograph and the broken-bar graph. The ability to read and interpret more complex graphs varies with the mental aptitude of the children and the teacher's skill in stimulating interest. The teacher needs to point out the practical value of graphs. He should guide the pupils step by step from the reading of simple pictographs and broken-bar graphs to the more complex graphs. The construction of simple graphs seems to aid in the reading and interpretation of others. Earnest Horn says, "Training in the construction of graphs might well go hand in hand with their interpretation since the purposes they serve, the standards that they should meet, and the related skills are much the same in either case."[1]

TYPES OF GRAPHS

The Pictograph

The pictograph is the simplest type to read. In it the quantitative units are represented by conventionalized pictorial symbols. The symbol should be easily identified with the subject. For instance, if corn production is the subject an ear of corn may be used as the pictorial symbol. Each symbol must be used consistently and represent the value indicated in the key. For example, in a pictograph

[1] Earnest Horn, *Methods of Instruction in the Social Studies* (New York, Charles Scribner's Sons, 1937), p. 454.

Graphs and Statistics in Geographic Education

```
North America  ))))))))))))))))))))))))))))))))))
Asia           )))))))
Europe         )))))
South America  )))))
Africa         )))
               ) = 100,000,000 bushels
```

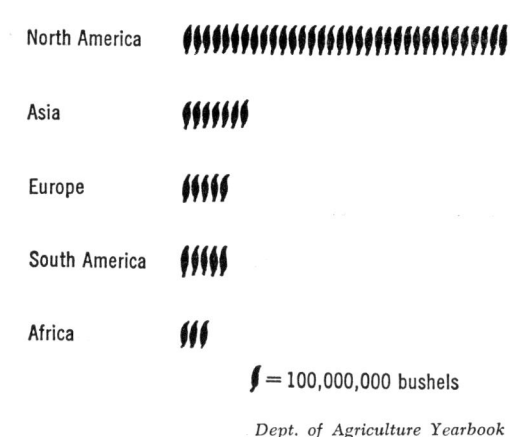

Dept. of Agriculture Yearbook

Fig. 15. Corn production by continents, 1952.

(Fig. 15) showing the production of corn on the continents in 1952, thirty-four ears of corn in a row represent the total number of bushels of corn produced in North America, Europe's production is represented by five ears, Asia's by seven ears, Africa's by three, and South America's by five. The key states that one ear represents 100,000,000 bushels. Such a graph can be read at a glance.

In making pictographs round figures are used, and in reading them this fact must be understood. Pictographs are often criticized on this basis, but for the average person round figures give a sufficiently accurate idea. For instance, one may state that he lives approximately a mile from a shopping center, although the actual distance is 5846 feet. One mile is easier to remember and sufficiently accurate for practical purposes.

Pictographs are used to make comparisons and show relationships between approximate quantities. They tell a story in a simple, informative, arresting manner and often raise questions in the reader's mind. The corn production graph would suggest several questions to the thoughtful reader: Why is North America's corn production so enormous? Europe and Asia are far more densely

```
Livestock feed  ■■■■■■■■■■■■■■■■■■■■■■■■■■
Manufactures    ■■■
Export          ■
Seed            ■
                ■ = 100,000,000 bushels
```

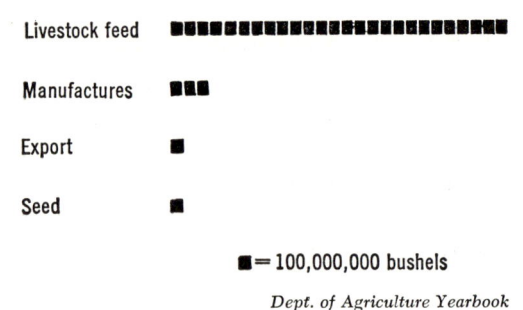

Dept. of Agriculture Yearbook

Fig. 16. Use of corn crop in the United States, 1952.

populated than North America, yet their production of corn is lower. Why?

The Broken Bar Graph

The broken-bar graph is perhaps the next easiest graph to read. It is more abstract than the pictograph in that squares represent the quantitative units. For example, in a graph showing how the corn crop of the United States is used, each square representing 100,000,000 bushels, twenty-six squares represent the amount fed to livestock, one square the amount exported, one square the amount used for seed, and three squares the amount used for manufactured products.

The Bar Graph

The bar graph is not as easily read as the pictograph or the broken-bar, but it is easier to construct and has more possibilities. The bars may be either horizontal or vertical, for instance, in a rainfall distribution graph the bars are usually vertical. In the construction of a bar graph, graph paper is used in order to determine the scale.

A simple bar graph may be used to show rank, for instance, the ten leading cotton producing states, or it may be used to show the annual distribution of rainfall by months.

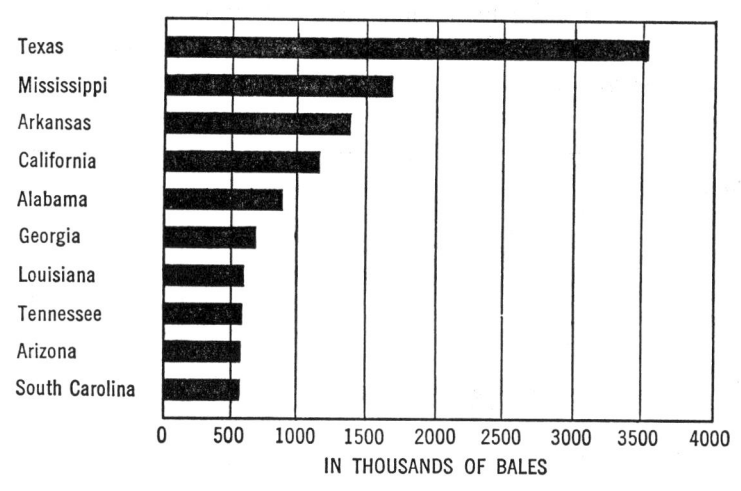

Fig. 17. Ten leading cotton producing states, 1954.

A double bar graph contains two sets of related statistics which are united by some characteristic they have in common. The two sets of bars may be placed side by side and distinguished by different colors or hatchings. In another form the center is the common factor and bars on either side of it represent amount, value, or character. Alice Foster[2] uses the double bar graph effectively to show the contrast in the seasonal characteristics of two branches of the wool trade—the movement of domestic wool from the United States shipping ports to United States receiving ports, and the movement of foreign wool destined for either United States or European ports.

The common factor is the wool trade. The solid bars represent the monthly movement of foreign wool through the Panama Canal; the hatched bars represent the movement of United States domestic wool from one United States port to another.

[2] Alice Foster, "Use of Statistics in Geographic Education," *Geographic Approaches to Social Education,* Nineteenth Yearbook (Washington, D.C., National Council for the Social Studies, 1948), p. 154.

Such graphs tell a more complicated story, contain more information, and stimulate more thinking than the pictograph and simple bar graph.

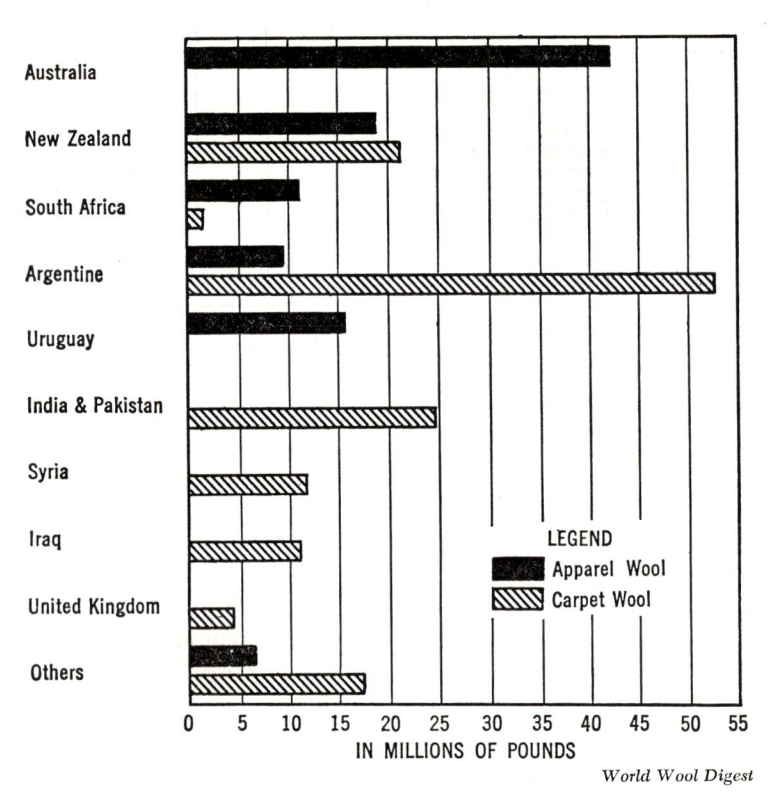

Fig. 18. United States imports of wool for consumption, 1956.

The Line or Trend Graph

In a line or trend graph, various types or colors of lines are used to show trends over a period of time with both time and amounts shown. The climatic chart shows the mean monthly temperatures by a line graph. See Fig. 20—Climatic Graph for Charleston, South

Graphs and Statistics in Geographic Education 119

Carolina—for an example. The vertical scale gives degrees of temperature and the horizontal scale gives the months of the year. Thus the trend of average monthly temperatures through the year may be noted.

This climatic graph also shows the average monthly rainfall at Charleston by use of vertical bars. One may note a relationship between the temperature and rainfall indicating maximum precipitation during the months with the highest temperatures.

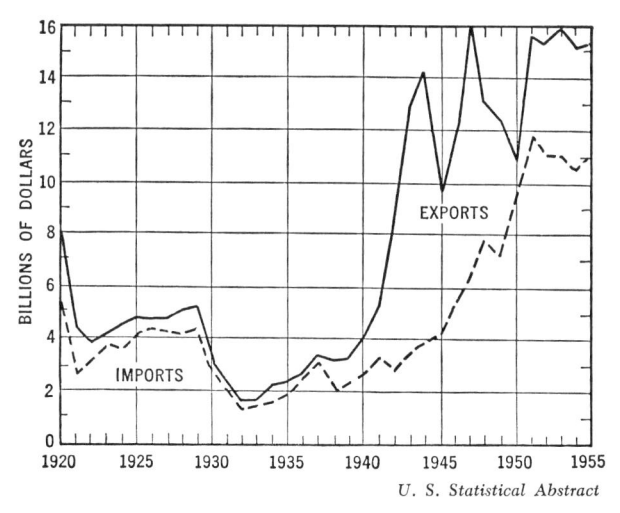

Fig. 19. United States exports and imports of merchandise, 1920–1955.

The Circle Graph

The circle or pie graph is not used as much as it formerly was, because its value in geographic education is limited. The division, or sectors, of the circle show a relation between each item and the whole. The statistics used must be converted into percentages and computed to the arc of a circle they represent. Although a circle graph is easy to read, it is difficult to construct.

There are many variations of these basic types. Both in using and in constructing graphs the teacher should select the graph that best emphasizes the data under discussion. Furthermore, the important point both in using graphs and in making them is that the information gained must function in geographic training.

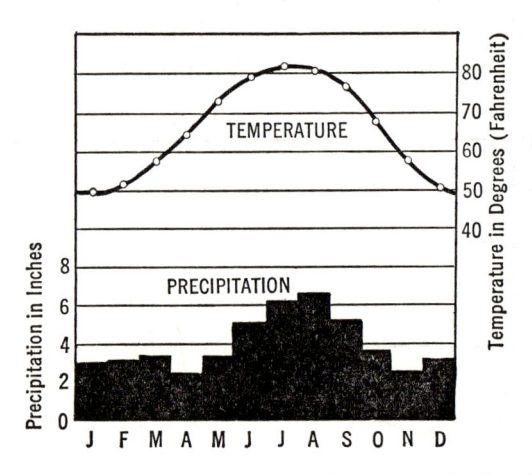

Fig. 20. Climatic graph for Charleston, South Carolina.

CONSTRUCTION OF A GRAPH

The construction of a graph involves the following steps:
1. *The statistical material.* The location and selection of up-to-date statistics on the specific topic or problem is the first step.
2. *The selection of a unit of measurement.* This can best be done by considering the largest and smallest amount involved. For most graphs round figures are used. Then, select a unit which will represent the smallest amount adequately and yet allow for the representation of the largest amount within the limits of the size of paper chosen. The selection of a satisfactory unit takes careful consideration. Note the units selected for Figures A, B, and C.
3. *Arrangement.* Since quick readability is a primary factor, the statistics should be arranged in ascending or descending order, if possible.

4. *Symbols.* The symbols chosen should be easily differentiated. Complicated symbols are difficult to make or reproduce. The symbols should be large enough to be easily seen and yet not so large that they distract the reader from the main purpose of the graph.
5. *Key.* The key or legend is a statement of what each symbol represents. It should be placed below the graph on the left side, if possible.
6. *Numbering.* Sufficient numeral guides should be put in so that the amount can be read. A graph has two axes, and each should be labeled to tell what it represents. For example, the horizontal axis may represent years, and the vertical axis tons of rubber.
7. *Title.* The title should be as brief as possible and yet make the meaning clear. Sometimes, in addition to the main title, there should be a subtitle to state the length of time, the date, or other pertinent information.
8. *Source of material.* Below the graph, credit should be given for the source of the statistics used.

STEPS IN LEARNING TO READ A GRAPH OR A STATISTICAL TABLE

In training students to read graphs and statistical tables, the teacher should guide them with specific questions and directions. At first the graph or statistical table is surveyed to get the general idea. The teacher may use such questions as the following:

What is the main subject or topic?
What specific information is given?
What symbols are used?

Study the column headings. What does the left hand or vertical column (scale) represent? What does the horizontal scale represent? In the majority of tables and graphs, the vertical scale is the key to the items which are to be compared or to the relationship to be established, and the horizontal scale shows the actual relationship which may exist. For instance in Fig. 15, Corn Production by Continents, the vertical scale states the continents to be compared, and the horizontal scale states that bushels of corn are being compared.

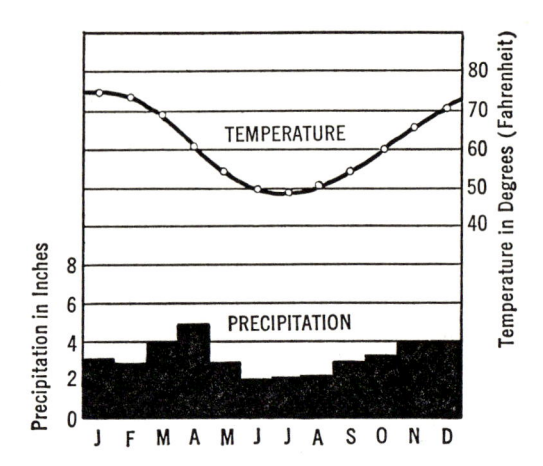

Fig. 21. Climatic graph for Buenos Aires, Argentina.

In the case of a line graph or a combination line and bar graph, additional directions and questions are necessary. In Fig. 21, Climatic Graph for Buenos Aires, Argentina, the part of the graph indicating rainfall should be examined first, noting that the vertical scale represents inches of rainfall, and the horizontal the months of the year. Next study the temperature section, in which the vertical scale represents degrees of temperature Fahrenheit, and the horizontal states the months of the year. The common factor of the two is months of the year. In this case, the teacher should point out that different symbols are used—a bar for rainfall, a line for temperature. Then the source of the statistical data used should be noted.

After the general survey, the students should read the graph or table for specific detailed information on the subject or topic. For instance, with reference to Fig. 15, Corn Production by Continents, ask the students the following:

What continents are named? How many bushels of corn does each symbol represent? What continent produces the most corn? How much does it produce? What continents produce the same amount? How much does each one produce?

With reference to Fig. 21, Climatic Graph for Buenos Aires, ask the following:

What month has the most rain? What month has the least rain? What month has the highest average temperature? What month has the lowest average temperature?

The teacher should discuss with the class the information gained from the graph or statistical table until he is sure that the majority understands the main facts.

In addition to reading the facts given on the graph, the student should learn how to interpret these facts and raise questions concerning them. Examples of how students may be guided in the interpretation of graphs and statistical tables are given in the illustrative units at the end of this chapter.

USING GRAPHS AND STATISTICS IN DEVELOPING A UNIT

Graphs and statistics are valuable tools in the development of a geographic unit. They are a source of information which may be used to introduce or motivate a unit by arousing curiosity and stimulating questions. They may also be used to gain a general impression of a nation or a region, its people and their activities.

Teacher and pupils may consult statistics to bring facts up-to-date, to prove a point, or to bring new evidence to bear upon a topic or problem. An ingenious teacher can use both graphs and statistical tables to check the students' knowledge and understanding.

Motivation

In the upper grades and high school, teachers have found graphs and statistics excellent tools for motivating or introducing a unit. Linnie B. James[3] describes an introductory lesson using a statistical

[3] Linnie B. James, "The Mystery Country," *Journal of Geography*, Vol. 51 (September, 1952), pp. 231–235.

table to present information and stimulate curiosity concerning the country.

The following survey of Colombia, South America is another illustration of the use of graphs, statistics, and maps.

A SURVEY OF COLOMBIA, SOUTH AMERICA

Today we are going to visit Venezuela's western neighbor. Turn to the physical-political map in the textbook. What country is west of Venezuela? Trace the boundary of Colombia with your finger. Judging from the map, how do you think Colombia and Venezuela compare in size?

A graph will give us a better idea of the size of the two countries.

1. Draw a bar 4½ inches long and 1 inch wide. Write "Area of Colombia" to the left of this bar. (The actual area is 461,000 sq. mi.)
2. Draw a bar 3½ inches long and 1 inch wide. Label it "Area of Venezuela."
3. Make a key. Draw a 1-inch square. Label it "About 100,000 square miles." About how much larger is Colombia than Venezuela? (About 100,000 sq. mi.)
4. In the bar that represents Colombia place 12 dots, separated by even spaces. (The population in 1952 was 11,768,430.)
5. In the dots that represent Venezuela place four evenly spaced dots.
6. In the key write "One dot equals (approximately) 1,000,000 people."
7. Write a title for the graph. What story does the graph now tell? What question comes in your mind immediately? (Why does Colombia, which is only a little larger than Venezuela, have twice as many people?) We shall look for reasons as we study.

Turn to the population map in the textbook. Is the population of Colombia spread evenly over the country or does the density vary from place to place? (It varies from less than 1 per square mile to 128 per square mile. On the blackboard the teacher should write the word *Colombia* as a heading, and below it, "1. Variety in Population Density.")

Judging from what you have learned of people in other South American countries, would you expect Colombia to have only one group of people within its borders or many groups of people?

After discussing this question write these statistics on the board:

Mestizos 68%
Whites 20%
Indians 5%

Do the statistics prove that you are right or wrong?
(On the blackboard under the heading "Colombia," write "2. Variety of people.")

COLOMBIA'S LEADING EXPORTS (1952)

Commodity	Value in dollars
Coffee	949,704,000
Petroleum	178,678,000
Bananas	23,715,000
Platinum	7,804,000
Tobacco	4,084,000
Cattle	2,622,000
Cattle hides	1,347,000
Sugar	1,327,000

Source, *Foreign Commerce Yearbook,* 1955

How does this table of Colombia's exports suggest the variety of work activities in the country? (During the discussion of this question the class mentioned farming, mining, and ranching. Several in the class suggested that some of the products might be raised on plantations, such as coffee and bananas, while others were products from small farms, such as tobacco. The class decided that "Variety of exports," and "Variety of products" should be added to the list on the blackboard.)

Study the following table of the leading crops of Colombia.

LEADING CROPS BY ACREAGE

Maize (corn)	844,000
Coffee	800,000
Potatoes	540,000
Wheat	188,000
Bananas & plantains	174,000
Rice	166,000
Sugar cane	149,000
Beans	92,000
Barley	51,000
Cacao	32,000
Tobacco	20,000

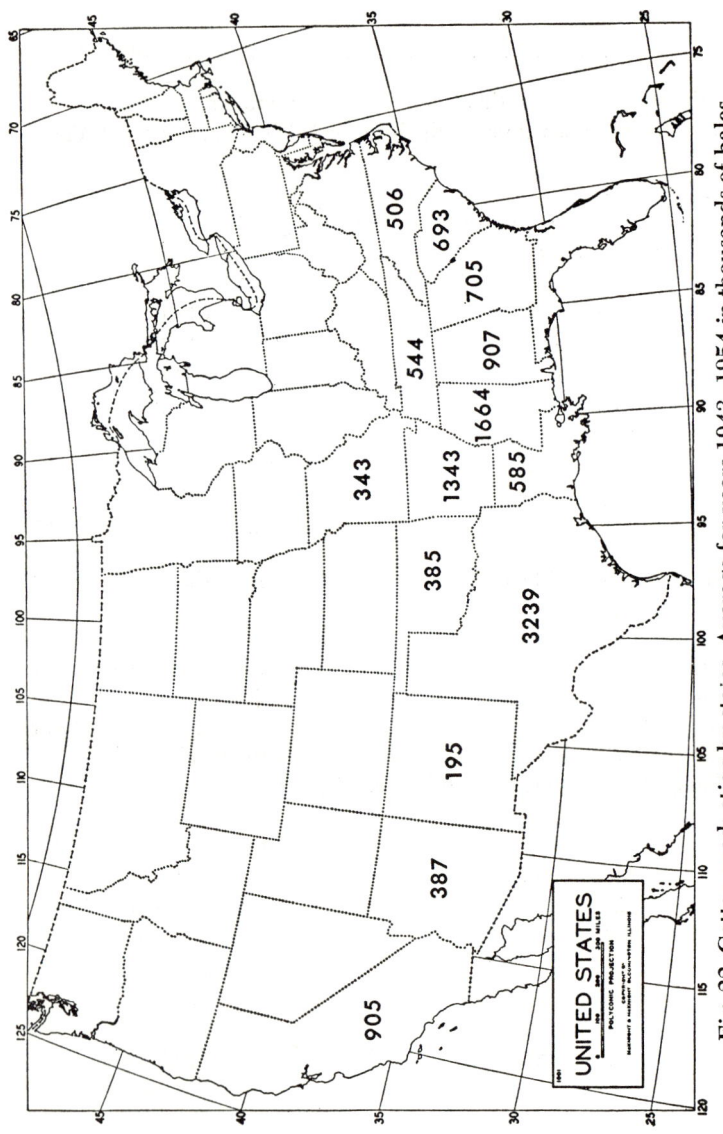

Fig. 22. Cotton production by states. Average for years 1943–1954 in thousands of bales.

Graphs and Statistics in Geographic Education

Does this bear out what you have said about the products of Colombia?

How does it suggest a variety of climate?

Examine the physical-political map of Colombia. How does it also suggest a variety in climate? What does the annual rainfall map suggest? (Precipitation ranges from less than 10 inches to over 80 inches. To the blackboard list was added "Variety of climate—(a) temperature, (b) precipitation.")

What different kinds of surface are shown on the physical-political map? (Delta plains, coastal plains, river valleys, interior plains, mountain slopes, and high mountain ranges. To the blackboard list was added "Variety of surface or topography.")

Read our list on the blackboard. What word is the keynote to Colombia's geography? (*Variety.* The teacher may wish to introduce the term *diversity* at this point.)

Colombia has been called a "land of contrasts" because there is such differences in topography, climate, products, people, and work activities. How can we learn more about these contrasts and why they exist? (A discussion of sources of information and topics to be explored followed, then, the class began their reading. They now had a definite aim and plan of work.)

Assimilation

During this stage in the unit, graphs and statistics may be used to settle an argument, provide additional facts, or clarify a distribution pattern. For instance, during the study of the cotton industry, one of the students brought in a news item stating that our import of raw cotton should be prohibited since the United States produced such a surplus. The teacher suggested that the United States *Statistical Abstract* be consulted to find out how much the United States exported and how much was imported. The class found that in 1954 the United States:

produced	16,317,000 bales
consumed	8,576,000 bales
exported	3,760,000 bales
imported	142,000 bales

The amount imported was so little that it could not affect prices or our production. But then they wanted to know from where we imported, the reasons, and to what countries we exported. They found some surprising facts.

Often a class may gain a better idea of the distribution of a crop or product if the statistical data are placed on a map. For example, if each state's cotton production by number of bales is written on the state, a very simple and general pattern of the distribution may be seen at a glance. Shadings may be added to make the pattern stand out. See Fig. 22—Cotton Map.

Application

There are a number of ways in which statistical data may be used for application and testing activities. This does *not* mean that the pupil should memorize lists of statistics, because they go out of date too quickly. However, general ideas, impressions, and geographic understanding can be tested. Alice Foster gives some excellent examples in her article.[4]

After studying a number of countries, the students may be given a test using export statistics of several of the countries. They are asked to identify the countries and explain their selections. The following was used after a study of the countries of South America.

TEST—LATIN AMERICA

Fill in the correct name of the country belonging to each one of the following sets of exports. The exports are arranged in order of importance.

1. *Principal exports from*
   _____.
   Cotton
   Sugar
   Mineral concentrates
   Petroleum
   Copper
   Wool

2. *Principal exports from*
   _____.
   Wheat
   Meat
   Wool
   Hides and skins
   Linseed oils and flaxseed
   Quebracho extract

[4] Foster, *op. cit.*, pp. 171–174.

Graphs and Statistics in Geographic Education

3. Principal exports from _____.

    Coffee
    Cotton
    Cacao
    Tobacco leaf
    Hides and skins
    Vegetables oils & wastes

4. Principal exports from _____.

    Tin
    Lead
    Zinc
    Silver
    Wolfram
    Copper

5. Principal exports from _____.

    Copper
    Nitrate
    Wool
    Iron ore

6. Principal exports from _____.

    Petroleum
    Coffee
    Cacao
    Gold

In a brief statement explain in each case the reason or reasons for your choice of country.

In such a test the student has to think in terms of the total list as well as individual items, and also recall total impressions of the country. In some instances there may be a key export, as "nitrate" in number 5, that identifies the country, but in numbers 1 and 3 cotton is an important export in both countries so the student has to think in terms of the whole list. If he should name Brazil for number 1 and Peru for number 2 the teacher knows that he does not have an understanding of the characteristics of the two countries.

Climatic statistics can be used to check a number of geographic concepts as illustrated by the following tables and accompanying questions.

TEST

Station No. 1

	Jan.	Feb.	Mar.	Apr.	May	June	July	Aug.	Sept.	Oct.	Nov.	Dec.
Temp.	68	63	61	58	56	52	52	53	54	57	60	62
Rain	0.0	0.0	0.4	0.6	3.8	5.7	4.0	2.6	1.3	0.4	0.3	0.2

Average yearly precipitation 19.3 inches

Station No. 2

	Jan.	Feb.	Mar.	Apr.	May	June	July	Aug.	Sept.	Oct.	Nov.	Dec.
Temp.	53	53	55	58	60	63	66	66	65	62	58	55
Rain	3.5	3	2.9	0.5	0.0	0.0	0.0	0.0	0.1	0.6	1.4	2.3

Average yearly precipitation 14.78 inches

Answer the following questions concerning these two stations:

1. What station has its rainy season from October to May inclusive?
2. Are these winter or summer months at this station? How do you know?
3. Which station has its rainy season from April to September inclusive?
4. Are these winter or summer months at this station?
5. How do you explain the fact that the seasons differ at these two places?
6. Is station number 1 in the low, middle, or high latitudes? How do you know?
7. Are these stations probably on west coasts or east coasts? Give a reason for your answer.
8. Agriculture is carried on in both regions; what adaptation might be necessary? Why?
9. From the following list of crops, check those that might be raised:
    a. wheat
    b. sugar cane
    c. bananas
    d. citrus fruits
    e. coffee
    f. olives

   Give reasons for your discarded list.

Pupil Activities

Individual students should be encouraged to construct graphs to supplement both oral and written reports. Oftentimes one can select items from a long statistical table to summarize information gained from a discussion or from his reading. Items in a long statistical table sometimes can be arranged more purposefully to point up a specific topic. For instance, export and import tables are very long and often should be summarized in a shorter and more pertinent table. A student may study the original table, choose larger categories such as *food, raw materials, fuel,* and so forth, add up

Graphs and Statistics in Geographic Education

the totals of the individual items usually given, and make a shorter table, or convert the statistics into an easily read graph.

In the junior and senior high school, a worthwhile group activity is the construction of climatic and other graphs for class use. These should be large enough as to be easily read from across the room. Adding to these from year to year, a valuable permanent file of worthwhile graphs for class discussion may be built up. Furthermore, this activity has a social value, for the individual or committee is contributing to the whole class.

SOURCES OF STATISTICS

There are innumerable sources of statistics, but in the following list are those most accessible and worthwhile for the average school.

1. *The World Almanac* is an invaluable source of data for geography and social studies teachers. It is published annually and may be purchased at most drugstores. The use of it gives pupils an opportunity to select information functional in any unit.

2. *The Statesman's Yearbook* contains data according to countries. It is a rich source of information and although too expensive for teachers to purchase, most libraries have available copies. It is published annually.

3. *Agricultural Statistics* is published annually by the United States Department of Agriculture. Often it may be obtained through a personal request to your local Congressman. It includes farm and crop statistics, not only for the United States but for many other countries.

4. *The Foreign Commerce Yearbook* is compiled by the Bureau of Foreign and Domestic Commerce. It contains data on all foreign countries. It is available in most libraries, but may also be purchased from the United States Government Printing Office.

5. *The Statistical Abstract of the United States* is compiled by the United States Bureau of Census. It is published annually and contains statistics on the industrial, social, political, and economic

organization of the United States. Almost anything statistical about the United States may be found in it. Its purchase about once in five years is worthwhile, although it may be found in most libraries. It is for sale through the Superintendent of Documents, U.S. Government Printing Office, Washington, D.C.

6. *The Commodity Yearbook* gives a brief account of leading world commodities and statistics on production and trade in them. It may be consulted in most libraries.

7. *Orbis* gives a variety of statistics on all countries of the world. It is in two volumes and is available in many libraries.

SUMMARY

Statistics have a definite, functional place in geographic education. They may be used to arouse curiosity and to stimulate questions. They give concreteness to general statements, and often they serve to prove or disprove a careless statement or impression. If graphed, the visual image aids memory and often clarifies a point. They are a means of keeping up to date on many changing conditions in peoples' activities such as trade, production, land use, and resources.

However, statistics should not be used as an end in themselves, for like maps and pictures they are tools in gaining geographic knowledge and understanding.

ILLUSTRATIVE LESSONS

A Lesson in the Reading of Graphs and Statistics

The pupils are given a set of the following statistics and a physical-political map of the world. They need to have access to a seasonal precipitation map of the world and a globe to which they can refer. The work of the teacher is to lead the pupils through a study of these statistics to find the country to which the statistics belong. As the pupils give clues, they are written on the board by the teacher.

Graphs and Statistics in Geographic Education 133

CAN YOU NAME THE COUNTRY
Prepared by Linnie B. James

I

AREA AND POPULATION

Area .... 483,000 square miles
Population 9,000,000
Density of population .... 19 per sq. mile

II

LAND USE

	Acres	Percent
Land area	309,000,000	
Arable (including fallow) and orchards	4,000,000	1
Permanent meadows and pastures	37,000,000	12
Forests and woodlands	173,000,000	56
Built on areas and wasteland	95,000,000	31

III

PRODUCTION OF PRINCIPAL CROPS

Forage crops	4,049,000	metric tons
Potatoes	1,315,000	" "
Cane sugar	598,000	" "
Maize	321,000	" "
Sweet potatoes, manioc	303,000	" "
Barley	217,000	" "
Wheat	162,000	" "

IV

LIVESTOCK

Sheep	17,750,000	Horses	432,000
Cattle	2,825,000	Donkeys	416,000
Goats	2,210,000	Mules	156,000
Pigs	995,000	*Others	3,025,000

* Llamas—To reveal this animal in the table would be indicating location of the country.

V

MISCELLANEOUS STATISTICS

Railways	2,350 miles
Roads suitable for motor vehicles	15,000 "
Motor cars	37,526 "
Trucks	28,985 "
Buses	2,943 "
Telephones	33,000 "

VI

EXPORTS

Total exports	$253,000,000
Cotton	85,400,000
Sugar	34,000,000
Lead, concentrates and refined	25,000,000
Petroleum and petroleum products	17,400,000
Zinc, concentrates	15,600,000
Copper, concentrates and refined	14,300,000
Wool and other animal fibers	14,000,000
Fish and fish products	5,570,000
Silver bars	5,280,000
Gold bars (re-export),	3,600,000

VII

IMPORTS

Total imports	$279,000,000
Iron and steel	17,800,000
Gold bars	17,750,000
Automobiles and parts	17,000,000
Trucks and buses	12,500,000
Machinery and parts	11,100,000
Pharmaceuticals	7,500,000
Electrical machinery	7,113,000
Chemicals	5,945,000
Paper manufactures and newsprint	5,120,000
Mining machinery	5,020,000

Source of statistics:
 Foreign Commerce Yearbook, 1951
 Encyclopedia of Extra-European Countries—Orbis
 Statesman's Yearbook, 1956

Graphs and Statistics in Geographic Education

After giving the set of statistics, the teacher introduces the work with the following statements:

Have you noticed how many of the television programs are detective stories? It must be that people enjoy them or they wouldn't give them. How many of you like detective stories? We usually have to wait until the last few minutes for the final clue to be brought out, don't we? Today we are going to be geography detectives in search of a country. Let's not decide which country it is until all possible clues have been given. In working out these clues you may study any maps or the globe in addition to the statistics.

Next, the teacher guides the pupils in examining the statistics to find clues as to what country they belong.

1. Look at the first sheet of statistics. What is the area of this country?
2. How does the area of this country compare with the area of Pennsylvania? (Compare area with an area with which the pupils are familiar.) We could say that the area of this country is three times that of California.
    a. (Teacher writes on board) Large country ten times size of Pennsylvania.
3. How does the population of this country compare with that of Pennsylvania?
4. What is the density of population? How does that density compare with the density of population of the United States?
5. Is this a densely or sparsely populated country?
    b. (On board) Sparsely populated.
6. Look at Table II which tells how the land is used. What percent of their land can be cultivated?
    c. (On board) About 1 per cent of the land is cultivated.
7. For what is the largest part of the country used?
    d. (On board) Over half of this country is in forest.
8. What part of the country is wasteland? What kinds of places are considered wasteland? Perhaps some of these will be found in this country.
    e. (On board) May have large areas of swamp, desert, or stony mountain land.
9. From the land-use figures what do you judge might be an important industry?
    f. (On board) Grazing might be important.

10. What is meant by "permanent meadows and pastures"? On what type of surface might permanent pastures be found?
11. What clues does this table give as to the type of surface in some parts of this country?
    g. (On board) Some of the land is mountainous.
12. About 1 per cent of the land can be cultivated. Perhaps Table III on Production of Crops will give us some clues. What crops are most important? What are forage crops? Name some. In what type of climate do these grow well? If they have to raise crops for animals, what does that imply? (Not enough pasture land because so much is wooded.)
13. Look at Table IV to see whether or not much livestock is raised. Notice how many more sheep than cattle are raised. Which need better pasture, cattle or sheep?
    h. (On board) Necessary to provide feed for animals.
14. What crop is second in importance? What type of climate do potatoes grow best in?
    i. (On board) Some parts of this country have a cool, moist climate.
15. What does the growing of sugar cane tell us about the growing season of some part of this country?
    j. (On board) Some parts of this country must have a frost-free climate.
16. What is manioc? What conditions does manioc require?
    k. (On board) Some parts of this country have a tropical climate.
17. What conditions does corn require? Barley? Wheat? You can see that this country has several different types of climate.
18. Let's examine these climatic graphs and see if they will give us some clues as to where this country is located. These three places are located in nearly the same latitude across this country. They are located as they are placed: A is in the western part, B in the central part, and C in the eastern part

Chiclayo

	Jan.	Feb.	Mar.	Apr.	May	June	July	Aug.	Sept.	Oct.	Nov.	Dec.
Temp.	76	78	77	72	69	64	64	65	66	69	72	70
Rain	0.1	0.2	0.5	0.0	0.0	0.0	0.0	0.0	0.1	0.0	0.0	0.0

Cerro de Pasco

	Jan.	Feb.	Mar.	Apr.	May	June	July	Aug.	Sept.	Oct.	Nov.	Dec.
Temp.	44	43.5	44	44	43.5	41	41	41	42	43	43	42.8
Rain	4.6	4.5	3.8	3.5	2.4	0.9	1.2	1.5	2.8	3.2	3.4	3.8

Graphs and Statistics in Geographic Education

Iquitos

| Temp. | 78 | 79 | 77 | 77 | 76 | 74 | 74 | 76 | 77 | 77 | 79 | 78 |
| Rain | 10.0 | 9.0 | 13.0 | 6.6 | 9.0 | 7.0 | 6.5 | 4.2 | 8.0 | 7.1 | 8.2 | 11.4 |

19. Are these three places in the northern or southern hemisphere? What tells you that?

    l. (On board) In the southern hemisphere.
20. Are they near or far from the equator? (Not much seasonal curve to temperature line.)
21. What might account for B's temperature being lower than that of the other two places? (Higher elevation.) If this is true where might some of the mountains be?
22. Notice the great difference in the amount of rainfall, yet these places are in nearly the same latitude. What wind belt is a little south of the equator? (Southeast trades.) What could cause the differences?

    m. (On board) The eastern part has heavy rainfall, the central and higher part has less rain, and the western part is a desert.
23. Let's check our clues. I'll read them as you study the physical-political and rainfall maps. (Teacher reads the clues slowly so as to allow time for pupils to draw certain conclusions.)
24. Now let's look still further for additional clues to strengthen our opinion as to the country. Look at Table V. What does the low mileage of railroads and motor roads tell you about the country? (Railroads must be costly to build or there is little need for them.)
25. Look at Table VI. These are the exports of this country. What industries seem to be important?

    n. (On board) Mining is important in this country.

    o. Cotton might be a cash crop.
26. What does the export of fish and fish products tell us?

    p. (On board) This country may have a seacoast.
27. What clues does the list of imports give you?
28. How does the total amount of exports compare with the total imports? Is this a good trade condition? Why?

In conclusion, the teacher tests the validity of the pupils' choices with references to the statistics given by providing additional information relating to the country.

Now we are ready to check our clues again. As I read, check to see if these facts could be true of the country you have decided must be the one to which the statistics belong.

a. Nearly ten times the size of Pennsylvania.
b. Sparsely settled.
c. About 1 per cent cultivated.
d. Over half of this country is covered with forest.
e. May have large areas of swamp, stony mountains, or desert.
f. Grazing is important.
g. Some land in this country is mountainous.
h. Necessary to provide feed for animals.
i. Some parts of this country have a cool, moist climate.
j. It is in the southern hemisphere, near the equator.
k. The eastern part has heavy rainfall, the central part is higher and has less rain, the western part is desert.
l. Surface may make the building of railroads and roads costly.
m. Mining is important.
n. There may be a seacoast.

To what country do you think these statistics belong? That's right! PERU!!. Now we must check our clues and learn if we drew correct conclusions. We have much more to learn about how the people live in the different parts of this interesting country.

REFERENCES

ARKIN, Herbert, and COLTON, R. R., *Graphs: How to Make and Use Them* (New York, Harper and Brothers, 1936).

BARROWS, H. H., and PARKER, Edith, "Some Critical Problems in Teaching Elementary Geography," *Journal of Geography,* Vol. 30 (December, 1931), pp. 353–364.

BLOUCH, Adelaide, "Lake Cargoes as Graph Material on an Elementary Level," *Journal of Geography,* Vol. 48 (January, 1949), pp. 38–40.

FOSTER, Alice, "Use of Statistics in Geographic Education," Nineteenth Yearbook (Washington, D.C., National Council for the Social Studies, 1948), pp. 146–175.

HAAS, Kenneth B., and PACKER, Harry Q., *The Preparation and Use of Visual Aids* (Englewood Cliffs, N.J., Prentice-Hall, Inc., 1946).

HARPER, R. A., and OTTO, H. G., "Evaluation of Graphic Instructional Materials," *National Elementary Principals,* Vol. 13 (June, 1934), pp. 228–237.

HARVILLE, H., "The Use of Posters, Charts, Cartoons, and Graphs," *Audio-Visual Methods in the Social Studies,* Eighteenth Yearbook (Washington, D.C., National Council for the Social Studies, 1947).

HORN, Earnest, *Methods of Instruction in the Social Studies* (New York, Charles Scribner's Sons, 1935), pp. 386–388.

JAMES, Linnie B., "The Mystery Country: A Lesson in the Reading of Graphs and Statistics," *Journal of Geography*, Vol. 51 (September, 1952), pp. 231–235.

MCKOWN, A. B., *Audio-Visual Aids in Instruction* (New York, McGraw-Hill, 1949), Chs. 6, 7, and 8.

MIKESELL, Ruth, "Geographical Activities Involving the Use of Maps and Graphs," *Journal of Geography*, Vol. 33 (March, 1934), pp. 105–113.

STRICKLAND, Ruth G., "A Study of the Possibilities of Graphs as a Means of Instruction in the First Four Grades" (New York, Bureau of Publications, Teachers' College, Columbia University, 1938).

STUTZ, F. H., and others, "Interpreting Material Presented in Graphic Form," *Skills in Social Studies*, Twenty-fourth Yearbook (Washington, D.C., National Council for the Social Studies, 1953), Ch. 9.

THOMAS, Kathryne C., "Ability of Children to Interpret Graphs," Thirty-second Yearbook, National Society for the Study of Education (Bloomington, Ill., Public School Publishing Co., 1933), pp. 492–494.

THRALLS, Zoe A., "Graphs and Museum Materials," *N.E.A. Journal* (January, 1933), pp. 9–10.

VAN TUYL, G. H., "Teaching Graphs," *Fifth Yearbook* (Philadelphia, Pa., Eastern Commercial Teachers Association), pp. 317–323.

VINCENT, H. D., "Use of the Graph," *National Elementary Principals*, Vol. 14 (October, 1934), pp. 23–26.

WHITTLESEY, Derwent, "Current Statistics as Fresh Test Materials," *Journal of Geography*, Vol. 31 (February, 1932), pp. 79–83.

5

Reading the Landscape

LEARNING HOW TO STUDY the landscape is essential in functional geographic education because the landscape is the basic source of all geographic knowledge. Thus every school has a ready-made geography laboratory in the landscape of the local community, whether the community is a city, a town, a village, or a rural area. It is at hand if the teacher knows how to use it. In the landscape of the local community the geographic facts, concepts, and interrelationships may be observed directly in life situations. Geography is not confined within the walls of a building nor within the cover of a book. Through field work in their own community, the students gain a realization that all the world and all of man's activities contribute to their education.

VALUES OF LANDSCAPE STUDY

Provides Direct Learning

A study of the local community is a direct learning experience in which the child is the active agent. Through his own observation he is discovering facts, gaining impressions, developing concepts, and noting interrelationships between man and the physical environment. In a sense he is working out the geography of his own community. Through this direct observation of the natural features and the cultural (man-made) features of his own community and noting their interrelationships, he learns how the geography of other regions has been gradually worked out.

Encourages Spirit of Exploration

A study of the local community helps to keep alive the child's spirit of exploration and investigation. He is an explorer as truly as Columbus or Magellan, in part because he knows so little about his own community. Guided, well-planned trips make the child conscious of the actual landscape. He discovers things that he did not know existed, and a multitude of features in the landscape take on more meaning. Most of us are among those "who have eyes but see not," because so many things around us have no meaning for us. Following a study of Oak Park,[1] two boys expressed the idea tersely. "I didn't know there was so much to see right here in Oak Park," remarked James. "We see what we learn to see," replied Bill.

Once the child discovers how interesting such exploration is he is likely to continue to explore. Our individual efficiency depends on our willingness to explore and investigate, and this spirit is worth cultivating in our students.

Aids Visualization

Another value of the geographic study of the local landscape is that it contributes to the ability to visualize landscape features in other areas. Students cannot directly observe the geography of the various regions of the world. They must gain their visual imagery and understanding from textbook descriptions, yet as L. C. Davis[2] says: "Concrete imagery resulting from field work affords experiences for building comparisons of local conditions with conditions elsewhere in state, nation, and the world."

---

[1] Mamie L. Anderzhon, "Geographic Field Work in Community Study for Junior High Level," *Journal of Geography*, Vol. 51 (November, 1956), p. 325.

[2] L. C. Davis, "Field Work in Geography," *Educational Method*, Vol. 17 (March, 1938), pp. 293–296.

The ideas gained from a study of the local landscape provide a background for the study of other regions. As Edna Eisen says:[3]

> For example, having seen outstanding landscape features which indicate functions carried on in Milwaukee and the site on which they have developed, students have less difficulty in visualizing city landscapes in other places. To be sure, grain elevators on the Buenos Aires waterfront are not identical with those of Milwaukee. However, the pupil who has seen those, who knows how the railroad cars bringing in grain are emptied on one side of the elevator, and how the grain is sent through long spouts into the holds of large lake carriers, has something to make real to himself the work in Buenos Aires.

Of course the teacher must be alert to point out, or lead the student to note, comparisons between the features or conditions in the local landscape and the region under discussion.

One of the most useful subjects for study in the local community is the climate. Climatic conditions in all regions are outstanding geographic factors. To understand other climates, constant comparisons with local rainfall, temperatures, winds, and storms should be made. Only through such comparisons do the climatic conditions and their effects become significant to the student.

Assists Comprehension

One of the chief complaints of teachers of geography and social studies is that the student does not understand what he reads. He reads words which are signs only, but the words have no real meaning to him because no image or concept lies behind the symbol. Correct ideas are built on the reader's experience by the exercise of constructive imagination. This inability of the child to translate word symbols into images or concepts seems to be due, in part, to a narrow environment and lack of meaningful contact with the environment.

Teachers have difficulty in realizing that the environment of many children is narrow. This is true of city children as well as rural. Many city children have never been beyond a few blocks

[3] Edna E. Eisen, "Field Work in Junior and Senior High School," *Journal of Geography*, Vol. 37 (February, 1938), pp. 77.

of their homes. They have never seen an airfield, a depot, or a railroad train, have never seen corn or wheat growing. Plowing, cultivating, and harvesting are unknown activities. Of course, they can pronounce the words glibly, but behind the words there are no real concepts. The teacher has to supply some background before the child can read the text material successfully. The field trip or excursion, both in the city and in the country, broadens the child's background and aids him in building meanings.

The lack of meaningful contact with the environment is another barrier to comprehension.

The environment may be rich in content but the child may have had no real contact with it. In western Pennsylvania where coal mining is an important activity, a teacher was astounded to discover that only a few of the children knew what a coal tipple was, or a shaft, a drift, and a number of other terms connected with the industry. Most of the children had seen all of these but they had never identified and understood their function. Consequently, when they read the material in their textbook they did not connect the words with their physical referents.

An elementary principal was astounded to discover that 90 per cent of his sixth-graders had never seen a river, although the school was in a city located on a river. The class was reading about this river, yet few made any connection between what they were reading and their own river. He took the class to the river and they discussed it and how it was used, and on their return they read their textbook with real interest and understanding. Thus, field experience makes "the obvious meaningful."

Furthers Understanding of the Community

The study of the local community contributes to the development of an understanding of their own community and its problems. As the students analyze the local landscape, becoming familiar with its natural features and man's activities as he has made use of the land, they become aware of the individuality of the community. They note what activities are carried on, how they are carried on, and *why* they are carried on where they are and in the ways they are. They gradually gain an insight into the relationship of man's activities to the physical environment, the relation of one activity to another, and the interdependence of the various activities. For instance, in Pittsburgh, the student learns why the steel mills are along the Monongahela and Ohio rivers, why the railroads come into the city along the routes that they do, and why certain types of residential sections have developed in specific areas. They discover how climate and topography have caused serious problems in the construction of streets, homes, factories, and business structures.

Each community has its unique personality as a result of the interplay of man and nature. A study of any community today reveals the interdependence of all communities and nations. Of course, the extent to which the study of the local community is carried on into its national and international relations depends upon the maturity of the group. In the primary grades the chief objective in local community study is the development of basic concepts of natural and cultural features of the landscape. This study is mainly descriptive, with only simple relationships pointed out. In the upper grades and high school, a more intensive study of the local community is possible. The city or area is mapped according to man's use of it and man's adaptation to the environment is studied. The reasons for the development of the community, its prosperity or lack of it, are sought and its natural resources are studied. As Jensen says:[4]

> The pupil who has had an opportunity to learn facts and discuss problems of the home community from the viewpoint of geography, grows up into a citizen more likely to view the physical facts of problems objectively, and more likely to arrive at reasonable conclusions. Moreover, as the growing child discusses problems of geography applied to local community problems with his parents, the school geography class comes to influence the thinking of adults in the community.

[4] J. Granville Jensen, "The Home Community," *Geographic Approaches to Social Education,* Nineteenth Yearbook (Washington, D.C., National Council for the Social Studies, 1947), Ch. 16.

Reading the Landscape

Aids Map Interpretation

Field work aids in intelligent map interpretation by giving meaning to map symbols. As Edna Eisen[5] says "Through recording in map language their field experiences, the pupils develop an appreciation of what goes into map-making, and a greater ability to translate map language back into landscape features for which they stand."

Improves Community Relationships

Communities differ in the kind of opportunities for field work which they offer, but every community no matter how small contains much worth observation. If community study is planned and the excursions carefully organized, relations between school and community should be improved. As Jensen says:[6]

Use of the local community as a geography laboratory pays most dividends when local citizens, businessmen, and technical personnel are called upon to help carry out the field experience. Even though one may feel entirely competent to explain the interrelationships of the industrial plant, the water system, or the economic bases for urban development, it is far better to ask the manager of the industrial plant, the city engineer, or the Chamber of Commerce leader to join the party. By so doing, the members of the party come to know the leaders of the community and the community leaders in turn come to understand better the work of the school, and in particular, the significance of geographic instruction.

With such training, the individual student gains a sense of responsibility and a better understanding of his place in the community.

Forwards Personal Development

Aside from the geographic value of the field trip, the personal development of the child is forwarded. If the teacher carefully plans and guides the excursion, the children should learn the neces-

---

[5] Edna Eisen, "Field Work in High School," *Journal of Geography,* Vol. 37 (February, 1938), pp. 75–77.
[6] J. G. Jensen, *op. cit.*

sity of planning their work if a project is to be carried out successfully. They discover that there are many primary sources of information in addition to their textbook. They learn how to seek out these varied sources of information, how to question people, and how to listen in order to gain pertinent facts. They also should learn to evaluate information by weighing facts and becoming critical of conclusions. As they seek additional information, and summarize their findings, they have practice in rounding out and completing a definite piece of work. In noting interrelationships in life situations on their trips, the interdependence of all is driven home.

Using the local landscape and studying the home community is not an easy method of teaching but is rich in opportunities to learn. But "Geography is most interesting, most real, most vital, when the realities existing together in the home community are studied."[7]

THE ORGANIZATION AND CONDUCT OF A FIELD TRIP

To secure maximum results, the teacher must make detailed and careful preparations for the field trip. The teacher's planning includes a number of definite steps: preparing himself; planning the administrative details; preparing the class; conducting the trip, and finally evaluating and checking the results.

The Teacher's Preparation

In selecting the trip, the teacher needs to consider the age and maturity of his group and also what he wishes the children to learn. The trip should enable the children to observe specific natural and cultural features of the landscape, and note their interrelationships on the child's level of comprehension. In the primary grades, the trips should be for the observation of natural features— streams, ponds, lakes, rivers, hills, valleys, and such features as the local scene offers. In towns and cities, some of these may be ob-

[7] Jensen *op. cit.*, p. 190.

Reading the Landscape

served in parks or unused areas. Even in a short walk, the children may become acquainted with different trees, flowers, and plants, and note the signs of the seasons. There should also be trips to observe cultural features, such as an airport, railroad station, barns, silo, types of homes, factories, and many others.

For the middle grades, actual landscape reading becomes more meaningful. In connection with various units, worthwhile trips may be taken to different parts of a town or city to observe different types of residential areas, recreational areas, and manufacturing locations, noting where they are and why. Some plants and factories may be visited to secure needed information. In rural areas, trips may be made to note land erosion, and the different uses of land as affected by slope, soil, drainage, and so forth.

The trip should not be so long as to exhaust both the teacher and the children, nor should too much be attempted. A kindergarten teacher took her class on a visit to a dairy and a farm in *one* day. As a result, the five-year-olds were completely exhausted and they saw so much that they were confused. This can happen with older children also.

In planning the trip, the teacher must consider the cost, the means of transportation, size of the group, the willingness of the principal and fellow teachers to co-operate, and the attitude of the parents. If the trip includes a visit to factory or farm, permission of the manager or owner and his co-operation are necessary.

Many of the excursions in the primary and elementary school are within walking distance, for it is mainly the immediate environment that is to be explored. On longer trips, street cars, buses, trains, or private automobiles may be used. Some schools provide for the expenses of trips in their budgets, in others the PTA provides the money. A chartered bus or the school bus is the best method of transportation. A bus accommodates an average size class. Instructions and explanations can be given to the whole class, and observations by the children can be made more easily.

Arrangements must be made with the school principal in all cases. His permission and co-operation are essential. Also, if the trip involves two or three hours, the co-operation of other teachers in re-arranging schedules may be necessary.

Another of the essential details is that of communicating with parents, explaining the trip, and securing their permission. This permission should be in writing, unless the use of the excursion or field trip is a recognized and regular part of the school curriculum, as it is in some communities.

If a museum, factory, market, or farm is to be visited, the teacher must contact the manager or owner to secure permission for the class visit, and explain the purposes of the visit. He needs to obtain a definite understanding as to the size of the group that can come, arrange the time of arrival, the length of the stay, and arrange for a guide if one is necessary.

All of these necessary details take time and tact, but whether the trip is a success or failure depends upon the proper preparation of these details. Of course, after a series of trips have once been set up, in the following years these details are routine. In many schools all trips are arranged before school begins, for they are a part of the regular school schedule.

Personal Preparation of the Teacher

The teacher must become thoroughly familiar with the route and the place to be visited. In going over the route he should make notes on the natural and cultural feature to be observed in the order that they will be seen. He should note the geographic relationships which are to be pointed out and discussed. If the group is visiting a plant where a guide or guides are used, he should have a conference with the guide. A guide usually has a prepared speech to use with adults that may not be wholly suitable for the class. The teacher may be able to help the guide to adapt his usual patter to the class' interest and understanding, and also prepare him for the questions that the children are likely to ask.

After familiarizing himself with the trip, the teacher needs to make a definite lesson plan and prepare guide sheets for the use of the class. A map to accompany the guide sheet is a requisite. On

Reading the Landscape

the map, the route to be followed is marked. The guide sheet should list the natural and cultural features to be observed in the order that the students will see them. It should also contain brief explanations and questions.[8]

In making the guide sheet, the teacher must keep in mind the major purposes of the trip. He should keep out nonessentials and not try to cover too much. He should list the necessary material, if any, that each child should have, such as pencil, notebook, and sketching pad, in addition to the guide sheet. Finally the teacher should make a tentative plan for later evaluation and testing.

Preparation of the Class

The class should feel a definite need for the trip as an outgrowth of their class work. The teacher can arouse the interest of the students through class discussions by asking questions which arouse curiosity or which challenge. Through these means, the trip may be suggested as a means of securing more information, or for clearing up points that bother them. Frequently during class discussions of a topic or problem, both the teacher and the class discover that some students have hazy ideas concerning certain phases of a topic, or lack necessary visual imagery. For instance in a steel center, such questions as the following came up, "What does a steel mill look like? How do you recognize a blast furnace? What is a coal barge? How does a lock work?"

Adelaide Blouch of Lakewood, Ohio, states: "Our trips have definite purposes growing out of school work, such as finding answers to these questions, 'How is land used in the vicinity of our school? From what places do our winter fruits and vegetables come? How does our city get its water supply? What land forms may be seen in our vicinity?' "[9]

Then through teacher-pupil planning, a working organization is

---

[8] An example of a carefully prepared Guide Sheet may be found in *Audio-Visual Materials and Methods in the Social Studies*, Eighteenth Yearbook (Washington, D. C., National Council for the Social Studies, 1946), pp. 54–59.

[9] Adelaide Blouch, "Field Activities in the Middle Grades," *Journal of Geography*, Vol. 39 (September, 1940), p. 246.

developed, and during class discussion specific aims are set up. The teacher keeps the attention of the class focused on the specific problems. During this planning stage, he also builds the vocabulary that is needed for intelligent observation.

The administrative organization of the class should be considered. One effective way of organizing, is to divide the class into groups with a leader for each who is the director and spokesman of the group. There should be a discussion of group responsibilities, such as safety precautions, group and individual behavior, and courtesy to bus drivers, guides, and others. The pupils should understand that the trip is a privilege, and in visiting a factory, a dairy, or any other place they are guests. If standards of behavior are established by the group, the maintaining of discipline will be far easier.

The route and plan for the trip should be gone over with the class. The class may have some worthwhile suggestions which may not have occurred to the teacher. Finally, the class planning should include a discussion of why and how the trip should be evaluated.

Conduct of the Trip

If the procedure of the trip has been planned as outlined in the foregoing discussion, the actual conduct of the trip will proceed with a minimum of inconvenience and delay. The teacher should be in control at all times, but he should not be fussy over minor matters. He should keep in touch with all of the group, making necessary explanations, calling attention to pertinent points, and occasionally asking questions.

Follow-Up Activities

Time should be given for a thorough discussion of the trip, for verifying the information, and, in some cases, seeking additional information for questions that were not satisfactorily answered. Some type of summary should be made which may be in the form of a written or oral report of the findings.

Some activities that may be worthwhile, depending upon the

Reading the Landscape

type of field trip, are completing sketch maps, filling in outline maps, and organizing charts or posters illustrating some phase or topic or the relationships noted. The trip may be used to furnish an idea for an auditorium program, a radio or television presentation, a booklet, or an article for the newspaper. Oftentimes the trip leads into independent investigations by individuals in the class, and follow-up visits.

The class as well as the teacher should evaluate the trip not only in terms of information gained but also in terms of its social value. In the evaluation, such questions as the following might be discussed:

Why was the trip helpful in the study of —————— ?
Why did we waste time? How can we prevent this happening again?
Did we as a class live up to our responsibilities? Did we share necessary work? Did we look out for our own safety? Did we consider all the members of our group? Did we listen and act courteously to our guide and others, as well as to members of our class?

In looking back over the trip, the teacher should ask himself such questions as: "Has the trip motivated other activities? Did the class gain sufficient learning and understanding to make the trip worthwhile for the time involved? In what respects can my plans be improved?"

ANALYZING THE LANDSCAPE

The natural landscape is the foundation upon which the cultural landscape is built. It is the landscape to which man has had to accommodate himself as he has developed an area. In many areas, such as in cities and industrial and commercial districts, the cultural landscape is so prominent that the natural features are obscured. For example, one usually thinks of soil and rock in connection with farming, but both are important elements in cities. If a city is built in a hilly area where shale predominates, stable foundations are a problem in construction. A wet season or an unusually severe rainstorm could cause the slipping of hillsides, with the result that houses move down slope and low areas are flooded with silt. Consider the problems New Orleans has had because it is built on a low, flat, marshy flood-plain. New York's massive skyscrapers are possible to construct because granite bedrock supports their weight.

The cultural landscape consists of man's homes and buildings, cultivated land, transportation facilities—roads, bridges, railroads, canals—mines, manufacturing plants, recreational areas, and population distribution and density, in fact all that man is responsible for. Various arrangements of these features constitute types of cultural landscapes. Man may transform so many of the surface aspects of the natural landscape that after a time it becomes obscured or unrecognizable. Man may mine the minerals, cut down the trees, destroy the wild game, harness the streams for power, navigation or irrigation, and cover the surface with farms, towns, factories, and other manifestations of his culture. But still, certain areas seem to develop into regions of farming, others into regions of manufacturing or commerce. This happens regularly enough to lead one to suspect that even though man can and does transform or even obliterate the natural landscape, there are certain causal forces in existence which he cannot control, and which, in turn, while they do not control him, do certainly, set the broad limits to what he may do in any given area.[10]

In a field trip, the students make notes on the natural and cultural features, and draw sketch maps or fill in outline base maps locating the features on the map. During the trip, the class, with the help of the teacher, should note easily understood relationships between activities represented by the cultural landscape and the natural environment. Back in the classroom, through map work and class discussion based on their notes and sketches, the geographic landscape is developed. Such questions as follow, may be used to bring out the geographic relationships:

[10] C. Langdon White, and George T. Renner, *College Geography* (New York, Appleton-Century-Crofts, Inc., 1957).

Reading the Landscape

How have the people been affected by the terrain (topography) in laying out the community and the location of roads, streets, parks, harbor, air fields, and so forth?

What kinds of crops or other agricultural products are found in the community? How are these affected by soil, terrain, slope, drainage, climate, and so forth?

How are the industries affected by sources of raw materials, soil, water supply, terrain, transportation facilities, and others?

What changes in the physical environment have the people made in the construction of dams, irrigation, tunnels, drainage, the cutting of forests, and by mining or quarrying?

How are the activities of the community affected by climate—industries, sports, architecture, heating or cooling arrangements, drainage or irrigation, and so forth?

How has the physical environment affected the government of the community—budget demands for instance? Are irrigation or drainage authorities needed?

These are general questions to direct the students' attention to the effect geography has upon human affairs, which is the aim of a field trip. Such questions must be modified and made specific for each community. Finally, a summary of the outstanding geographic relationships illustrated in the community should be written or illustrated through maps, diagrams, and charts.

SUMMARY

Field trips for the purpose of reading the landscape are vital in geographic education. The teacher must select the trips carefully, with the aim of developing concepts and geographic understanding. Well-chosen and skillfully conducted trips give a strong concrete basis for geography work, but to secure such results requires careful preliminary planning of details. The class must be ready for the trip with guide sheets, maps, and other materials prepared and at hand for immediate use. The follow-up work should be interesting and worthwhile. Then both teacher and class will find the trip rich in opportunities to learn, and a source of personal growth.

ILLUSTRATIVE PLANS FOR FIELD TRIPS

A FOURTH-GRADE TRIP TO A NEARBY STREAM
Prepared by Ethel Mink

The fourth grade was ready to study how people lived along the Congo River. I knew that in reading about a trip on the Congo the children would encounter a number of new terms. In preparing the class I suggested that we visit a nearby stream and see what we could learn. We discussed some of the things we would look for:

1. Direction the stream flowed.
2. The movement of the water (the current).
3. The source of the stream.
4. The basin of the stream.
5. What a valley is.

The Trip Itself:

During our geography class we went on our journey. We walked from the school across the plateau and down the slope to the valley. We noticed gullys, slope of the hill, and the valley below. When we reached the creek the children stood along the bank, and I crossed over to the other side. Questions were asked, such as:

1. What direction is the water flowing?
2. Which way is downstream? Upstream?
3. Which way would we go to be going with the current?
4. Which way would we travel to reach the water's source? Its mouth?

Then we talked about where the water would be running more swiftly, and where the water would be dangerous to travel upon because of large stones in the creek. This brought out the danger of rapids and navigable and unnavigable waters. We were in the valley, and the land that was being drained by this stream was the stream's basin.

We were then ready to go back to our classroom and read about the Congo River. To the children the words had meaning, and they could readily understand why we had to take a train part way, and why it would be harder to get to the native village than to go back to the seaport.

Other Observations:

During the year we have gone outside and noticed the sun's position in the morning, noon, and evening. Then we have noted the sun's position in September and in December. We have drawn pictures of the

Reading the Landscape 155

sun in the sky in September; in the morning, noon, and evening. Then in December we drew pictures of the sun's position at different times. I do think that this helps explain the sun's position at different seasons and its effect upon the lands where it is high in the sky or low in the sky.

A BUS TRIP TO THE CLEVELAND FLATS
Field Trip and Observations for 5th Grade
prepared by Lucille Kenney, Hayes School, Lakewood, Ohio

I. CLARK AVENUE BRIDGE

This is the longest bridge in Cleveland. It is 6,687 feet in length and crosses the Cuyahoga Valley as well as the Cuyahoga River. Looking into the Cuyahoga Valley from Clark Avenue Bridge, you should see:

1. Cuyahoga River
    a. Are there any boats on the river?
    b. With what are they loaded?
    c. Where are they unloading their cargoes?
2. Blast furnaces and stoves
    The blast furnaces and stoves are on the west side of the river. The Otis Steel Co. furnaces are south of the bridge; the Corrigan and McKinney north of the bridge.
    a. How many blast furnaces do you see?
    b. Can you find the three materials put into the blast furnaces? What are they?
    c. Can you find the two materials that are taken from the furnaces? The slag may be drawn off into a slag pit, or may be carried away in ladles. Are they emptying ladles at any place? The pig iron may be taken away in ladles or may be cooled in molds.
3. Buildings with open hearth furnaces
    a. Can you find any scrap iron used in these furnaces?
    b. Can you find the steel caskets in which the scrap is carried to the furnaces?
    c. Can you find an electro-magnet handling the scrap?
4. Coke ovens
    a. Is the ram working? It pushes the coke from the oven.
    b. How does the coke look when it drops into the car?
    c. How is the coke cooled? The tall building with the cloud of steam coming from the top is the quencher.
5. Railroads
    a. Can you find the names of the railroads?
    b. Why are railroads necessary in this region?

6. Check each of the following that you have seen:

Blast furnace	Limestone	Coke ovens	Electro-magnet
Stoves	Slag	Coke	Lake freighter
Iron Ore	Pig Iron	Scrap Iron	Open hearth furnaces

II. Along Independence Road You Will See:

1. The Corrigan McKinney Steel Co.
    a. How many blast furnaces do you see?
    b. Notice the storage piles of pig iron. What will be done with the material?
    c. Notice the scrap iron.
    d. Notice the steel ingots.
    e. Notice the tall building that houses the Bessemer Converter. This is where pig iron is changed into steel in about 30 minutes. The process is best for heavy objects, such as rails for railroads, and car wheels.
2. The Dupont Chemical Company
3. The Sohio Refinery
4. The Illinois-Carnegie Plant of the American Steel and Wire Co.

III. At Collision Bend

1. Give reasons why it is a problem for boats to get around this bend in the river.
2. Notice: The Terminal Building, The Illuminating Company, The B&O RR. This railroad follows the Ohio Erie Canal bed.

IV. Along Canal Road

This road follows along the old Ohio Erie Canal. It goes under the tracks of the Terminal.
What large paint company do you pass on this road?
Check on the following that you have seen:

Pig iron
Scrap iron
Oil storage tanks
Ingots
Bessemer Converter
Collision Bend
Piles of sulphur
Old Ohio Erie Canal bed
Terminal Building
Baltimore and Ohio Railroad tracks

Reading the Landscape

V. On Merwin Street You Will See:
1. Large horizontal tanks filled with turpentine. In the nearby cans is resin.
   a. In what industry will these products be used?
   b. From what part of our country did these products come?
2. Erie Railroad Loading Docks
   a. How does the coal reach the docks?
   b. What is done with the cars of coal at this dock?
3. Irish Town Bend
   a. This part of the river got its name from the many Irish who worked and lived along the Ohio Erie Canal.
4. Sapphire Flour Co.
   Here it is possible to store 1,000,000 bushels of wheat. This year wheat is being shipped east from Cleveland through the New York State Barge Canal. Note the old mill stone beside the storage bins.
5. Booth Fisheries
   Here you should see nets drying.
   a. Where have they been used?
   b. Are there any tugs at the dock?

VI. Along Division Avenue You Will See:
1. Erie ore docks
2. Allied Oil storage tanks
3. Housing project
4. Filtration plant
5. American Shipbuilding Company
6. Sewage disposal plant

Check the following that you have seen:

Turpentine tanks	Wheat storage bins	Lake freighter
Cans of resin	Fishing nets	Tugs
Coal loading docks	Trains of coal	Ore unloader
Grain elevator	Oil storage tanks	Iron ore

VII. Pennsylvania Ore Docks
1. What is the name of the freighter?
2. From where did the boat come?
3. How much ore has been unloaded?
4. What is being done with the ore as it is taken from the freighter?

5. Where is the boat going after it has been unloaded?
6. What is the length of the freighter?
7. _____ and _____ routes meet at this dock.
List any other kinds of work you see going on in this valley.

REFERENCES

ANDERZHON, Mamie L., "Geographic Field Work in Community Study for Junior High Level," *Journal of Geography*, Vol. 51 (November, 1952), pp. 325–332.

ATYEO, H. C., "The Excursion in Social Education," *Audio-Visual Methods in the Social Studies*, Eighteenth Yearbook (Washington, D.C., National Council for the Social Studies, 1947), pp. 33–52.

BERRY, W. J., "Laboratory Work in Geography," *School Science and Mathematics*, Vol. 33 (June, 1933), pp. 596–603.

BLOUCH, Adelaide, "City Study in the Upper Elementary Grades," *Journal of Geography*, Vol. 47 (November, 1948), pp. 306–310.

―――, "Field Activities in the Middle Grades," *Journal of Geography*, Vol. 39 (September, 1940), pp. 246–248.

BROWNELL, Joseph W., "An Approach to Field Experience in Eighth Grade Geography," *Journal of Geography*, Vol. 55 (April, 1956), pp. 200–203.

BRYAN, H. E., "Out of the Classroom into Life," Thirteenth Yearbook, National Elementary Principals (Washington, D.C., Department of NEA Association, June, 1934), pp. 278–283.

CORFIELD, G. S., "The Out-of-Doors: Geography's Natural Laboratory," *Journal of Geography*, Vol. 38 (May, 1939), pp. 195–199.

DAVIS, L. C., "Field Work in Geography," *Educational Method*, Vol. 17 (March, 1938), pp. 293–296.

DEIHL, Ivan C., "Methods of Procedure for an Excursion," *Journal of Geography*, Vol. 39 (February, 1940), pp. 78–80.

DIFFENDERFER, N. R., "Junior High Field Trips in Geography," *Journal of Geography*, Vol. 54 (January, 1955), pp. 22–24.

DILLON, Jessie M., "Field Trips in the Elementary School," *Teaching of Geography*, Thirty-second Yearbook, National Society for the Study of Education (Bloomington, Ill., Public School Publishing Co., 1933), pp. 519–524.

EISEN, Edna E., "Field Work in Junior and Senior High School," *Journal of Geography*, Vol. 37 (February, 1938), pp. 75–77.

―――, "Geography Field Work at Junior High School Level," *School*

Science and Mathematics, Vol. 33 (December, 1933), pp. 929–940.
———, "Geography Field Work with Junior High Pupils," *Journal of Geography*, Vol. 30 (February, 1931), pp. 61–73.
FRENCH, W. W., "Outdoor Geography in the Classroom," *Journal of Education* (London, Eng.), Vol. 86 (September, 1944), pp. 429–431.
GREGORY, W. M., "Maps in Community Study," *Audio-Visual Methods in the Social Studies*, Eighteenth Yearbook (Washington, D.C., National Council for the Social Studies, 1947), pp. 131–144.
GROSS, H. H., "An Experiment in Home Community Geography," *Journal of Geography*, Vol. 54 (November, 1955), pp. 403–406.
HARDEN, Mary, "Going Places and Seeing Things," *Educational Method*, Vol. 14 (March, 1935), pp. 324–331.
JENSEN, J. Granville, "The Home Community," *Geographic Approaches to Social Education*, Nineteenth Yearbook (Washington, D.C., National Council for the Social Studies, 1948), pp. 176–190.
KENNY, Arletta, C., "Teaching the Wholesale Market in Grade Two," *Journal of Geography*, Vol. 51 (December, 1952), pp. 365–374.
KING, Gladys H., "The Teaching of Local Geography in the Fifth Grade," *Journal of Geography*, Vol. 51 (October, 1952), pp. 283–284.
KUSCH, Monica, "An Experiment in Fifth Grade Field Work," *Journal of Geography*, Vol. 35 (May, 1936), pp. 179–185.
LAINE, O. H., "Who Says That Geography Isn't Practical," *Journal of Geography*, Vol. 52 (May, 1953), pp. 210–215.
PACE, Ethel, "Constructive Activity—Follows a Field Trip," *Journal of Geography*, Vol. 52 (April, 1953), pp. 144–146.
PARKER, Edith, "Geography and the Community," *Journal of Geography*, Vol. 40 (March, 1941), pp. 98–108.
PREBLE, C. S., "Field Trips in Upper Grade Geography," *Journal of Geography*, Vol. 31 (October, 1932), pp. 296–304.
RIDGLEY, Douglas C., "Some Possibilities for Field Work in Elementary Geography," *Journal of Geography*, Vol. 34 (April, 1935), pp. 161–168.
RIGGS, Margaret, "Geography Work in the Small City," *Journal of Geography*, Vol. 37 (January, 1938), pp. 28–31.
SMITH, Villa B., "A Field Study from the Terminal Tower in Cleveland," *Audio-Visual Methods in the Social Studies*, Eighteenth Yearbook (Washington, D.C., National Council for the Social Studies, 1947), pp. 53–60.

VOUGH, Maude, "Adventures in Geography in Second Grade," *Journal of Geography*, Vol. 49 (January, 1950), pp. 26–29.

ZACHARI, Elizabeth D., "Field Trip Experiences in the Intermediate Grades," *Journal of Geography*, Vol. 33 (February, 1934), pp. 49–60.

6

Current Events in Geographic Education

WITHOUT QUESTION, current-events material is one of the geography teacher's valuable instructional aids. In modern geography we are endeavoring to discover how people in various regions of the world are trying to establish "workable connections" with the earth resources of their home region and with the world at large. Furthermore, such connections between man and the earth are constantly changing, taking on new meanings and values. Consequently, geography teachers are concerned with the three following problems: (1) What activities, both economic and cultural, is man carrying on in any given locality? (2) Why is he carrying on these particular activities? (3) What problems is he meeting? Any current event which deals with these problems involves geography.

An illustration of this fact was the hurricane which struck New England in September, 1938. The newspapers and magazines contained articles from day to day giving the progress of the storm and its effect upon New England. For several weeks articles continued to appear. Every phase of life in New England and for some distance in the interior was affected by this terrific storm which swept northward outside the usual path of hurricanes. Another newspaper heading, "The Soviet Will Build Arctic Fuel Bases," has reference to present-day geography. The Soviet is building air bases on the Siberian Coast. The reason for building air bases in these high latitudes with their severe climate lies in the shape of the earth, the severe climate, and other natural conditions which make land and sea transportation difficult or impossible. Air transportation is hazardous but is possible. Man meets numerous problems in building and maintaining air bases in such regions, and these problems are chiefly the result of the natural environment.

One can scan any newspaper and find several articles which deal with man's activities in some part of the world in their relation to the physical environment. Illustrations of such articles are the following headlines taken from newspapers at various times:

VENEZUELA PUMPS OIL PROFIT INTO IRON
ALUMINUM INDUSTRY SLATED FOR CANADIAN WEST COAST
U.S. UNIT TO STUDY ICE IN ANTARCTICA
TEXAS GULF CUTS PRICE OF SULPHUR
OIL CONCERNS CUT IMPORTS

None of these articles brings out geographic relationships directly, but the teacher's job is to help the children to analyze the event and see the geography behind it.

Furthermore, articles from newspapers and magazines dealing with current happenings should be used constantly in the schoolroom, because the school is as much a part of life as the home, the office, or the factory. The children are often as interested in current events as adults are. When children are uninterested, investigation usually discloses that they do not have access to such material. The number of families who do not take *any* newspaper or magazine regularly is astounding. This fact alone is a compelling reason for the school to use current events in connection with geography, and also other subjects in the curriculum.

THE "WHY" OF USING CURRENT EVENTS

Current events serve various purposes in geographic education. One function is to help the pupils to realize how geography is related to everyday life, in other words, "to make geography real." Many teachers and children think of geography as something between the covers of a book with no application or connection to the activities of people in general. A class may study Venezuela—the topography, the climate, the resources, the people and their work, the cities, and the rivers—yet Venezuela may not be a wholly real country of people to them. But a current news item about opening up the iron mines, building a port, dredging the lower Orinoco to open up a ship channel, the amount of ore shipped to the United States and its destination in the United States brings home to them the importance to themselves of that land and its people. It is possible for a child to note or read such a news item and not make the connection with the country he is studying about in school. The teacher's job is to bring the two together, to help the child to see the geography behind that news item and apply it.

Another important purpose in the use of current events is to develop a critical, thoughtful attitude toward current happenings as reported in newspapers. It is one thing to read a newspaper and quite another to read it with understanding. The majority of people read the headlines and note two or three facts which they accept without the slightest question. To illustrate this point consider the following headline in a newspaper after World War II:

ALLIES LET SOVIET DRAFT DANUBE PACT
Soviet Aides Speed Plan for Danube

The majority of readers glance at the headlines, skim the details rapidly and dismiss them. They remark, "What's up now? Where is the Danube? In Germany? Oh, well, it must be another one of those European rivers." Few if any will even look at a map to see where the river is, let alone try to think through some of the important questions involved. If the news item really enlightens the reader and affects his thinking, he will have to read the article carefully and think about the following points:

Where is the Danube located?
What countries does it border or flow through?

How important is it as a waterway?
Why are we interested in it?
Should the Soviet control it?
What does Soviet control imply as to the future of the Danube and the Danubian countries?

These are only a few of the questions and associations which should be considered and thought through if a person reads the article intelligently. As Ernest Dimnet, the great French scholar, says:[1]

> Few school books can sum up as many events of world wide importance as those which day after day have filled the newspapers since 1914. . . . Indeed the newspaper is richer than any textbook, and blind indeed must be the people who daily glance at it without realizing that if the quality of our thought depends upon that of the images we garner in, here is an incomparable chance. But blind indeed are most people, for the so-called wise and the foolish agree in speaking contemptuously of what they all read unintelligently.

Thus in using current events, the teacher trains his pupils in reading a newspaper with discrimination and intelligence. The pupils garner facts as materials for thinking.

The proper use of current events in the geography class should develop better understanding of other peoples and also of our part as American citizens in improving relations between nations, because the daily news gives a picture of the immediate yet ever changing relations between nations and peoples. News items such as the following focus our attention on international relations in a specific region, Saudi Arabia and the Middle East:

WORLD OIL STRUGGLE GROWS MORE INTENSE
WORLD OF SAND MOVES IN ON CITY OF OIL
SAUDI ARABIA AND OIL FIRM AGREE TO 50-50 PROFIT SPLIT
ARABIAN STATE FINDS OIL FIELDS STRONG BAR TO NEUTRALITY
MORE RENT FOR PIPE LINES

[1] Ernest Dimnet, *The Art of Thinking* (New York, Simon & Schuster, 1928), pp. 149–150.

Current Events in Geographic Education

LEBANON SNARES OIL PROBLEM AS IRAQI TROOPS STAND WATCH ON TWO FRONTIERS
FUSE TO MIDEAST OIL SPUTTERS

These were a few of the headlines from 1950 to 1956 on the oil fields and nations of the Middle East, but as far back as 1930 the oil of that area was making headlines frequently. To read any of these items intelligently requires historical and geographical background. One needs to know where the oil deposits are, what nations are involved, who is developing the oil, where it is marketed, under what agreements are the oil fields being developed, how is the oil being transported, and what are some of the handicaps, such as climate, topography, and so forth, that the oil companies have to overcome. Even the religion and customs of the Arabs are involved. For example, the oil companies had to agree to permit the Arab employees to stop work and pray, facing Mecca, at stated intervals.

The oil companies had to build towns, air-conditioned homes, and schools for their European and American employees. They also had to instruct them regarding Arab customs. Those American citizens who as children and as adults were familiar with the past events of the Middle East were better able to understand the world problem caused by President Nasser of Egypt's seizure of the Suez Canal and the ensuing events. As Marcus Aurelius of ancient Rome said, "He who knows not the world knows not his own place in it."

The study of current news concerning the United States gives the child a picture of the changing geography of his own country and also its problems. The newspapers tell of the growth of industries in the Far West and in the South, the building of dams and highways, the shifts in population, the problems caused by flood and drought, the farmers' problems, and so forth. All of these have a geographic base and cannot be understood without a knowledge of the geography of the various regions where the events are taking place. Even our political campaigns involve geography. The speeches and promises of both parties in most campaigns can be evaluated only if you know the geography behind the issues. For instance, in 1956 the declining income of the farmer, the problem of public versus private development of water power, and foreign policy were some of the issues, and to understand and evaluate the position of either party with respect to these problems was impossible unless one knew at least some of the geography that was basic to them.

The use of current events in the class also has some indirect values. One of these is the improvement in map reading and interpretation. In order to develop the geographic setting of current events, the teacher must guide the children in reading the newspaper map that often accompanies the article and also guide them in selecting and reading atlas or textbook maps needed for additional information. Often physical-political, rainfall, population distribution, and other distribution maps are needed. A physical map is necessary to give some understanding of the topography of a region. Topography frequently influences trade routes, the relative accessibility of a region, the success of the people in developing an area—in brief, what choices the people have in making a living in the region.

Climatic conditions always have a bearing upon man's life and activities. The amount and distribution of rainfall, the range of temperature, the length of the growing season, the winds, and types of storms characteristic of a region are important. Soil, minerals, and forests all play their part in human events. For instance, the following summary of an article describing a flood in India involves climate and topography:

In October, 1956, there was a disastrous flood in northwestern India. For a week, 7 to 12 inches of rain had fallen on the foothills of the Himalayas. This is more than New York City gets in two average months. The swollen waters of the Jumna and its tributaries poured over the flat farmlands and into New Delhi. Tens of thousands fled from the raging waters driving their cattle ahead. The Taj Mahal at Agra was cut off by the flood waters to the disappointment of hundreds of tourists. One official reported that in one state 300,000 homes were destroyed, 30 million dollars worth of crops ruined, and the irrigation work of ten years wrecked.

Current Events in Geographic Education 167

More details were given in the article. To really understand this disaster a physical-political map should be studied to locate the Jumna River, New Delhi, and Agra and also to observe their location in respect to the Himalayas, noting the topography which was one cause of the widespread destruction. A discussion of this article gives the teacher an opportunity to review or to explain the seasonal distribution of rainfall in India and the monsoons. This heavy rain is unusual for October in northwest India. Following the summer monsoon October is usually dry and clear, but this event illustrates how uncertain the weather is and how the monsoons affect India.

Nearly every current event of any importance is tied up with some of these natural factors. As the pupils use the various maps in getting information about some current happening, they see the functional value of maps and are more likely to habitually turn to a map when reading about world affairs.

Another indirect value is practice in different types of reading. As the children go through newspapers, they need to practice skimming as well as to read with comprehension. The greater part of a newspaper may be skimmed, for a quick glance at the headlines gives the reader the main points of the story. One can quickly note the articles that are worth careful reading and investigation. To learn what to skip, what to skim, and what to read in the true sense of reading are skills of permanent value to the child. Furthermore, the child is acquiring the skills through an ordinary everyday experience common to the majority of Americans.

The use of current events has a value in developing certain worthwhile social attitudes, such as: (1) interest in keeping up with the news; (2) overcoming prejudice; (3) intelligent attitudes toward political, economic, and social problems. These social attitudes are certainly needed in a democracy.

Finally, from the teacher's standpoint, as one teacher says:[2]

[2] Jane Ungashick, "The Use of Current Events in Geography Teaching," *Journal of Geography,* Vol. 39 (November, 1940), p. 319.

The use of current events in the manner discussed gives to the students a greater sense of reality, it provides an opportunity to review by enrichment, it provides interest leads resulting in more effective work. To these gains are added an increased interest in the news and increased reading and listening to news broadcasts. The students use the concepts gained in geography in making the news more meaningful, thus using these concepts in exactly the manner which is a major objective in worthwhile geography teaching.

THE SELECTION OF CURRENT EVENTS

In the use of current events, careful selection is necessary because there is such an enormous mass of materials flowing from newspapers, radio, television, and magazines. One is overwhelmed by its sheer bulk and has a feeling of frustration and confusion. Both the teacher and the students need guiding principles in the selection of what current materials are to be used.

A current event deserves a place in the geography classroom:

1. If it has geographic quality, that is, shows a fairly direct relationship between man's activities and the natural environment.
2. If it provides additional information which has a clear bearing upon the topic, country, or people that the class is studying.
3. If it clarifies a situation or helps to answer a question or problem under consideration.
4. If it is related to new discoveries and explorations.
5. If it reports major activities by nations or governments, because these usually involve geographic factors.
6. If it helps us to understand national and international affairs and problems.
7. If it illustrates or serves as an up-to-date example of basic geographical principles.

A current event that fulfills one or more of the above conditions is likely to be significant. The teacher must guide the students in setting up similar criteria so that they may develop discrimination in reading newspapers and in selecting items for class use. This takes time, tact, and patience, but it can be done through class discussion, pertinent questions by the teacher, and words of approval as the children improve.

SUGGESTIONS ON USING CURRENT EVENTS IN GEOGRAPHY UNITS

There are as many different ways of using current events as there are teachers. The selection of method depends upon the needs and interests of the student, the topics under consideration, the maturity of the students, and the teacher's preference.

The following general suggestions may be of assistance to the teacher in developing specific techniques in the use of current events.

1. Only a few outstanding events should be considered at any one time, for too many confuse the child. Time is required to read carefully, to think about an article, and to discuss it. Consequently, the article should be of national or world importance, and preferably should be related to the subject matter assigned to the particular grade level. Of course, news does not break in relation to the curriculum, but this problem can be solved by a combination of methods. One method is to permit flexibility in the order of taking up units. For instance, a unit on India may be scheduled for December. However, if in October, an important series of events take place in India; why not move up the unit on India to take advantage of the interest aroused by the newspaper articles?

Another method is to discuss with your class, at the beginning of school in the fall, the areas of the world which they will be studying during the year. Have the class examine the newspapers and note what articles about these regions are appearing. Start the students collecting and filing worthwhile articles which will be available for use when needed. Some type of committee organization may be developed to take care of the clippings as they come in.

2. Really significant news does not end with one event but has continuing chapters. In fact, any event of national or international importance has a past and will have a future; it doesn't just happen. Therefore, the teacher should help the children to see the event in its historical setting and to consider its possible future.

Oftentimes the historical background is the source of an emotional atmosphere which may surround the present event and affect people's attitudes. An illustration of this is the Israel-Arab problem which has been with us ever since the State of Israel was established in 1948. The long history of Palestine, going back to 1025 B.C., is such that Jew, Moslem, and Gentile are affected emotionally in their consideration of events there. If one is to understand, even on the level of a sixth-grader, the conflict in Palestine, one must know something of the history of that tiny strip of land on the eastern edge of the Mediterranean. Palestine has always been a land of conflict. It is a narrow highway between desert and sea, connecting the fertile valleys of the Tigris and Euphrates with the rich land of Egypt. Traders, pilgrims, and armies have met, passed, and fought in it and over it. The desert nomad has always eyed its streams and pastures hungrily. So the conflict of Arab and Jew today is only the present phase of an age-long conflict.

3. The geographic background of almost any current event is of equal importance, and in many cases of even more importance, than the historical setting. For an illustration of the importance of the geographic setting of a current event, take any one of many outstanding events of the past ten years, for instance, Egypt's seizure of the Suez Canal in 1956. One needs to know both the historical and geographic background of the Suez Canal if its vital importance is to be understood. The importance of the Suez Canal and its control is due to its location, connecting the Mediterranean and Red Sea on the vital trade route between Europe and the oil-rich nations of Arabia, Iraq, and Iran. It is also of importance to India and the Southeastern Asiatic nations as it is their shortest route to the nations of western Europe. Geographic factors also play a part in the running of the Canal. It lies in a desert region, and sand storms during certain seasons reduce visibility almost to zero. Constant dredging is necessary to maintain sufficient depth, and the channel shifts. Expert pilots and technical men are necessary to maintain navigation. At the time of Egypt's seizure of the

Canal, there was a serious question of whether Egypt could maintain uninterrupted navigation through the canal.

Some other geographic factors bearing on the Suez Canal were the location of the oil deposits, their development, why European nations were dependent on the Arabian, Iraquan, and Iranian oil, why South American oil could not fill the gap, and why India was interested.

4. Maps should be used constantly. Every event has a specific location that is significant, as well as a past and a future.

5. Every child should be held responsible for a contribution to the discussion of current events, just as in any other part of the curriculum. Furthermore, whatever system of credit is used in the school system should be applied to the study of current events.

6. The use of current-event articles should not cease with class discussion. Those articles which appear to be of permanent value should be preserved. One teacher used a method which built up a series of permanent reference books of great value. A committee from the class selected each week the articles of probable permanent value, while another committee mounted these in blank books. Articles dealing with certain nations of the world were placed together. At the end of the year a table of contents and an index were made. Each class was proud of its book, and tried to produce not only an attractive volume but also a usable one.

In following years, the new classes found these current-event books valuable. They were surprised to find that many of the same places and regions continued to be important in the news. They began to realize the continuity of history and of man's experiences in adjusting his activities to the physical environment. They began to ask *why* certain regions and certain problems reappeared in the headlines. They began to sense certain geographic principles, such as an event in one part of the world often affects man's life in practically every other part of the world. They also began to see the truth of the old saying that it is far better to work with nature than against nature.

7. New concepts and terms in current events must be brought

within the comprehension of the children. In order to read and listen to news reports, vocabularies must be kept up-to-date. Discuss with the class how we learn new words, and then put the suggestions into practice. List new words in a current-event article, discuss their meaning, and give illustrations of their meaning. Insist on the students using the new words in their discussions and written work.

SPECIFIC TECHNIQUES AND ACTIVITIES

There is an endless variety of ways to use current events in the geography class. The following discusses various ways teachers have used, and also projects or activities that they have found worthwhile.

In geographic education probably the best technique is to use current events in relation to the geography and social studies units in the regular course of study. In developing a unit, current events may be used at all stages of the unit. Many teachers have found a timely current event to be an excellent introduction to a unit. The following is an account by a teacher of how she used a news item to introduce a unit.

Several weeks ago a news reporter gave us an interesting item which stated that, in one month, exports and imports of both Switzerland and the Netherlands had decreased about 40 per cent. The children were intrigued by this article and wanted an explanation for this change in trade. In the 7th grades of our system we teach world industries. In beginning the teaching of this type of geography we study the geography of one region and then find similarities to other regions with the same kind of work. The exports of a country are usually a fairly good indication of the industries of its region and make a good starting point for their study. When my children exhibited an interest in why the exports and imports of Switzerland and Netherlands had decreased, I took advantage of this interest and set them to work at finding what those countries exported and imported and with whom they carried on their trade. After they found this material and had worked out tentative answers to their own questions, they were interested in finding out why the commodities exported were raised or manufactured in these countries. This was the starting point for a new unit of work and the interest lead was furnished in a news bulletin.[3]

A class studying South America had a news committee to collect worthwhile news items for each country. When the class was ready to take up Peru, the committee on that country looked over the items on hand. It had several and presented one for the class to discuss on a recent revolt in Peru. At first the teacher was doubtful of its value in a geography class but she said nothing, and one of the committee presented the main points to the class. Briefly, the points emphasized were: A revolt against the president, a dictator, had broken out in Iquitos, but had been suppressed by naval units based south of Iquitos; Peru is not a single nation but really three, geographically, politically, and socially; the country was usually controlled by the wealthy ruling class living in the coastal cities of the desert. Immediately the class wanted to know where Iquitos was, and what was meant by the statement that Peru was not a single nation but three? The textbook map was studied and the pupils readily noted the coastal region, the Andean Mountain region, and the Eastern plains region of the upper Amazon, and Iquitos was located. Someone turned to a rainfall map and called the class's attention to the great difference in rainfall along the Pacific Coast and on the eastern side of the Andes. Questions and possible answers flew about the class. The teacher broke in to suggest the class organize their study. The reference committee was asked to list reference material on the blackboard, the news committee was to post all news items on the bulletin board, and the vocabulary committee was to begin listing new words under the usual heading "Words to Keep in Our Vocabulary—Use Them." These words are suggested by the class as the unit is developed. A map committee was to make and post a large outline map of Peru, on which places and other items would be located. Finally, the class decided that they wanted to find out why Peru was divided

[3] *Ibid.*, pp. 318–319.

into three parts—geographically, socially, and politically. Then the unit was really launched.

During the development of a unit, news items help to bring the geography of a region or nation up-to-date. No textbook can be fully up-to-date, because a year or more elapses between the time it is written and the time it is published. It cannot be revised every year because of the expense; furthermore, schools cannot afford to buy a new edition every year. The class studying Peru found an item on new irrigation projects in northern Peru where a 15,310 foot tunnel under a section of the Andes diverted the Chotano River, draining into the Amazon Basin, into the Chancay River flowing into the Pacific, thus providing additional water for irrigation in the Chancay Valley in the desert. The class was especially interested when they found that an Idaho firm had completed the project.

As news items are used, the pupils not only eagerly watch the papers and magazines themselves but they enlist the aid of their families. Mother and father are forced to read more carefully the worthwhile articles.

The teacher can use old as well as recent articles in the summary and application step in a unit. For instance, during the summarizing and application step in a unit on Venezuela, the teacher placed this statement and question on the board for discussion: "A recent news item makes this statement, 'Although Venezuela has made important strides in developing its agriculture, it still imports large quantities of food.' What have we learned about the geography of Venezuela that helps to explain the above item?"

Another teacher used this headline, "450 Million Dollar Grain Crop Buried in Canadian Snow," and asked: "Where in Canada has this happened? Why do you think so? Why is this not an unusual occurrence in this part of Canada?"

Often weeks or even months after a unit has been finished, another news item comes up about the country or topic. Some of the children always notice this and are eager to bring it up in class again. They get a great amount of satisfaction out of proving their knowledge.

In addition to integrating news items with the unit, there are many other effective ways of using current events, especially in the junior and senior high school classes. One of these is to have individual progressive geography notebooks. This should be a loose-leaf notebook in which the student puts maps, pictures, and newspaper items illustrating the topics or units being studied. The teacher and class should discuss the criteria for a worthwhile notebook, suggesting such points as neatness, geographic value of the material, the use of the pupil's own comments, arrangement, and so forth. The teacher should make clear to the class that mere bulk or a fancy cover does not make a good notebook. From time to time the teacher should give specific directions. The date and source of every article, map, or picture should be stated, then some comments made as to how the article is related to the unit or how in the incident described man's activities were affected by natural forces. The following are examples of instructions to a class at various times:

TOPIC: WORLD TRANSPORTATION

The daily newspapers and current magazines publish many maps. Try to find one or more maps which show world transportation patterns. For example, an air transportation company has published a map showing the world pattern of its air routes. Paste the map in your notebook, and write a title for it if a printed one is not given. Give the source of the map, for example, *The New York Times,* and give the date when the map was published. Write a list of important facts which you can read from the map.

TOPIC: HOW MAN'S LIFE IS AFFECTED BY HIS PHYSICAL ENVIRONMENT

Find in a newspaper the report of a current event which shows how man's life is affected by his physical environment. For example, an article appeared in a newspaper which told how heavy snow tied up railroad traffic, cut down iron and steel production, caused a shortage of coal and food supplies in cities, and shut down flour and grain mills. Your article may be about a storm, a flood, an earthquake, a drought, or some other event. Be sure to give the source and date of the article. Write a set of statements explaining how, in the incident described, man's activities were affected by natural forces. Make a list of place names mentioned in the article and locate these on a map.

The teacher's instructions would vary with the units and the ability and interests of the class. The notebooks should be consulted frequently, for their contents should enrich and illustrate the topics being studied. Although some of the pupils may have the same article, there will be some different ones brought to class depending upon the newspaper the child has access to. Sometimes it is interesting to compare the reports from different newspapers of the same event. Such a progressive geography notebook may be an individual, committee, or even a class activity.

Mary V. Phillips, of New Kensington High School, in her high school senior class uses a written report frequently. The following is the form used:

Name _____
Class _____
Date _____

CURRENT EVENT ASSIGNMENT
HIGH SCHOOL GEOGRAPHY

I. Paper _____

II. Title of Article _____

III. Write a summary of the important items discussed in the article.

IV. What areas of the world are mentioned? Locate these areas on an outline map.

V. Vocabulary—List new words and their meanings.

VI. What cultural and natural items are mentioned in the article?

VII. Give your evaluation of the article.

With a class studying Mexico a teacher put a large map of Mexico on the bulletin board. As the pupils brought in articles on Mexico, each one located the place where the event took place by sticking a pin in the map, then a string was attached and led out to the edge of the map to where the article was posted. Each pupil, before posting his item, gave a brief report to the class of the main points in it and stated why he had selected it. The teacher found that the pupils became acquainted with many places in Mexico not mentioned in their text. At free periods there was usually a group at the map reading and discussing the items.

Some teachers prefer to have a weekly forum during which important current events are discussed, whether or not such items bear upon the unit being studied. Some current events remain of continuing importance, for example, the seizure of the Suez Canal, and the revolts in Poland and Hungary against the Soviets. When the forum plan is used, the class or teacher selects the important event, and the class not only brings in the items as they appear but reads background material on the topic or problem in preparation for the forum discussion. Such a forum is conducted by a chairman selected or elected from the class, and parliamentary procedure is followed during the discussion.

Another method of using current events, either in presenting them or in summarizing the events of a week or a month, is for a pupil to assume the role of a radio or television news commentator. A television receiver may be simulated by the use of a large box with 2 open sides, mounted on a table. Each pupil commentator steps behind the box and speaks as if he were appearing on a television screen. The following is an illustration of such a broadcast by Christobel M. Cordell.[4] A class or a committee could write a similar one using the material from their own selection of current events.

WORLD NEWS ROUND-UP

A Dramatized Radio Broadcast

Introduction:

The characters in the following script are fictional but the facts presented are accurate. The broadcast as presented, however, does not re-

[4] Christobel M. Cordell, "World News Round-up," *Colorful Geography Teaching*, edited by J. Weston Walch (J. Weston Walch, 1954), pp. 155–166.

178 *The Teaching of Geography*

fer to specific events of a particular date. This script can be used in a variety of ways. The entire script might be presented as an assembly program or PTA program to illustrate some of the material covered in geography class. The script could be presented "live," that is, with all characters actually appearing, or it could be produced as an actual broadcast over a PA system, or recorded and then played back.

For classroom use the separate scenes of the script might be presented individually either as a preview of the unit to be studied or as a review after the unit has been studied. Another possibility is to present each scene to the class as a quiz-skit. In this event the name of the place or region involved would be omitted and the students would be required to determine in what part of the world the event described took place. Still another way to make use of the script is to present it in class, either completely or in part, and then assign groups of students to prepare a similar broadcast based on other events such as a tornado, blizzard, earthquake, flood, drought, and others.

This script is based on a variety of sources including newspaper and magazine descriptions of the events involved.

    Scene I: A London hotel lobby
    Scene II: Broadcasting studio, Mexico City
    Scene III: Broadcasting studio, Tripoli, Libya
    Scene IV: Main lobby, North Station, Boston, Massachusetts

Characters:
NARRATOR
NEW YORK ANNOUNCER
LONDON ANNOUNCER
MEXICO CITY ANNOUNCER
TRIPOLI ANNOUNCER
BOSTON ANNOUNCER
MR. LLOYD BARTON, a London businessman
ANNE HUMPHREY, a young woman
MR. R. H. MONTAGNE, a meteorologist
JOSE JIMINEZ, a Mexican farmer
MR. ROBERT LANCASTER, an explorer
WOMAN
MAN
BOY

NARRATOR: We're going to present to you today a radio broadcast based on events that actually have happened in different parts of the world. The broadcast is imaginary and the events described didn't happen all on the same day, or perhaps not even in the same year. But such things have happened and will undoubtedly happen again.

Scene I

NEW YORK ANNOUNCER: Good Afternoon, ladies and gentlemen. It's time once again to bring you our weekly on-the-spot eye witness accounts of unusual and interesting happenings around the world. This week, nature makes news in a number of different ways and in widely scattered places. First we take you to our London reporter. Go ahead, London.

LONDON ANNOUNCER: London reporting. People in this city are talking about only one thing today—fog—or to be more accurate, smog. Fog is common in London, the silvery mist that limits visibility to about 100 yards. Londoners are used to that kind of fog and it doesn't bother them too much, but this is something different. We'll talk more about that difference later. Right now we want to tell you what's happening here. We have set our microphone up in the lobby of a downtown hotel where a number of stranded Londoners have sought refuge. I'm going to let you hear the first-hand experiences of a couple of these people. Here's Mr. Lloyd Barton, who has told me that he's planning to sleep right here in the lobby. Is that right, Sir?

MR. BARTON: I don't see any alternative. That's a fact.

LONDON ANN: Is your home outside London?

MR. BARTON: No sir. Right in the city. Only 12 blocks away, in fact, but it might as well be 12 miles. Out there on the street you can't even see your feet. I'd be dead lost before I went a block.

LONDON ANN: I know what you mean. It's even difficult to see people here in the lobby. There's no transportation available, I suppose, Mr. Barton?

MR. BARTON: None but the subway, which doesn't go near my home. And even if it did there'd be no chance of getting in. They tell me they had to close the gates a while ago because the platforms got so crowded. Long lines there are, of people waiting to get in.

LONDON ANN: How do you usually get home?

MR. BARTON: I drive my own car. I started out from the office in my car but after half a block I just left the car where it was. I couldn't see where I was going and I was afraid I'd knock somebody down. So I'm just going to wait out the fog right here.

LONDON ANN: Thank you, Mr. Barton. We hope it won't be too long before you find your way home. Here's a young lady just coming through the door. Let's find out how she managed to find her way here. Excuse me, Miss, may I ask you a few questions?

MISS HUMPHREY: Yes, of course.

LONDON ANN: First, what is your name?

MISS HUMPHREY: Anne Humphrey . . . Miss Anne Humphrey.

LONDON ANN: Are you also looking for a place to wait out the fog, Miss Humphrey?

MISS HUMPHREY: No, as a matter of fact, I'm staying here in the hotel for a few days. I've just returned from the theater.

LONDON ANN: You're home from the theater so early?

MISS HUMPHREY: There wasn't much point in staying. No one could see the stage except those in the first few rows. I don't believe even the actors could see each other very well.

LONDON ANN: How did you find your way back to the hotel? Were you able to get a taxi?

MISS HUMPHREY: Gracious, no. I'm sure there isn't a taxi left running.

LONDON ANN: You mean you found your way here on foot?

MISS HUMPHREY: I'll tell you what happened, although it will sound quite unbelievable I know. When I came out of the theater I didn't know which way to turn. I just stood there for a minute trying to get my bearings and then I started in what I thought was the right direction. I'd only gone a few steps when I bumped into a gentleman. I asked him if he could tell me whether I was headed in the right direction for the hotel and he said I was going in just the opposite direction.

LONDON ANN: There was a man with a good sense of direction.

MISS HUMPHREY: But wait until you hear the rest. He offered to lead me back to the hotel and he did, without even hesitating. I was utterly amazed and when I asked him how he could do it he said, "It's simple for me. You see, I'm blind." Apparently he had spent the whole day guiding people.

LONDON ANN: That's a remarkable story. Thank you for telling us, Miss Humphrey. . . . I think you're getting an idea, ladies and gentlemen, of the difficulties people are having in London today. Unfortunately, however, there is a much more tragic aspect to this situation than just inconvenience. All over London people are literally choking to death. Most of the deaths are among elderly people and those with bronchitis or asthma. The doctors have no way of getting to all the people who need attention and the hospitals are already overcrowded. But perhaps you're wondering why this "smog" is so much worse than the usual London fog which I described at the beginning. By a fortunate coincidence, one of the fog refugees here in the hotel is an eminent meteorologist, Mr. R. H. Montagne, and he has agreed to answer a few questions. Mr. Montagne, just what is fog?

Mr. Montagne: Fog is a condition that develops when a body of moist air becomes cool and condenses into very tiny drops of moisture which collect particles of soot and smoke.

London Ann: But why is fog so much denser and blacker and more persistent at certain times?

Mr. Montagne: Usually fog is quickly dissipated by the movement of the air. It takes only a faint current to disperse it. Even if there isn't even a slight breeze, however, fog generally rises into the cooler layer of air that is above it. Then it's high enough so that it isn't bothersome.

London Ann: Obviously there hasn't been enough movement of air to dissolve this fog, but why hasn't it risen as you say it usually goes?

Mr. Montagne: Because at this time there's a rare meteorological condition existing. The air above the fog is not cooler, as is commonly the case, but is warmer. We call this condition an "inversion roof." The warmer air up above acts like a cover holding the fog down.

London Ann: That accounts for the fog hanging on but why is this fog denser and blacker than usual?

Mr. Montagne: Simply because the longer it lasts the more soot and smoke it collects. London, as you know, is a coal burning city. Not only the factories but probably two million homes burn soft coal. With the inversion roof that I mentioned there is no way for that black smoke to escape, so it mixes with the fog and we have smog.

London Ann: Is there any way to prevent a smog like this from happening again?

Mr. Montagne: These smogs have been occurring at intervals for hundreds of years. There is no way to eliminate fog as yet, and the only thing to keep it from becoming smog is to reduce the volume of smoke and soot in the air. Before that can happen Londoners will have to change their way of living. From the time of Queen Elizabeth the first, the government has been trying to persuade people to abolish the soft-coal, open fires. But they still burn.

London Ann: Thank you, Mr. Montagne. This has been the London report, ladies and gentlemen, and in London the news can be summed up in just one word, "Smog." We return you now to New York.

New York Ann: Thank you, London. We take you now to our reporter in Mexico City.

Mexico City Ann: Good evening, ladies and gentlemen. The big news in Mexico is that everything is quiet. This may not seem like news to you but it is big news at Paricutin, where it has not been quiet for several years. But Paricutin is still. The big volcano has died and residents of nearby villages are offering prayers of Thanksgiving. We have with us in the studio today, Jose Jiminez, who was once a resident of the village of Paricutin. I don't suppose you've grieved much over Paricutin's death, have you, Jose?

Jose: If I could only believe that Paricutin was really dead, I would be most happy and thankful, Senorita. But with the volcano one is never sure. Dead one minute, yes, and the next—pfft—she is alive again.

Mexico City Ann: Tell me, Jose, do you recall the day that Paricutin first erupted?

Jose: Never will I forget. We were at work in the village when one of the farmers came running in from his fields two miles away. He was out of breath and very frightened. At first we thought he was trying to fool us when he kept talking about smoke coming from out of the ground in his cornfield. But we told the Padre and he went out with some of us to see what had happened.

Mexico City Ann: And did you find the hole with smoke coming out of it?

Jose: That is right. But already it was a bigger hole than Jose had said. And not only smoke but ashes and stones were flying out from the hole. The Padre knew at once what was happening and he told us all to take our belongings and to move away from Paricutin.

Mexico City Ann: Did you do that?

Jose: Not at once. We did not think that such a small hole could do harm two miles away. But in only one week the cone was 500 feet high and the ashes were falling on our village. By then we were all very frightened and in a short time the whole of the village was abandoned.

Mexico City Ann: And Paricutin kept right on growing. Isn't that right?

Jose: In one year it was 1500 feet high and still growing. Everything was destroyed for miles and miles. Lava was coming from the top and from the sides, and some of it flowed for twenty miles. Many villages were completely destroyed. More and more farms and villages were deserted.

Mexico City Ann: It must seem very quiet now that Paricutin is dead.

Jose: Oh, yes, Senor. She was a noisy one, that Paricutin.

Mexico City Ann: How often did it explode?

Jose: Every six minutes was a big bang and red hot rocks and lava would fly into the air thousands of feet. Then would be smoke and ashes.

Current Events in Geographic Education

You would think the whole world was blowing up. But after a while we got used to all that and we didn't pay so much attention. We had settled far enough away so we hoped we would be safe.

MEXICO CITY ANN: And now at last it's quiet again.

JOSE: Let us hope it will stay like that, Senorita. Already Paricutin has done damage enough. Hundreds of farms destroyed and worst of all, the good land is gone. Even if she never erupts again the land is ruined for our lifetimes. But for one thing we are grateful, Senorita. Paricutin took no lives. We had time to escape so we do not complain.

MEXICO CITY ANN: There is good reason to be grateful. Some volcanoes, like Mt. Pelee and Vesuvius, killed thousands of people. Thank you, Jose Jiminez, for telling us your story. That's all from Mexico City today, ladies and gentlemen. Everything is quiet, including Paricutin.

NEW YORK ANN: Thank you, Mexico City. We go now all the way to Tripoli in Libya, on the edge of the Sahara desert. Take it away, Tripoli.

TRIPOLI ANN: This is your Tripoli reporter. Here in this part of Africa the big news is the safe return of a party of American explorers after they were caught in a furious desert sandstorm. The leader of the expedition, Mr. Robert Lancaster, is here to tell something of the party's experiences. Did any of your group suffer any serious injuries, Mr. Lancaster?

MR. LANCASTER: Fortunately we all came through the storm in good shape, but it isn't an experience any of us would care to repeat in a hurry. Now that it's over, however, we're glad that we were able to get a first hand record of the effects of the *gibli*.

TRIPOLI ANN: What was your biggest problem during the storm, Mr. Lancaster?

MR. LANCASTER: Believe it or not one big problem was keeping warm. But the thing that really worried us was that we would lose our bearings when the storm was over. We knew that those storms can change the whole desert landscape by filling up valleys and flattening hills.

TRIPOLI ANN: Since you arrived here safely I can assume that that fear didn't materialize.

MR. LANCASTER: No. We were lucky. The route wasn't quite the same as our chart showed and some of the wells had been filled in, but we were able to make our way out all right.

TRIPOLI ANN: Do you want to tell us a little something about your feelings during the storm? Were you really frightened at any time?

MR. LANCASTER: I don't mind admitting that it was a very uncanny and frightening experience. In almost any other sort of storm or dangerous situation there is at least the consolation of being able to see what's happening and of being able to talk things over with your companions. But in a sandstorm you feel that you're completely isolated, even in a crowd.

TRIPOLI ANN: How's that, Mr. Lancaster?

MR. LANCASTER: In the first place we had to keep our eyes completely covered to avoid the danger of blindness. Until you experience it yourself you can't believe how that sand can cut your skin. If it reached the eyes it would be disastrous. But, believe me, it's a terrible temptation just to take a quick look to see what's happening.

TRIPOLI ANN: But why couldn't you talk to each other?

MR. LANCASTER: Because, if a man opened his mouth he could easily choke to death on the sand he would swallow in just a few seconds. So we just sat huddled together, with sand in our hair and sand in our clothes. We couldn't eat anything of course, and we couldn't even eat much when the storm was over because there was more sand in the food than there was food. If the storm had lasted a few days instead of a few hours I doubt that we would have made it back. And those *giblis* sometimes do blow for several days at a time.

TRIPOLI ANN: I think you were indeed fortunate, Mr. Lancaster. I have heard many reports of travelers who weren't so lucky. There's one more thing I would like to know, though. How do the camels manage to survive in a storm of that nature?

MR. LANCASTER: The camel is an excellent illustration of the marvels of creation. He is destined to live in the desert and nothing has been overlooked to make it possible for him to survive the hazards of the desert, including sandstorms. Everybody knows, of course, about the peculiar arrangement of the camel's stomach . . . that he has cells in which he can store an extra supply of water.

TRIPOLI ANN: Yes, I understand that a camel can go from three to five days without water. But what else is there about a camel that's much different from other animals?

MR. LANCASTER: For one thing he can close his nostrils tightly during a sandstorm and so keep from choking. He just barely opens them enough to breathe and does it so quickly that no sand can enter. And to protect his eyes he has double lids. One is a very thin but strong membrane. This can be closed to keep out the sand and the glare of the sun but he can still see through it.

TRIPOLI ANN: In other words, you might say that the camel comes equipped with his own smoked glasses.

MR. LANCASTER: Exactly. And it's a very fortunate thing for humans that camels are built as they are, for men couldn't live in the desert very comfortably without the camel.

TRIPOLI ANN: Thank you very much for your interesting report, Mr. Lancaster. . . . That's all from Tripoli, ladies and gentlemen, where the big news today is sand.

NEW YORK ANN: Thank you, Tripoli. . . . Nature certainly seems to be making it difficult for people in various parts of the world. There is one place, however, where nature seems to be in a more benevolent mood. Up in New England they're having one of the mildest winters on record. We'll let our reporter up in Boston tell you about it.

BOSTON ANN: This is Boston reporting. It's quite true that New Englanders are lucky this winter. There has been only an inch or two of snow and to date the temperature has been well above normal. In fact, there's nothing to complain about. We've set up our microphone in Boston's North Station and we're going to ask a few of the people passing by for their reactions to the unusually good weather. We'll start with a young lady here. Are you enjoying this fine winter weather?

WOMAN: Fine weather nothing! I think this is a terrible winter.

BOSTON ANN: Now that's a surprise. You mean you'd rather have lots of snow and cold?

WOMAN: I certainly would. My husband and I run a ski resort up in New Hampshire and if we don't get a lot of snow in a hurry we won't make enough money this winter to pay our expenses.

BOSTON ANN: I can see how this weather wouldn't look so good to you. I was just thinking how nice it is not to have to shovel snow. But for your sake I hope that it'll snow soon, and hard.

WOMAN: Thank you. I hope so too.

BOSTON ANN: Now let's see what a man has got to say about the weather. They're the ones that have to do the shoveling and the driving usually. Excuse me, sir, but how do you feel about this mild winter? Are you enjoying the absence of snow?

MAN: Don't talk to me about this weather. If it keeps up much longer I'll be bankrupt.

BOSTON ANN: Oh, you don't like it either. May I ask what your business is?

MAN: I'm in the fuel business . . . coal and oil.

BOSTON ANN: I guess that explains everything. Thank you, sir. . . . I thought we were going to bring you some happy New Englanders but it seems I was mistaken. At least so far. I'll try once more. Here's a very young man. Hello, young fellow. How old are you?

BOY: Eleven.

BOSTON ANN: Pretty good winter we're having, isn't it?
BOY: Phooey. It's an awful winter.
BOSTON ANN: Another one who doesn't like it.
BOY: Who would like it? No snow for coasting. No ice for skating. And that's not the worst of it. We haven't had one day off from school because of storms all winter. Phooey!
BOSTON ANN: There you are, ladies and gentlemen. The big news in New England is weather. I was going to say "good weather," but I guess the adjective you use depends on your point of view. To the people you've just heard "good weather" is bad news, which just goes to prove that no matter what the weather is you can't please everybody. We return you now to New York.
NEW YORK ANN: Thank you, Boston. That completes our weekly news round-up. Join us again next week for firsthand reports on interesting and unusual items in the news. Your New York announcer. . . .

SOURCES OF GEOGRAPHIC NEWS ITEMS

A problem that many teachers face is where to find worthwhile news items. Our daily newspapers have improved and carry more important national and world news than they did before World War II, but there is still room for continued improvement. In nearly every section of the United States there is one or more newspapers that carry worthwhile national and world news. The reports are usually well written and authentic. Among such papers are: *The New York Times, The Christian Science Monitor,* the *Kansas City Star and Times,* the *Cleveland Plain Dealer,* and *The Minneapolis Star.*

There are news weeklies such as *Time* and *Newsweek,* and in addition there are current event papers written for children and often subscribed for by the school, such as those published by the American Education Press, Columbus Ohio, and the *Junior and Senior Scholastic* published in New York.

In the newspaper and the news weeklies some of the best articles are found on the financial pages, and in port cities such as Boston, New York, and Cleveland in the "Shipping News." The financial pages often carry articles on the industrial development of various regions, the building of dams, and stories of new industries and new products.

Other sources, especially for junior and senior high school students, are publications by the state and national governments, and the publications of the National Geographical Society and the American Geographical Society. In addition to its monthly magazine, the National Geographic Society publishes a small weekly bulletin for schools which is inexpensive and suitable for all grades. It contains four articles with pictures each week. The American Geographical Society publishes *Focus* monthly. Each issue deals with one country or topic bringing the reader up-to-date on conditions. It is inexpensive and valuable to a teacher, and high school students also find it of great value.

Many school libraries subscribe to one or more newspapers, news weeklies, and other magazines that the pupils can read and summarize articles or follow an event. However, the children should be encouraged to read newspapers and magazines in their home.

Of course there is radio and television, but the news commentator of these mediums has time to give only one or two high points, and, if the news is worthwhile, reading of the newspaper or magazine is a necessary follow-up to get the complete picture.

To use current events effectively, the teacher must read at least one good newspaper and news weekly regularly. Unless he does this, he is not able to take full advantage of current events in his teaching. If the teacher is acquainted with world activities he can anticipate news to be given and is prepared to use it to introduce a new unit, or to review or illustrate a principle or point already discussed.

The teacher should collect and file worthwhile articles for future as well as immediate use. Often such an article has a bearing on a present event or illustrates a topic, especially the effect of unusual weather, storms, floods, and earthquakes on man and his activities. Again, an article may give the teacher background material or information he may need weeks or months later in another unit. For instance, in August, 1956, an article in the *Christian Science Monitor*, "New Rail Line Follows Marco Polo's Track to Open Northwest China," contained a map, a full description of a new railroad line, and descriptions of the farms, villages, and people of Northwest China. Whenever China was studied the teacher would have up-to-date information to enrich the textbook. Such items help to make geography live for the pupils.

If the teacher of geography uses current events with discrimination, guiding his students in reading intelligently the current newspaper, he will be training his students in the art of thinking as well as in geography. He will be helping to make their lives richer by broadening and deepening their interest in world affairs. They will also become more intelligent citizens *not* through being preached at which does little good but through becoming more interested in and more intelligent concerning national and international events.

As Thomas Jefferson wrote: "If a nation expects to be ignorant and free in a state of civilization, it expects what never has and never will be."

REFERENCES

ANDERSON, H., "Magazines and Education," *School Review*, Vol. 62 (December, 1954), pp. 511–517. A general discussion that is worth reading.

CHAMPLAIN, C. D., "Learning to Read Current Events," *Education*, Vol. 73 (October, 1952), pp. 79–90. Discusses the importance of current events in education.

GATHANY, J. Madison, "Teaching Pupils to Think for Themselves," *Social Studies*, Vol. 42 (February, 1951), pp. 78–81. Contains some excellent suggestions on developing the power to think; uses current events as illustrations.

GRAHAM, Marie C., "Geography in the News: The Partition of Palestine," *Journal of Geography*, Vol. 37 (November, 1938), pp. 318–329. An excellent and very full discussion of how a current event was used as a basis to develop a unit.

HARTSHORNE, M. F., "Teaching Contemporary Affairs," *Social Education*, Vol. 14 (October, 1950), pp. 245–246. States some important aims in the use of current events.

Current Events in Geographic Education

MILLER, W. H., "Modern Geography and Current Events," *Journal of Geography*, Vol. 35 (October, 1936), pp. 279–284. This article is addressed to the college teacher, but others may get some ideas from it.

PICKEL, Robert D., "The Joy of Teaching Current Events," *Social Studies*, Vol. 45 (April, 1954), pp. 139–141. Discusses methods of teaching current events which may be adapted by a geography teacher.

REPASS, F. C., "An Experiment in Teaching Current Geography," *Journal of Geography*, Vol. 36 (November, 1937), pp. 321–324. Emphasizes the use of maps in teaching current geography.

SHINN, R. F., "The News: Six Nations' Viewpoints," *The Clearing House*, Vol. 28 (May, 1954), p. 558. Description of a panel discussion. Written for history teacher, but a geography teacher could adapt the idea to his class.

SNEED, Alma S., "The Use of Current Events in Grade Four," *Journal of Geography*, Vol. 47 (March, 1948), pp. 92–95. A description of how a teacher used Byrd's Antarctica expedition. Very good.

THRALLS, Zoe A., "Geography and Current Events," *Journal of Geography*, Vol. 39 (May, 1940), pp. 200–202. Discusses relation of current events to geography, and the purposes of teaching current events.

TORRENS, Hazel L., "Current Events in the Ninth Grade," *Social Education*, Vol. 10 (October, 1946), pp. 255–256. An illustration of the use of the open forum in teaching current events.

UNGASHICK, Jane, "The Use of Current Events in Geography Teaching," *Journal of Geography*, Vol. 39 (November, 1940), pp. 315–319. An excellent article on ways of using current events and the attainments of the pupils.

WEST, Emma F., "The New Geography and Newspaper Clippings," *Journal of Geography*, Vol. 22 (May, 1923), pp. 176–182. An old article, but has some excellent suggestions.

7

Reading as a Tool in Geographic Education

IMPORTANCE OF READING

READING IS AN essential tool in the study of geography because pupils must gain a large part of their knowledge of other lands and peoples from books. Much of the stimulation to their thinking also comes from books. The successful use of reading as a tool depends upon their knowing how to read geographic materials to arrive at the major objective of geographic education: which is a knowledge and an understanding of how man has adapted his ways of living to the natural environment in specific regions of the world.

Reading of geographic materials involves the ability to read maps, pictures, graphs, statistics, and the landscape as well as textual materials. The use of the above tools has been discussed in previous chapters. In this chapter we are particularly concerned with the effective reading of geographical textual materials.

The use of the various tools mentioned increases the need for efficiency in reading. Their use involves reading skills because maps, graphs, pictures, and statistics have *keys* and explanations which must be interpreted through reading verbal materials. For instance, a picture has a location indicated in the title, a map has

Reading as a Tool in Geographic Education

a title, and a table of statistics has certain explanatory facts which must be read. The reading and interpretation of the above learning aids raise questions or problems. As Edith P. Parker[1] says:

> Reading matter contributes in some measure in all of the aforementioned ways [use of maps, pictures, graphs and statistics] and may have high utility as a tool for directing the use of the materials presented. It is valuable as a check on information gained from other sources; it supplements information acquired elsewhere; and it aids in unifying, summarizing and fixing groups of impressions gained by various means.

The ability to effectively read geographic textual materials is also necessary because in certain situations textual materials are the only sources of information available. A teacher does not always have at hand a picture which shows the desired geographic relationships. Some ideas cannot be mapped, photographed, nor shown graphically, as for example the characteristics of the people.

Reading is an essential tool in geography as well as other subjects, because of the close relation between reading, thinking, and studying. Lyman expresses this intimate relationship as follows:[2]

> ... the activities of reading, of thinking, and of studying are considered as aspects of the one process by which we learn to use materials which we find in printed form. All are activities of the mind. We *read* serious books to get ideas; we *think* about them to see what these ideas mean; we *study* ideas and their meanings, endeavoring to make them our permanent possessions and to get ready to use them in problems of our own.

The very nature of geography makes reading especially important. Dealing as it does with man's activities in the specific natural environments of the varied regions of the world, the only way the child can acquire a knowledge of these regions is through vicarious experiences. He cannot visit, see for himself, and study each spe-

---

[1] Edith Putnam Parker, "The Teaching of Geography," *The Teaching of Reading: A Second Report,* Thirty-sixth Yearbook, National Society for the Study of Education, Part I (Bloomington, Ill., Public School Publishing Co., 1937), p. 162.

[2] R. L. Lyman, *The Mind at Work* (Chicago, Scott, Foresman & Co., 1924), p. 14.

cific cultural and physical landscape. Consequently to become acquainted with them, to learn *how* and *why* the people live as they do and to gain a feeling of reality, he must depend upon the writings of others.

First hand experiences are impossible for each student. Well-written accounts of the findings of accurate observers in the field help to make vivid to the learner the significant types of adjustments of human activity to the natural environment, and at the same time help the individual to project himself into these regions in imagination.[3]

Reading is an important tool in geographic education, also, because apparently many failures in geography are due at least in part to the child's inability to read geographic materials. H. H. Hahn diagnosed 283,000 answers written by children who took the preliminary test for the construction of the Hahn-Lackey geography scale. He also used hundreds of answers by others. He summarizes his findings as follows:[4]

Many children fail, in part at least, because they do not possess all the reading abilities essential to the successful study of geography. To be successful they should be able to read accurately and rapidly informational subject matter for the following purposes: finding the topic sentence of paragraphs; finding the main points of a selection; giving a coherent reproduction; giving an accurate summary; finding answers to questions; working out solutions to problems; exploring for directions to carry out activities; discovering and formulating questions, problems, and activities.

Our study shows clearly that reading disability in one form or another is one of the causes of failures. In cases of trouble, teachers should have no difficulty in determining which in the above list of skills is lacking. Each one can be tested directly in daily work or by means of more formal tests. Having discovered a specific reading disability, it should be easy to work out and apply remedial measures. This one thing is cer-

---

[3] Mary Logan, "Techniques of the Reading Tool in Reaching Worthwhile Geographic Understandings," *Journal of Geography*, Vol. 33 (January, 1934), p. 10.

[4] H. H. Hahn, "Why Failures in the Study of Geography," *Journal of Geography*, Vol. 35 (September, 1936), pp. 225–226.

tain, every minute the teacher spends in teaching children how to read and study geography saves hours for both the teacher and her pupils.

Finally, in geography as in other fields of knowledge the adult's knowledge of geography and his geographic thinking are based largely on reading matter. Numerous problems faced by businessmen and others can be solved only by taking into consideration geographic factors as well as other factors. Such problems as the following are typical: How to vote on certain political issues; where to establish a particular type of factory in relation to transportation facilities, sources of raw materials, markets, and so forth; where to find needed raw materials; where to find markets for products; even where and how to build a home. Possible solutions of such problems can be arrived at only through thinking based on geographic facts. The necessary facts can be gained through intelligent reading of printed matter, maps, graphs, statistics, and pictures, as well as personal study of the landscape.

THE RESPONSIBILITY OF THE TEACHER OF GEOGRAPHY

Since reading is such an essential tool in geographic education the teacher of geography should be responsible for developing the children's skills for the reading of geographic materials. The reading teacher cannot do this. For one reason she has a big job to build the general reading skills. In the second place, the reading teacher does not know what reading skills are needed in geography. Even if she is conscious of those needs she does not have the time. Her time must necessarily be devoted to the development of general reading skills. Furthermore, she does not have the type of geographic materials for the use of the pupils nor is the general reading class situation suitable for the functional development and use of geographic reading skills.

As Gray says: "Each field has its own vocabulary, concepts, and ways of organizing and presenting ideas. Children need specific help in grasping the meaning of new words, in interpreting the language used, and in acquiring new understandings, interests, attitudes, and patterns of behavior."[5]

Geography, as other subject-matter fields, has its own vocabulary, its own type of organization, and its own distinctive pattern of thinking. Therefore, the best place to teach the geographic vocabulary and pattern of thinking is in the class situation where these function.

One result of the growing realization of the importance of relating training in methods of study to the specific needs of each field of the curriculum has been to place the responsibility for the efficient study of a subject squarely upon the teacher of that subject. In effect, every teacher becomes a teacher of reading. Such a plan has distinct advantages, not only for the motivation of drill in reading skills, but also for guidance in the application of the skills to specific fields.

Introducing skills when they are needed leads children to appreciate their usefulness and provides an immediate check on accomplishments.[6]

THE PATTERN OF READING, THINKING, AND STUDYING IN GEOGRAPHY

Since it is the responsibility of all teachers of geography to guide their students in developing the necessary skills essential to the effective reading of geographic materials, what are those skills? Modern geography teaching is based on the use of facts about man's activities and the natural environment in such a way as to recognize geographic relationships and to develop geographic understandings. Mary Logan says, "Geographic relationships are the warp and woof out of which the fabric of geography is made."[7] It involves a critical attitude toward facts and an ability to evaluate

[5] William S. Gray, "Reading as an Aid in Learning," *Reading in the Elementary School,* Forty-eighth Yearbook, National Society for the Study of Education, Part II (Chicago, University of Chicago Press, 1949), Ch. XI, pp. 239–240.

[6] Mabel Snedaker and Earnest Horn, "Reading in the Various Fields of the Curriculum," *The Teaching of Reading: A Second Report,* Thirty-sixth Yearbook, National Society for the Study of Education, Part I (Bloomington, Ill., Public School Publishing Co., 1937), Ch. V, p. 151.

[7] Logan, *op. cit.,* p. 10.

Reading as a Tool in Geographic Education

them. In reading geographic materials one must not only grasp the meaning of the contents of the printed page but use these materials in thinking. A formula for reading geographic materials might be expressed as follows: *Facts and Ideas + Thinking + Study = Geographic Understandings and the Application of These Understandings to Solve Problems.*

J. Russell Smith expresses much the same idea: "When geography is well taught we have an evolutionary process somewhat as follows: At the basic level, geographic facts, from the facts ideas, from the ideas objectives, from the objectives conduct, from the conduct legislation, convention, literature, art, and new ideas of right and wrong."[8]

Therefore guidance in reading geographic materials must be aimed toward developing geographic understandings. The gaining of such understandings from reading involves a number of abilities.

Geographic Reading Skills

The basic geographic reading skills are as follows:

1. Ability to recognize in reading material and to visualize (*a*) man-made features and conditions; (*b*) natural features and conditions. In order to understand and to visualize the cultural and the natural conditions in a region, the individual needs to know many facts about the kinds of people living there, the kinds of work, how the people live and work, and the kind of land in which they live.

2. Ability to recognize direct and indirect relationships between the cultural conditions and the physical conditions or in other words, why the people live and work as they do and also what problems they face due, in part, to natural conditions. The geographic relationships may be stated in the reading material or may be inferred from the statements in the material.

3. Ability to use reading material to solve problems, to answer

---

[8] J. Russell Smith, "Geography: A Group of People in a Place," *Education*, Vol. 60 (December, 1939), pp. 195–200.

specific questions, and to check information gained from other tools, such as maps, graphs, and so forth.

4. Ability to grasp the main and subordinate ideas in a paragraph and a chapter, and to recognize the relationship of the modifying ideas to the main idea.

5. Ability to associate meanings with technical words and to attach geographical meanings to familiar words such as "plain," "cape," "a divide," and others.

6. Ability to think in terms of location as one reads, because where people live and where a land is are important in geographic thinking.

7. Ability to associate new understandings with previous experiences.

8. Ability to use a geographic vocabulary.

9. Ability to retain a series of related ideas which have been read.

10. Ability to adapt rate and technique of reading to varying purposes. For instance, skimming to find a specific fact or the answer to a question.

11. Ability to use the atlas and the index, table of contents, and statistical tables of his text and reference books.

TECHNIQUES FOR IMPROVING ABILITY TO READ GEOGRAPHIC MATERIALS

If reading geographic material is to be effective the student must be prepared to read for a specific purpose. The teacher must create a desire in the child to read the particular materials at hand. There are many ways of interesting the pupils in reading geographic materials. However, arousing interest in attacking a problem or topic should be a co-operative affair, the teacher and pupils working together. Of course, the basic responsibility is the teacher's. He must plan and prepare the materials and he must so guide the class activities that the pupils co-operate in stating and organizing problems and questions.

Reading as a Tool in Geographic Education

Motivating Interest in Reading

One method of arousing interest in a new topic is to help the class by means of questions to recall what they already know about the topic or the new region. For instance, the new region might be the Amazonia region in South America. Some pupils may know something about the Indians of Amazonia, the rubber gatherers, the animals, Brazil nuts, blow guns, and so forth. As they tell what they know, others in the class may raise questions and want to know more about the topics mentioned. The teacher may inject questions and direct the pupils' attention to important points, especially guiding the class to the "why" of the people's activities in the region.

The teacher may use a set of pictures, pictures in the textbook, or a film to stimulate interest. Several illustrations of the use of pictures to motivate a unit are given in Chapter 3. In examining and discussing pictures the teacher should give definite instructions. These questions will vary, but however stated the following points should be kept in mind: (1) Location of the scene; (2) Who the people are; (3) How the people make a living; (4) How the people in the various pictures are alike or different; (5) What you learn about the recreation, the homes, and other things concerning the people; (6) What relationships between the people's ways of living and the natural environment you notice. The questions and directions, of course, are adapted to the region or topic, and the maturity and background of the child. Then through class discussion, the pupils and the teacher work together to state and organize the questions to be answered, the information or the inferences to be verified through reading. Through such an attack the class should have definite purposes in reading.

Frequently a current-news item brought in by the teacher or a pupil, or a television program, or radio newscast dealing with the new region or topic may be used to stimulate interest, and to raise questions and problems. The use of these in motivating a unit is discussed in Chapter 6.

The class might pretend that they are news reporters or special correspondents sent to gather additional information for a story. How would they go about such an assignment? What questions would they ask? The class suggests possible questions and the teacher should make sure that such questions as these are included: "How many people live in this place? How do they earn their living? How well do they live? Why do many people live here, or why do so few people live here? Why do they earn their living as they do? [farming, herding, mining, lumbering, fishing, trading, manufacturing, and so forth] Why do they live as they do?"

An exhibit of objects from a region stimulates interest and questions about a place and the people. For instance, a sixth-grade teacher put up an exhibit of articles from India a week before she expected to introduce the unit. She said nothing about the articles, but of course the children were curious. Some were labeled, some were not. They looked, felt, and discussed the objects, and they asked questions. The teacher did not answer their questions fully, but suggested that each pupil write his question and put it in the question box. Sometimes she said just enough to arouse the pupil's curiosity even more. By the end of the week, some of the students were bringing in additional material, and everyone was ready for opening the question box. At first, the discussion was enthusiastic but rambling. However, soon the teacher was able to guide the discussion until a well-organized series of questions were developed to guide the pupils' reading. They turned enthusiastically to their texts, reference books, and maps to learn about India and its people.

Oftentimes a teacher can find a catchy title, a striking statement, or an unusual question to introduce a class discussion. For instance, in a class studying the climatic regions of the world, the teacher introduced the low latitude (tropical) wet and dry region by writing on the board, "Lands of Alternate Feast and Famine for Man and Beast." The class discussed the meaning of *feast* and *famine,* and also the term *alternate,* for many did not know what

Reading as a Tool in Geographic Education

it meant. After the class decided that in these lands there must be some years when there was plenty of food and other years when there was little or none, the question "Why" was asked, and suggestions followed and were written on the blackboard. Someone said that perhaps it was a land like our "Dust Bowl." These suggestions and questions prepared the class to read the chapters on the world's vast tropical wet and dry regions.

Other striking statements or questions which may be used in a similar fashion are the following:

> Why has Denmark become the world's teacher in dairying?
> Why is Portugal called "The Garden by the Sea"?
> Brazil—the South American "Treasure House of Raw Materials."
> The Chinese, Farmers of Forty Centuries, and their Land.
> China, Land of Contrasts.

Sometimes a headline in a current newspaper suggests to a teacher a statement that he can use to start a class discussion. As Loula Upton says:[9]

> If we can make a connection between the subject matter of the lesson and some recent movie, current happening, or a story familiar to the class, we find that the text becomes a living subject. Recently my fifth-grade class studied Mexico rather indifferently in the textbook. We turned aside for a few days to read the story of "Manuel in Mexico" and then went back to the text for a review. The children were greatly interested in discovering similarities between the two accounts, and would frequently exclaim, "Why that's just like Manuel," or "Manuel rode a burro," or "Manuel ate tortillas," and so forth. They did not find the text the least bit dry or uninteresting.

A teacher may read a story or an interesting account from a book or magazine article that can be associated with the region or topic. Such contacts require careful selection of the literature in order to stimulate interest in reading geographic materials. Their use also requires skill on the part of the teacher in guiding the class to the desired objective. The following is a descriptive selection that the teacher could read to the class to interest them in a study

---

[9] Loula Upton, "How To Use the Textbook," *Journal of Geography*, Vol. 32 (December, 1933), p. 360.

of Indonesia and to develop a purpose for reading geographic material on Indonesia. The teacher could introduce the reading in the following manner.

We are about to visit a new country in southeast Asia. It is a young republic and consists of two large islands and a number of small islands southeast of Asia. What is the name of this young country? (If no one can name it, the teacher tells the class and has the pupils locate it on their maps, noting the names of the main islands.)

Now, I am going to read a traveler's account of what he saw when he visited Indonesia. "To visit one of the big native markets in Java, we took a bicycle chair. It is a three-wheeled vehicle with a chair in front, and a Javanese man's bare legs propels it. At the market we found a jumble of crude bamboo and wooden stalls huddled together along both sides of narrow, twisting lanes. In these little shops are offered a great variety of articles—rusty nails, screws, cloth, fruits, vegetables, goat meat, birds, bananas, American cigarettes, rice, and fish. The lanes were crowded with jostling bargain hunters. When we tired of the noise and smells, we took a one-horse, two-wheeled carriage back through the city.

"Next morning, early, we took a drive through the country side. As the sun was not yet up, we saw hundreds of candles twinkling at market places and food stalls along the road. We met men, naked except for shorts, carrying heavily loaded baskets on bamboo shoulder sticks, on their way to the city market. In some of the baskets were live, squealing pigs.

"These slender little brown men carry loads of 150 pounds or more for 50 miles. Others were pushing or pulling great, clumsy two-wheeled carts loaded with fire wood or big bamboo poles. Occasionally an ox or small horse, instead of men, would be pulling the cart.

"Along the road were fruit and nut bearing trees. Every tree furnished either food or some valuable raw material. Among these trees were oil and coconut palms, banana plants, mango, bread fruit, rubber, and kapok trees, just to name a few.

"As our car climbed the mountain slopes, we saw tea plantations clinging to the steep mountain slopes, and everywhere people at work. Men and women were carrying golden sheaves of rice on shoulder sticks. Others were setting out young rice plants in muddy fields.

"After lunch we visited a village school. The teacher's home was a small, clean, well-built house with lattice-work sides to let the breeze through. It was in the midst of a tree-shaded village. The other houses were similar to the teacher's. Nearly every home had a neatly swept and sanded yard and its own little fish pond. Also in each village there was a public storehouse in which is kept the seed-rice for next year's planting. This storehouse is carefully guarded by village officials.

"The school was in a small one room house without any furniture. The teacher and pupils sat on the floor with their legs crossed under them. They had only a few books and writing materials, but they were eager to learn. So anxious are the children to learn that in Sumatra we saw children building their own school. They were carrying rocks from a hill-side for the walls. At this stage the school house was only an open shelter with a tin roof. The teacher said, 'We are *gotong-rojong* that is, helping each to help the other.'

"In Sumatra, we also saw busy oil drillers at work. All were Indonesians working together under the supervision of an American oil expert. The young men were learning the oil industry from the discovery, drilling, bringing in the oil well, and transporting to the final refining of the oil. Here again we saw *gotong-rojong* at work as American and Dutch experts worked together.

"Next we took a wood-burning train across the low lying, northern coastal plain of Java. Everywhere, toward the sea on one side and to the mountains on the other, stretched green, flooded rice fields. Grazing or wallowing in streams or mud holes were many herds of water buffalo. Always, with each herd, was a small boy astride one of the animals. He was responsible for the animals. Usually the buffalo is gentle and docile, working willingly in the muddy rice fields. But during the middle of the day when the almost vertical sun beats down, its skin dries out and it becomes dangerous unless permitted to go to the water. But the buffalo is the farmer's most prized possession and he does not grudge him several hours of leisure in a tree-shaded pool."

After reading the selection, have the class list important items of information they have learned from this traveler. If necessary ask for questions. If the class is slow in making comments or asking questions, the teacher should ask such questions as the following:

What kind of climate do the fruits and crops suggest? Why?
What does the school suggest about the people?
Have you seen a picture of a water-buffalo?
Discuss his appearance. Why is he so important?

The discussion of these and other questions serves as an introduction or stimulus for reading about Indonesia to find out more about this young yet old land.

Guidance in Vocabulary Building

Arousing interest to read geographic material is only a part of the program. Even though eager to read, the pupil will be frustrated if he encounters many unknown words, words without meaning to him. In some cases he knows the word, but does not know its geographic meaning. Geography has a language of its own as do all fields. One cannot read intelligently and with ease about the geography of any region without an understanding of the language of the subject. There are numerous geographic terms that must be learned and understood such as *delta, tributary, navigable, growing season, precipitation, source, port,* and many others. Then there are terms familiar to the pupil in a different context, for instance, the child knows a meaning for the word *divide,* but probably does not know what a *water divide* is, nor what *the continental divide* refers to. There are also concepts of distance, of quantities, and of size which must be developed.

If the teacher introduces new terms gradually and thoroughly during the motivating activities, much of the difficulty in reading geography may be decreased. In planning the unit, the teacher should check all the reading material that he expects the class to use for vocabulary and concepts. He should list words and concepts that he knows are new to the class. These terms should be listed on the board and then presented with as many meaningful connections as possible. The teacher should use pictures, illustrations in the textbook, diagrams, and sketches to aid the child to visualize the term and gain an understanding of it. Many terms may be developed by means of local field trips, for instance, a river system may be illustrated by visiting a local stream and noting the area it drains, and its tributary streams. *Island, delta, falls,* and *rapids* are other terms that often may be illustrated on a small scale in the local community.

If the word is in the dictionary, its various meanings should be

Reading as a Tool in Geographic Education

discussed, its geographic meaning illustrated, and its use in context found. If the word is derived from one or more other words, the teacher would do well to discuss the various sources, for instance, the word *hydroelectricity*. They probably know what *electricity* means, so the teacher should explain *hydro*, and then combine the two meanings—"electricity made through the use of water power." Thermometer is derived from *thermo*, meaning "heat," and *meter*, "to measure." Most children like to know how words have been formed and the meaning of their components.

With some groups, the teacher may find it necessary to read to the class, explaining and interpreting as she goes along. As Ruth Strickland says, "Content materials need to be read with children so that the teacher can help them to build clearer mental pictures than they could conjure up for themselves. Children need help to put meaning into material, to react to it, to fit it into the mass of their previous experience and knowledge, and arrange it all in proper perspective."[10]

As new words and concepts are developed the class should make a class dictionary, also individual dictionaries if they wish, explaining and illustrating the terms geographically. If a committee is given the task of keeping the class dictionary, it should also plan review, checking, and drill exercises so that a real mastery is gained. Every pupil should be working constantly to improve his vocabulary.

In summarizing the problem of developing a geographic vocabulary these rules may be suggested:

1. Introduce each new word or concept *as needed* in meaningful discussion.

2. Use the new word orally as often as the opportunity arises so that the pupils become familiar with the sound symbols and with its meaning in relation to geography.

3. Provide accurate concrete imagery of the word through the

---

[10] Ruth Strickland, "The Relation of Reading to Development in Language Arts," *The Reading Teacher*, Vol. 9 (October, 1955), p. 37.

use of the local landscape, pictures, diagrams, sketches, specimens, and so forth.

4. Write the word on the blackboard as you discuss it.

5. Provide opportunities for the pupils to read textbook sentences containing the word or phrase.

6. Ask questions which require the use of the word in oral and in written situations.

Vocabulary Drills and Checking Exercises

As in the teaching of arithmetic, much drill and review must be provided if the pupils are to retain the new words and concepts. Children enjoy drill and review exercises if they are varied, and contain a puzzle or game element. The pupils often suggest or invent games and puzzles if given the opportunity.

Virginia Schauer suggests the following exercises for drills on vocabulary.[11]

GUESSING GAMES

Purpose: To provide drill to help the child connect the sound symbol of a word with its sign symbol.

Materials: The words printed on the blackboard, on a chart, or on flash cards.

"It" chooses mentally a word from the group and asks, "Which word do you think I have chosen?" He calls on some member of the class who asks, "Did you choose 'desert'?" pointing to the word as he pronounces it. "It" says, "No, I did not choose 'desert,'" pointing to the word, also. This continues until one member selects the word "It" had chosen and then becomes "It."

I AM THINKING

Purpose: To provide drill on the sign symbol, the sound symbol, and imagery.

Materials: A set of word cards and a set of pictures.

Place the word cards on the chalk rail. Put the set of pictures on the bulletin board. The teacher may begin the game by saying, "I am thinking of a word which refers to ———," giving two or three descriptive

[11] Virginia Schauer, "Teaching Children to Read the Textbook," *Journal of Geography,* Vol. 44 (October, 1945), pp. 281–282.

Reading as a Tool in Geographic Education

ideas about the word. "What word is it? A child chooses the word from those displayed, and matches it with a picture showing the item. This child is then "It."

MATCHING GAME

Purpose: To help the child connect the printed symbol with the pictured feature.

Materials: A set of word cards and a set of pictures. The teacher or a pupil points to a feature in a picture, calling upon some member of the class to choose the word to fit the feature.

USE OF SLIDES

Select a slide showing a number of features on which the class needs to be drilled. Type the names of these and a few others not shown on the slide. The list of words is projected on the screen first. The class is given time to read the words. Then the picture is shown. The children are asked to point to features in the picture which were listed on the first slide and to name the item. To make sure it isn't a lucky guess, the vocabulary words are shown again and each child is told to point to the word he named.

Other reviewing and checking vocabulary exercises are the following, which may be adapted to various grade levels. In each case the words would be from the class's vocabulary list.

DEFINITION GAME

The teacher selects a member of the class, who gives the definition or explains the meaning of one of the words in their vocabulary list and then calls on some other member of the class to pronounce the word defined. The second person then defines a second word, and so on.

A PAPER AND PENCIL RACE

Be in condition for the race. Learn the meanings of the words in the vocabulary list. When it is time for the race, copy the words below in a column on the left hand side of a sheet of paper. Write on only every third line to allow space for the definition. When the teacher gives the signal "go," write the definitions as quickly as you can. As soon as one member of the class finishes, the teacher will call "stop." Exchange papers and mark them. What is your score? Where do you stand in your class?

MATCHING

Try to find a picture to illustrate each of the following words. If you cannot find a picture, perhaps you can draw one. Then four or five suitable words that can be illustrated follows.

CHECKING TEXT AND VOCABULARY LIST

Locate each of the following words or phrases in Chapter ——. Read the sentence in which each one occurs. Then give an explanation in your own words of the vocabulary word or phrase listed here. (The teacher lists the words and phrases which the pupils are to check.)

A SCRAMBLE VOCABULARY

This is a scramble vocabulary. Unscramble the words below. The explanatory phrases give clues. After unscrambling the words, write the corrected list of words. For example, *cheal*—"dissolve minerals out of soils." The word is *leach*. The teacher makes a scrambled list of words from the unit or topic being studied with explanatory phrases for the class.

NEW WORDS

Make a list of five words in this chapter which are new to you. Have other members of the class explain the words or use them in sentences. Perhaps you can invent a game using all the new words listed by the class.

RELATING CHARACTERISTIC WORDS OR PHRASES TO A SPECIFIC REGION

Explain how each of the following is related to the mountainous land in this region, or to the Mediterranean type of climate: (*a*) terraced slopes; (*b*) irrigation; (*c*) flat or nearly flat roofs; (*d*) raising of olives; (*e*) zonal agriculture; and others. The teacher's list would depend upon the unit or region being studied.

ASSOCIATION

Associate each of the following words with either soil, topography, or native grass, and tell why you make this association: (*a*) *coulies;* (*b*) *leach;* (*c*) *playa;* (*d*) *wash.*

Use each of the following words correctly in a sentence which applies to the steppes and deserts of Argentina: (*a*) *Mendoza;* (*b*) *vineyard oasis;* (*c*) *pass city;* (*d*) *Patagonia;* (*e*) *canyon.*

Reading as a Tool in Geographic Education

Checking the understanding of terms, such as export and import. Pretend you are a visitor on the docks at Guayaquil, Ecuador. As you look over the crates, boxes, and barrels lined up at the docks, see whether you can place the proper label (Import or Export) on the products

sewing machines	coconuts	gasoline pump	cacao
balsa wood	straw hats	bananas	fire arms
outboard motors	cotton cloth	nut oil	wheat
medicine	rubber	baskets	

These exercises are only a few of the many that teachers and pupils have developed and used. A teacher can find others in textbooks and teacher's manuals which can be adapted to the materials and the educational level of the class.

The development of vocabulary skills does not cease in the elementary grades. It must be continued on through the junior and senior high school and into the college.

Guidance For Developing Effective Reading in Geography: The Assignment

The next and most critical step is to provide effective guidance in reading and study activities in order that the pupils will gain the desired geographic understandings. The teacher must make well-planned assignments which will challenge a maximum of good thinking while the pupils are in the act of reading. The assignment must be motivated and focalized. As Paul McKee says:[12]

> Each assignment to reading must be built with care. Through preliminary discussion of the topic (or problem) to be attacked, the pupils and the teacher work together, think out, state, and organize questions to be answered. This co-operative action stimulates the pupil's interest in reading on the problem, encourages him to read with definite purpose and aggressive interest, and directs his attention to important matters.

The co-operative work of the teacher and pupils during the introduction of the unit should contribute directly to the assignment.

---

[12] Paul McKee, *Reading in the Elementary School,* Forty-eighth Yearbook, National Society for the Study of Education, Part II (Chicago, University of Chicago Press, 1949), Ch. VI, p. 145.

In many cases even the specific problems and questions used in the assignment grow out of the introductory activities. The teacher needs only to refine the questions and direct the class in organizing the questions, either in better order than originally suggested or under a few large topics or problems. The teacher usually needs to add directions or questions for the use of maps, pictures, and other tools.

In the assignment there should be questions or directions which cause the pupil to recall past experience or learnings that are related to the new topic. Very few students are in the habit of consciously recalling related experiences or knowledge about a problem or topic before turning to the text or references for information. The teacher can give questions and directions in the assignment to train them in this worthwhile habit. The following is an example of such an exercise:

Have the class find in a paragraph items typical of some far-off land which can also be seen from the school windows, or on the way to school, or as you drive on the highway from the local community to a certain point. For example, an assignment might be. "Today we are going to read about an important manufacturing district in Germany. As you read you will find many things in this far-off landscape that can be seen here at home. Make a list of these items." If you choose, you may allow the class to list items which cannot be seen at home. The lists are not the end. To explain the likenesses and differences, or the *why* of the landscape is the reason for listing the facts.[13]

In an assignment for the study of Ecuador the teacher added some directions to the class list of questions:

You studied about the raising of cacao and coffee when we were working on Brazil. As you read about raising cacao in Ecuador, compare it with the same industry in Brazil. How are the two alike? How different? Coffee raising in Ecuador is also somewhat different than in Brazil. Note the differences and try to discover the reasons for the differences.

[13] Virginia Schauer, "Teaching Children to Read the Textbook," *Journal of Geography*, Vol. 44 (October, 1945), p. 285.

Such exercises will train the children in the habit of using information already acquired and personal experiences in the mastery of new subject matter. In the introductory or motivating step, in the assignment, and in the final checking up of a unit, the teacher should see that the pupils use the old in discovering the new.

The assignment should also provide for individual differences in the reading ability of the pupils. There is a wide range in the reading abilities of every class. In a sixth-grade class, individuals may vary in reading ability from second-grade level to eighth-grade. Such a problem may be taken care of by providing reading materials of different levels of difficulty. The teacher, or the teacher and a committee, can collect and list references to be read. The teacher can direct the pupils to the books or articles within their individual abilities. The teacher can also use questions which are graded as to difficulty. Virginia Schauer gives some examples of such gradation:

A. Use questions which have answers that fairly leap from the page to the eye. Such answers usually begin with capital letters or are written in italic print. It is evident that one could not plan an entire reading-geography lesson using only this type of question. Any one page or even several pages has at most only a few basic facts recorded in this style. But, if the teacher uses this type of question at every opportunity afforded by the text and reserves this type of question for the poorer reader, she can help the poorer reader increase his ability to read with understanding.

B. Use questions which are phrased like the answer to be found. For example, a sentence reads, "Grass had been planted on the dunes to keep the sand from being blown away by the wind." Phrase the question like this, "Why has grass been planted on the dunes?" Seven of the words to be read from the text are found in the question. These seven words appear at the beginning of the answer to be located.

C. Use questions phrased unlike the answer to be found. The class will read, "The salmon industry is not carried on the year round because the fish swim upstream only during the spring and summer months."

The question is phrased something like this, "Why do we say that salmon fishing is seasonal work?"

D. Use questions which require several answers. "Why is Birmingham the leading iron and steel center of the South?" "How is lumbering carried on in the Pacific States?"[14]

The teacher may ask questions which require explanations of what the pupils are reading, such as "Describe in your own words what you might see from a train window as the train crosses from the Guayas River to the base of the Andes Mountains in Ecuador. If you prefer, you may draw pictures of typical scenes along the railroad line." Such a question makes demands upon the students to interpret and attempt to visualize what they have read about in their geographic source materials.

A series of questions may be used to lead the pupil to a conclusion. For instance, of what material are the houses, barns, and fences in Norway made? What is the raw material used in making paper? Why does Norway have many wood pulp and paper mills? These and other questions lead the children to realize that the forests of Norway are one of the nation's important natural resources.

The assignment should provide periods for checking progress of individuals, committees, and of the class as a whole. Through such checking up, the class and the pupils have a greater sense of responsibility, gain a sense of security and satisfaction from their accomplishments. Teachers use a variety of ways for progress reports. Eugenia Baxter and Katherine Montgomery tell how their class committees report:[15]

After working for a time in committees, the pupils usually encounter trouble. They should then assemble for a first progress report and for suggestions for further refinement of their work.

[14] *Ibid.,* p. 284.
[15] Eugenia Baxter and Katherine Montgomery, "Environments For Geographic Education," *Journal of Geography,* Vol. 55 (September, 1956), p. 276.

CHART SHOWING PROGRESS REPORT ON PROBLEM

Problem	Stage at which we have arrived toward solving the problem	New Problems	Suggestions by class and teacher to solve new problem
What is the geography behind the industries in the Ruhr Valley?	We are writing a report. We want to make geographic relationships. We have this started.	Where can we find material for this problem? Most geographies have just general information.	Best source, *Focus*. Read Lutz's letter to 7th grade. He tells of the industries.

Such problems as, "We want to make a chart of the products of New South Wales and the geography behind these products. We don't have enough material. Where can we find more?" will arise.

Annice Elkins reports on a work sheet which serves as a guide for both superior and slow readers. It is a plan that must be made specific and adapted to each unit.

SUGGESTED PLAN FOR GUIDE SHEET

1. Vocabulary helps. Identify the following by matching:

   Words and Geographic Terms   *Definitions*
   1. _____   ( ) _____
   2. _____   ( ) _____
   3. _____   ( ) _____
            etc.   etc.
2. Guide questions for reading (taken from preview and tentative statements).
3. Map questions (assigned from study aids in text).
4. Relationship outline (assign certain paragraphs from text to be outlined under the following headings):
   Man's Activities   *Natural Features*
5. Make a bar graph representing the following table of statistics. (Teacher should give table.)
6. Reading supplementary material, taking notes, and preparing report to present before the class.

7. Problem-solving (report may be oral or written). Gather together information from pictures, maps, verbal material, and other sources to find some reasons which help explain man's activities in relation to his environment.

This worksheet offers guidance to both slow and independent readers. Slow readers will work through only the first few parts, while the superior reader has a challenge in the remaining parts. As the class works, the teacher has an opportunity to help children solve their individual reading problems. The sheets require careful preparation on the part of teachers, but results are rewarding.[16]

The class discussion may be used to guide and improve the reading abilities of the class. During class discussions of the topics or problems, misconceptions may be corrected by explanations and the rereading of sections. Often some pupils will have vague ideas concerning some concepts and interrelationships; the teacher and class can co-operate to clarify these. The class discussion period is also the time to organize the information gathered. During this period the pupils should be required to report accurately and give sources of the information being reported. If opinions are given, they should state the reasons for their opinions. The organizing, checking, and evaluating of information should stimulate and direct further reading.

The assignment should also provide for recording and using the results of the pupils' reading and study. The teacher and pupils should work together in suggesting and deciding how the results of their reading and study are to be recorded, by individuals, committees, or the class as a whole. Such recording and application activities supply an opportunity for display of individual interests and abilities. The expression activities may be stories written by a pupil or committee, pictures collected and arranged to illustrate the natural and cultural conditions of the country or region, drawings, puzzles, and games, an outline of the problem or topic, an exhibit, a dramatization, a mural, or a booklet.

[16] Annice Davis Elkins, "The Problems of Reading Geography," *Education*, Vol. 77 (September, 1956), p. 43.

The Idea Line suggested by Virginia Schauer is an excellent means for a class to organize its findings:[17]

Draw six columns on the blackboard. Head the columns—*What, Where, How, How Much,* and *Why.* The children read about one major type of work in a region and report findings which fit into the columns. The teacher records each of the findings in the proper column.

What	Where	When	How	How Much	Why
Fishing for salmon.	Near coast of northern California; cool waters farther north; streams of Washington and Oregon.	Between March and September.	Fishing vessels. Seines. Trap nets. Trolling.	The most valuable.	Salmon live in ocean most of time. Swimming upstream.

But whatever the means used to record the information found and the understandings gained, both the teacher and the class should evaluate the procedure in terms of geographic understandings and social value. By recording their findings in some definite concrete manner, the pupils gain a feeling of accomplishment, a pride in a task well done. A class once told a supervisor that they did not like either geography or history because they never knew when or what they knew, in other words, the class never had a feeling of accomplishment. That situation was soon remedied, and by the end of the year those children liked both geography and history.

Through clear, definite, well-motivated assignments which include specific questions, directions, checking up exercises or progress reports, selected references, class discussions, and finally worthwhile, interesting expression and recording activities, the teacher not only can further the pupil's reading abilities but also develop a feeling of responsibility and accomplishment on the part of the children.

The Teaching or Reteaching of Certain Basic Reading Skills

The teachers of geography must recognize that often basic reading skills should be taught or retaught. The children may have

[17] Schauer, *op. cit.,* p. 286.

used these skills in other situations but do not know how to apply them quickly to their geography work. The class may not know how to use the index in their geography texts, or cannot organize geographic materials, nor adjust their rate of reading to study needs and purposes. In teaching or reteaching these skills, the teacher should use the exercises in situations where they meet specific needs of the pupils as they read and study geography.

Use of the Index. Skill in the use of the index is one of the basic reading skills, indispensable in the study of geography. Even though the pupils are accustomed to using the index in their readers and other books, they usually need some practice in the use of the index of their geography text. The index of a geography text is rather complex. It contains special symbols referring to maps, pictures, and graphs, and in each text these symbols are likely to be different. In some situations a class may need direct teaching with special lessons on the index.

Marion Anderson has listed ten of the abilities which contribute to efficient use of an index:[18]

1. Ability to locate words in alphabetical order to the fourth letter.
2. Ability to recognize the sequence of letters in the alphabet from *a–z* and from *z–a*.
3. Ability to select the key word in a question or topic.
4. Ability to recognize additional entries that may yield further information.
5. Ability to understand the use of the comma and the hyphen in an index.
6. Ability to understand and use cross references.
7. Ability to recognize and use typographical aids, such as italic type for map references.
8. Ability to use both topics and sub topics in an index.
9. Ability to turn quickly to a reference.
10. Ability to skim a page rapidly to determine whether it contains information on the problem.

[18] Marion Anderson, "Learning to Read in the Social Studies," *The Sixth Annual Conference on Reading* (Pittsburgh, Pa., University of Pittsburgh Press, 1950), p. 96.

Reading as a Tool in Geographic Education

The teacher can make exercises to check abilities which will give practice in the use of the index. The following are only suggestive of types of exercises.

Use the index of your text to locate information on the following:
1. What is the work of the forest ranger?
2. What is the Tennessee Valley Authority?
3. Give the pages on which you will find maps which help you to locate the following places:
    Boston, Mass.
    Portland, Ore.
4. On what page is there a picture of Chicago; of farm machines?
5. Which of the topics listed below do you find in the index of your book? Draw a line under the topics you find, and give pages on which they are discussed:
    (a) forage crops   (c) timberline
    (b) textile mills   (d) roads in South America

Often the key word is not definitely stated, or children have difficulty in deciding on the key word, necessitating special help and exercises. A class discussion should be the first step. For instance, a class wanted to find what were the industrial regions of the United States. The teacher asked the class what they considered the most important word or words to look for. The answer was, *Industrial regions of the United States.* There was no such topic in their index. The teacher then asked for suggestions. A pupil suggested looking for *industry* and for *manufacturing.*

Another class had trouble in finding information on transportation in Africa. They thought the key word would be *transportation,* as it should have been, but it was not listed in the index. The class discussed their problem and the following possibilities were suggested: *camels, railroads, airplanes, air routes, navigable rivers,* and *highways.* In checking the index they found some of these listed, but not *highways* or *navigable rivers.* They decided that they would probably have to check the larger rivers—the Nile, Congo, and Niger. They checked the index for the topics suggested and then quickly skimmed the pages indicated to see if the information was given. In checking the Congo River they found the paragraph heading was *highways,* and not only was river transportation discussed but also land roads. As a rule, children enjoy running down information in this manner, probably because of the puzzle element and the challenge. Practice exercises, such as the following, help those who need individual attention.

In the questions listed below, draw two lines under the important key word which you find in the index; draw one line under the less important key words or subtopics. What are the important industries of Europe? Describe the coastline of Spain.

Giving special exercises is not the end, the teacher must watch to see that the pupils use the index in real study situations. Only through use will the children learn to appreciate the value of the index as a practical learning tool.

Organization Skills. These are helpful in outlining and summarizing. Mabel Snedaker has developed what she calls "A Ladder of Organization Skills" with types of exercises for the six skills. Miss Snedaker's outline and exercises should be helpful to a teacher of geography in training a class that lacks such skills. A teacher of geography would use a geography textbook or other geographic materials in planning these exercises.

A LADDER OF ORGANIZATION SKILLS WHICH HAS BEEN HELPFUL IN DEVELOPING THE ABILITY TO OUTLINE AND TO SUMMARIZE

These six skills should be developed in the order listed:
1. Skill in selecting paragraph headings.
   Exercises to be used in developing this skill:
   a. Choose the best of several suggested headings.
   b. Match paragraph headings with paragraphs.
   c. Rearrange, in proper sequence, paragraph headings listed out of order.
   d. Choose the topic sentence in a paragraph.
   e. Make paragraph headings.

Reading as a Tool in Geographic Education

2. Skill in asking a question which covers all the important ideas in a paragraph.
    Exercises to be used in developing this skill:
    a. Change paragraph headings made by the class into questions.
    b. Choose the best of several questions, as suggested under 1.
    c. Decide upon and list the important question for each paragraph in a selection. Check back through these questions to see whether you can answer them adequately. Use the questions as a guide in deciding where you need to reread the material, and as a check upon how well the selection is prepared.
3. Skill in distinguishing between the main idea and supporting details.
    Exercises to be used in developing this skill:
    a. Choose from a list of sentences the topic or paragraph heading, and then decide which of the remaining sentences should be listed as important subtopics.
    b. From an unorganized list that contains both steps in a process and supporting details, choose and arrange in proper sequence the important steps in the process of making or doing something. (For instance, in geography, steps in raising cotton or some other crop.)
    c. Choose the steps in a process (or the steps in doing some type of work) from a written account, and then list the supporting details for each step.
4. Skill in dividing material into sectional headings.
    Exercises to be used to develop this skill:
    a. Decide in turn the number of paragraphs in a section that tell about each one of sectional headings listed in order.
    b. Match sectional headings with sections of material.
    c. Divide material into sectional headings.
5. Skill in outlining.
    Exercises to be used in developing this skill:
    a. Fill in a paragraph heading for each paragraph of a selection under the sectional headings recently made by the class.
    b. Fill in skeleton outlines when the paragraph heading is given.
    c. Fill in a skeleton outline when the paragraph heading must be supplied.
    d. Use outlines which the class has made for various purposes: (1) as an aid to remembrance in giving a report; (2) as a basis for a summary of a paragraph; (3) as a guide in reviewing important points.

Note: Begin with one step outlines of single paragraphs that are easily organized. Do not proceed to more complex outlines until students can make one-step outlines with facility.

6. Skill in summarizing.
Exercises to be used in developing this skill:
  a. Change outlines recently made by the class into summary statements.
  b. Choose the best of several suggested summary statements for a paragraph.
  c. Match summary statements with paragraphs.
  d. Make summary statements for paragraphs.[19]

Adjusting Rate of Reading. Another skill to be taught, or retaught, is how to adjust the rate of reading to study needs and purposes. Some children seem to know how to do this without any special teaching or practice. Others, usually the less able readers, read everything at the same rate of speed regardless of the purpose for which they are reading. The following procedure is suggested as one way of helping students to adjust their rate of reading to study needs and purposes, for instance, to answer a direct question, to gather information for the solution of a problem, or to find proof for a statement.

1. Select a section or chapter in the geography textbook, or give each pupil a mimeographed copy of a selection from a geography reference book.

2. Make up a list of questions, some calling for skimming, some for careful reading, and some for more careful reading or even rereading.

3. Help the pupils decide which questions can be answered by skimming, which by careful reading, and which by careful, thoughtful reading and rereading. This discussion is very important. The pupils should discover that the answers to "what," "where," and "when" questions can be located by skimming. But "how" questions usually require slower and more careful reading, while "why" questions often require not only thoughtful reading, but often rereading, for one needs to interpret and relate various facts.

[19] Mabel Snedaker, "A Ladder of Organization Skills which Has Been Found Helpful in Developing the Ability to Outline and to Summarize," *Teaching of Reading: A Second Report,* Thirty-sixth Yearbook, National Society for the Study of Education, Part I (Bloomington, Ill., Public School Publishing Co., 1937), pp. 180–181.

Reading as a Tool in Geographic Education

4. Give plenty of time to the introduction of the material, using maps, pictures, or graphs.

5. Introduce in context any new and technical words, write the word on the board, and explain the meaning of the term.

6. Have the pupils work with the skimming questions first. Help them to decide on key words or phrases to look for, and also under what topic the answer is likely to be found. Have them skim, watching for variations in their speed. Give help to those needing it, and check each child's progress.

7. On another day, work on the questions requiring careful, rather slow reading.

8. Finally, work with the "why" questions which require thoughtful reading and rereading.[20]

Reading is an essential tool in the study of geography, as in other subject-matter fields. The development of reading skills in geography is the responsibility of the teacher of geography. It is not an easy task, but an enthusiastic, skillful teacher can so guide a class that they will tackle reading with pleasure and enthusiasm. But the development of these skills must not be left to chance. Careful and systematic practice is necessary if the children are to gain and retain the essential reading skills needed in the study of geography.

REFERENCES

ANDERSON, Marion A., "Learning to Read in the Social Studies," *The Sixth Annual Conference on Reading* (Pittsburgh, Pa., University of Pittsburgh Press, 1950), pp. 90–100.

BAXTER, Eugenia, and MONTGOMERY, Katherine, "Creating Environments for Geographic Education," *Journal of Geography*, Vol. 55 (September, 1956), pp. 271–278.

BEERY, Althea, "Development of Reading Vocabulary and Word Recognition," *Reading in the Elementary School*, Forty-eighth Yearbook, National Society for the Study of Education, Part II (Chicago, University of Chicago Press, 1949), pp. 184–186.

[20] Adapted from "Reading and Listening Skills," *Skills in the Social Studies*, Edited by Helen M. Carpenter, Twenty-fourth Yearbook (Washington, D.C., National Council for the Social Studies, 1953), Ch. VI, pp. 114–115.

BRINKMAN, A. R., "Reading Improvement in Geography for Retarded Readers," *Journal of Geography*, Vol. 46 (September, 1947), pp. 234–240.

BURTON, William H., *Reading in Child Development* (New York, Bobbs-Merrill Co. Inc., 1956).

EISEN, Edna E., "Reading Materials," *Geographic Approaches to Social Education*, Nineteenth Yearbook (Washington, D.C., National Council for the Social Studies, 1948), Ch. X.

ELKINS, Annice D., "Efficient Use of Geography Texts," *N.E.A. Journal*, Vol. 44 (February, 1952), pp. 81–82.

———, "The Problems of Reading Geography," *Education*, Vol. 77 (September, 1956), pp. 37–44.

GOODYKOONTZ, Bess, "Teaching Pupils to Organize What They Read," *The Elementary English Review*, Vol. 7 (April, 1930), pp. 87–90.

GRAY, William S., "Reading as an Aid in Learning," *Reading in the Elementary School*, Forty-eighth Yearbook, National Society for the Study of Education, Part II (Chicago, University of Chicago Press, 1949), Ch. XI, pp. 233–253.

HARBESON, Mrs. Cordelia, "Intermediate Geography: A Reading Problem," *Journal of Geography*, Vol. 50 (January, 1951), pp. 21–24.

HUTSON, Percival W., "Reading Purposes in Geography," *Journal of Geography*, Vol. 25 (December, 1926), pp. 321–330.

LOGAN, Mary, "Techniques in the Use of the Reading Tool in Reaching Worthwhile Geographic Understandings," *Journal of Geography*, Vol. 23 (January, 1934), pp. 10–16.

LORD, F. E., "Diagnosing Study Difficulties in Elementary Geography," *Educational Method*, Vol. 17 (March, 1938), pp. 273–277.

LUCAS, W. C., "Making Geography Teaching Click," *Journal of Geography*, Vol. 38 (December, 1939), pp. 349–354.

MEIGHAN, Mary, "Training Children to Use Their Geography Books Efficiently," *Journal of Geography*, Vol. 38 (November, 1939), pp. 330–339.

PHILLIPS, Mary Viola, "Methods to Improve Skill in the Use of a Geography Vocabulary at the High School Level," *Journal of Geography*, Vol. 55 (November, 1956), pp. 369–374.

ROBINSON, Ruth M., and Committee, "Skills in the Social Studies," *Reading and Listening Skills*, Twenty-fourth Yearbook (Washington, D.C., National Council for the Social Studies, 1953), Ch. VI.

RUTAN, Edward J., "Learning the Language of Geography," *Journal of Geography*, Vol. 45 (May, 1946), pp. 204–206.

SCHAUER, Virginia, "Teaching Children to Read the Geography Text-

Reading as a Tool in Geographic Education 221

book," *Journal of Geography*, Vol. 44 (October, 1945), pp. 279–287.

SNEDAKER, Mabel, and HORN, Earnest, "Reading in the Various Curriculum Fields," *Teaching of Reading: A Second Report*, Thirty-sixth Yearbook of the National Society for the Study of Education, Part I (Bloomington, Ill., Public School Publishing Co., 1937), Ch. V.

TAYLOR, Catherine R., "The Vocabulary Problem in the Intermediate Grades," *The Third Annual Conference on Reading* (Pittsburgh, Pa., University of Pittsburgh Press, 1947), pp. 127–130.

UPTON, Loula, "How to Use the Textbook," *Journal of Geography*, Vol. 32 (December, 1933), pp. 359–364.

WHIPPLE, Gertrude, "Language Activities in the Social Studies," The Sixth Annual Conference on Reading (Pittsburgh, Pa., University of Pittsburgh Press, 1950), pp. 101–106.

8

Geographic Reading Materials

BOTH THE STUDENT and the teacher acquire most of the experiences that are basic to the gaining of geographic knowledge, abilities, attitudes, and appreciations through reading various kinds of geographic materials. Reading materials of value in geographic instruction may be classified as follows: (1) geographic informational materials such as textbooks, readers, and both general and specialized references; (2) travel books, scientific reports, magazine and newspaper articles; (3) recreatory materials such as fiction, essays, and poetry. Each one of these has its place in geographic education. The value of varied and wide reading is well expressed in a brief essay by the great polar explorer, Vilhjalmur Stefansson:[1]

Armchair Exploration

Indeed, I rather think that the armchair explorer—the alert reader whose distant journeys are made exclusively on the wings of the printed word—often sees in better perspective frozen seas or splash through steaming jungles than do the adventurers themselves. A certain kind of Arctic expedition, for instance, will devote months or years to attaining a single geographical dot on the map; during the same period the armchair explorer can, through varied reading, range far and wide over the

[1] Vilhjalmur Stefansson, "Armchair Exploration," *Reader's Digest*, Vol. 18 (March 1931).

whole surface of the globe, enjoy the most diverse experiences, and come back from his many trips with a harvest of stimulating ideas.

Now *ideas*, after all, are the only things that count in any form of exploration. The discoverers of islands or continents are finders and temporary figures; the discoverers of ideas are creators and long revered. Of that in our own time Darwin is the perfect example. His trips to the *Galapagos* (Gä lä pä gos) and to Tierra del Fuego would have been of little more than curious interest to his family and friends had he not also been an explorer in the realm of thought. It was his discovery of an idea that made the voyage of the *Beagle* one of the greatest adventures in history. And while Darwin may have discovered the germ of his idea in the Galapagos Islands, he was able to establish his views finally by tireless mental journeys through stacks of books, pamphlets, and fragmentary reports. The result was his epochal work, *The Origin of Species*.

But epoch-making ideas are not the only fruit of exploration in the realm of thought. To him who nourishes his mind, in every spare moment, with absorbing reading, all the swift events of our time take on more thrilling interest. The day's news will seem dull and ephemeral or dramatic and significant according as we observe it with inert minds or with minds that are tinglingly stocked with the thoughts that we have found on the printed page. The discovery of the bodies of Andree and his companions was little more than a passing sensation unless you looked upon it through eyes familiar with the lore of Arctic travel. Then it became a far more absorbing mystery than met the casual eye—a mystery challenging one to pursue interesting speculations to a poignant climax.

The like holds true in all daily affairs. The unread man may have the wildest adventures yet live a shallow and disappointing life. But each experience to a well-read man is so broadened by association with his previous mental adventures that it partakes of all the experience of the race.

GEOGRAPHIC INFORMATIONAL MATERALS
Textbooks

The modern textbook is an important and desirable source of information for both teacher and pupil. The textbook, with its pictures, maps, diagrams, statistics, and subject matter, constitutes a valuable geographical resource for classroom use. With a common textbook all pupils have at hand the basic geographic tools for learning. In general, the subject matter in geography texts is well organized. This is important, because not all teachers have the ability or the time to select materials from a large number of sources and organize such materials for teaching. If the teacher does have the training and time to select and organize geography subject matter, the textbook gives a starting point and also provides the maps and pictures needed for effective study.

The teaching helps in the modern textbook are also an aid and stimulus to both teacher and pupils. They save time for the busy teacher and aid the pupil by emphasizing the important facts and ideas and by stimulating him to think about what he is reading. The study helps and suggestions are usually prepared by experienced teachers.

Of course textbooks often are not properly used, and such misuse reflects on the intelligence of the teacher, not on the value of the textbook as a geographic tool. In the hands of a skillful, trained teacher the textbook is an important tool, a reliable source of basic information, a stimulus to further reading, and a guide. For those reasons, a textbook should be chosen with care after careful study and evaluation.

For those teachers and committees who have the responsibility of selecting textbooks, the following list of questions may be of assistance in evaluating geography texts:

I. What are the qualifications of the author or authors?
   A. Is he a recognized geographer? If there is more than one author, one of the two should be an educator or a classroom teacher who knows children and the psychology of learning.
   B. Have they the modern viewpoint of geography?
II. Is the publishing firm known as a reliable, up-to-date company? Geography textbooks are the most expensive textbooks published. Maps and pictures are expensive to make or buy, and also to print. In a single book, the original cost of these two items alone runs into thousands of dollars. The text must be revised almost continuously, which means that a company must have a capable, well trained

Geographic Reading Materials

editorial and research staff. A text is no sooner off the press until the process of revision is under way. Few people realize the time, expense, scholarship, and painstaking care that goes into the publishing of a series of geography textbooks, or even of a single junior or senior high school geography textbook.

III. Has the subject matter been selected and organized with regard to the modern viewpoint of geography and to modern educational aims and practices? Have the relative and shifting values of geographic facts been considered? Is there sufficient vivid detail to build meaningful geographic understandings, to build up images, and to develop appreciations? Has the age level and interests of the children been considered in the selection and organization of the subject matter?

IV. What teaching and study aids are provided?
    A. What type of map studies and map problems are given?
    B. Are there thought-provoking questions and problems to stimulate the pupils and to aid in seeing the application of the subject matter to life situations?
    C. Are there questions and activities which would appeal to children of varying abilities and interests?
    D. Are there worthwhile summaries and reviews which require the reorganization of the subject matter, or a new view of what the child has been studying?
    E. Are teaching suggestions or helps provided in the text or in a manual?

V. Does the text contain sufficient maps in color and in black and white? Are the maps suited to the age level? Are they as accurate (in proportion as well as content) as possible? Are they clear, pleasing, and effective in color?

VI. Are the pictures (both colored and black and white) clear, attractive, and worthwhile? Are they of sufficient size to be read? Are they integrated into the text and thus contributing to building imagery and understandings?

VII. Is the mechanical make-up satisfactory? The textbook should be attractive with clear print. The binding should be strong to withstand use. The arrangement of pictures, maps, and text should be attractive.

VIII. Does the table of contents give an adequate idea of the contents of the book?

IX. Is the index so arranged that a topic may be easily located, and is it in sufficient detail?

The chapters on maps, pictures, and graphs in this book will aid a teacher in evaluating the items in a textbook.

Geography Readers

The geography reader supplements the text. It may enlarge upon topics which are briefly discussed in the textbook or it may discuss topics not treated in the text but which are of geographic value and interest. It may give more details than the text which add vividness and create interest, thus enriching and broadening the understandings gained from the text. Frank Carpenter's geographical readers published in the early part of this century were of this type. Children enjoyed them, although they were not easy reading. They were not ideal by any means, but children would read and reread them. Unfortunately, during the past thirty years there have been very few of the true informational type of reader published. Instead, a new type has sprung up—the supplementary recreatory type.

The supplementary recreatory type of informational reader is a mixture of information and fiction. There is a story, usually an account of a family or a child on a trip, and the story thread is very thin and artificial. The information is given in answer to the children's questions. Some children's reaction to this type is summarized in one boy's statement, "I have to read too much to find what I want to know." Others read the books but are unable to pick out the important points. However, this type of supplementary reader has improved as publishers have become more selective in their choice of writers. In selecting such readers, however, as in selecting textbooks, the teacher or selection committee should set up some criteria for evaluating them. The following list of questions may be of assistance.

1. Is the author qualified to write about this region, nation or work?
2. Does the book present accurate information?
3. Is it unbiased and constructive in its presentation of ways of living, customs, and so forth?

Geographic Reading Materials

4. Does the book present materials which clarify, enrich, and give more reality to the geographic region or topic presented?[2]

Reference Materials

Reference materials include encyclopedias, yearbooks, government reports, professional magazines, and other magazines and newspapers. Pupils read from this group of materials as a result of interest created in the classroom and from the need of additional information. Such reference materials are of value to both teachers and pupils.

The most used encyclopedias are: *Compton's Pictured Encyclopedia*, *The World Book*, and *The Junior Britannica*. These furnish definite additional information to supplement the text. However, the teacher must guide the children in evaluating the information and relating it toward the development of geographic understandings. Facts alone do not have geographic significance, but facts are necessary as a basis for thinking.

There is an enormous amount of excellent material hidden in government reports and documents. When in need of materials for special units and projects the teacher should investigate these sources. The material is worthwhile, interesting, and up-to-date. Government journals containing material for the geographer are: *The Commerce Weekly*, *Foreign Agriculture*, *Foreign Crops and Markets*, and the *Monthly Weather Review*. These contain excellent articles on countries, industries, construction projects, new discoveries of minerals, in fact on almost every topic that a geographer or a teacher of geography would be interested in. Other documents are vital reference tools, such as:

Clayton's World Weather Records
Climatic Summary of the United States

[2] Excellent examples of the better type of supplementary readers are: Jack Bechdolt, *Oliver Becomes a Weatherman* (New York, Julian Mesner, Inc., 1953); G. W. Hoffman, and V. Hoffman, *Life in Europe—Switzerland* (Grand Rapids, Mich., The Fideler Co., 1955) [There is a series of these books on various countries.]; *The Young Travellers* (New York, E. P. Dutton & Co., 1955).

The Industrial Reference Service
Census Atlas Maps of Latin America

Two other reference books should be mentioned—*Webster's Geographical Dictionary* and *A Dictionary of Geography*.[3]

Only a few of the many valuable magazines can be discussed here. *The National Geographic Magazine* is well known for its pictures as well as for its articles. The *Geographic News Bulletin*, also published by the National Geographic Society, is a small weekly publication for children. It is worthwhile because it brings up-to-date information into the classroom. It is brief with attractive pictures. The *Journal of Geography* is a professional magazine for teachers, but it also contains well-written articles which can be read by pupils from the fifth or sixth grades on up. Such articles as "A Tourist-Geographer Visits Iquitos, Peru"[4] and "Sleepy Orinoco Valley Comes to Life"[5] are read and enjoyed by both teacher and pupil.

Focus, published by the American Geographical Society, provides background facts and geographical interpretations of current world problems and problem areas. It costs $1.00 for ten issues. Not only the geography, history, or social studies teachers, but every teacher should subscribe to *Focus.*

The Geographical Review is a magazine for professional geographers, but a teacher should know it because it frequently has articles of interest to the junior and senior high school teacher. When a teacher is looking for special or uncommon materials on a specific country or continent, he will find geography magazines for almost any country, such as the *Australian Geographer, The Canadian Geographical Journal, Malayan Journal of Tropical Geography, The Geographical Magazine, The New Zealand Geog-*

---

[3] Webster's *Geographical Dictionary* (Springfield, Mass., G & C Merriam Co., 1949); W. G. Moore, *A Dictionary of Geography,* Penguin Books.

[4] Elizabeth Eiselen, "A Tourist-Geographer Visits Iquitos, Peru," *Journal of Geography,* Vol. 55 (April, 1956), pp. 176–181.

[5] C. Langdon White, "Sleepy Orinoco Valley Comes to Life," *Journal of Geography,* Vol. 55 (March, 1956), pp. 112–121.

rapher, and many others. Many of these magazines may be found in college and university libraries, and in large city libraries.

TRAVEL BOOKS AND SCIENTIFIC REPORTS

Travel books and books reporting on scientific expeditions are worthwhile to give vivid detail and reality to distant places. Of course, these vary greatly in value depending upon the author. Some writers emphasize the unusual or bizarre and do not give a true picture, but this type is less common than was formerly. Such books as Anne Lindberg's *North to the Orient,* Richard E. Byrd's, *Little America;* Henrich Harrer's, *Seven Years in Tibet,* Robert L. Stevenson's, *In the South Seas,* are of value.[6]

Then there are two anthologies, *Splendor of the Earth: An Anthology of Travel, Outside Readings in Geography,* which are also of value.[7]

Such books give both teacher and student experiences that they cannot otherwise obtain because of the limitations of time, space, safety, and, perhaps, finance. For instance, the following description of a tropical desert sandstorm is worth reading to any geography class above the fifth grade:[8]

December 7th provided us with a *gibli,* a strong wind laden with sand, which nearly tore up our tent pegs and covered everything with a thick coating. Hair, eyes, and skin were full of sand. Everything we ate was flavored with it. It oozed from the pillows and every article of clothing. It penetrated every box and bag. . . . That night we all sat around a fire with a cold wind freezing our backs.

[6] Anne Lindbergh, *North to the Orient* (New York, Harcourt, Brace and Co., Inc., 1940); Richard E. Byrd, *Little America,* (New York, G. P. Putnam's Sons, 1930); Henrich Harrar, *Seven Years in Tibet* (New York, E. P. Dutton & Co. Inc., 1954); Robert L. Stevenson, *In the South Seas* (Philadelphia, Eldon Press, Ltd., 1937).

[7] Margaret S. Anderson, *Splendor of the Earth* (London, George Philip and Son, Ltd., 1954); F. E. Dohrs, L. M. Sommers, and D. R. Petterson, *Outside Readings in Geography* (New York, Thomas Y. Crowell Co., 1955).

[8] Rosita Forbes, *The Secret of the Sahara* (New York, George H. Doran Co., 1921), pp. 60, 66. An account of a trip to the oasis of Kufra in the Sahara.

Another passage, from T. E. Lawrence, gives the feel of the tropical desert heat,[9]

The rocks on which we flung ourselves . . . were burning, so that they scorched our breasts and arms, from which later the skin drew off in ragged sheets. . . . It was a breathless wind, with the furnace taste; and as the day went on and the sun rose in the sky it grew stronger, more filled with the dust of the great sand desert of northern Arabia. . . . By noon it blew half a gale, so dry that our shrivelled lips cracked open and the skin of our faces chapped; while our eyelids, gone granular, seemed to creep back and bare our shrinking eyes. The Arabs drew their headcloths tightly across their noses, and pulled the brow-folds forward like viziers with only a narrow loose-flapping slit of vision.

Then there are such books as William Beebe's *Edge of the Jungle,* with its vivid descriptions of the insects and other life of the wet tropics. For instance, the following description of the Attas ants helps one to realize some of the difficulties of living in the wet tropics.[10]

There are three dominant labor unions in the jungle, all social insects, two of them ants, never interfering with each other's field of action, and all supremely illustrative of conditions resulting from absolute equality, free-and-equalness, socialism carried to the ant power. The Army Ants are carnivorous, predatory, militant nomads; the Termites are vegetarian scavengers, sedentary, negative and provincial; Attas, or leaf cutting ants, are vegetarians, active and dominant, and in many ways the most interesting of all.

The casual observer becomes aware of them through their raids upon gardens; and indeed the Attas are a very serious menace to agriculture in many parts of the tropics, where their nests, although underground, may be as large as a house and contain millions of individuals. While their choice among wild plants is exceedingly varied, it seems that there are certain things they will not touch; but when any human-reared flower, vegetable, shrub, vine, or tree is planted, the Attas rejoice, and

[9] T. E. Lawrence, *Revolt in the Desert* (New York, George H. Doran & Co., 1927).
[10] William Beebe, *Edge of the Jungle* (New York, Henry Holt & Co., 1925), p. 154–155.

Geographic Reading Materials

straightway desert the native vegetation to fall upon the newcomers. Their whims and irregular feeding habits make it difficult to guard against them. They will work all round a garden for weeks, perhaps pass through it en route to some tree that they are defoliating, and then suddenly, one night, every Attas in the world seems possessed with a desire to work havoc, and at daylight the next morning, the garden looks like a winter stubble—a vast expanse of stems and twigs, without a single remaining leaf. Volumes have been written and whole chemists' shops of deadly concoctions devised, for combating these ants, and still they go steadily on, gathering leaves which, as we shall see, they do not even use for food.

Passages from such books help to create vivid mental images, and in the creation of such mental pictures lies the secret of real and lasting instruction.

For what purposes may these be used? Such materials may be used to introduce a new topic or unit by creating interest or raising questions. Descriptive passages such as the two quoted, on sand storms and desert heat, provide details and the atmosphere or "feel" that makes teaching more effective, and also aid in the development of concepts and understandings, merely hinted at or only mentioned in the textbook. Such materials extend the child's interest beyond the classroom and his immediate locality.

In presenting such material, the teacher should read it to the class at the right time, taking time to discuss the article with the class, calling attention to new terms and vivid picturesque words, and leading them through questions to relate the content to the unit or topic the class is studying or has studied.

For instance, after reading Lawrence's description of the heat of the desert and its effects, ask such questions as this: "What are the actual desert temperatures which produce such effects? How does this account show why the Arabs dress as they do?" If the account is read before a study of Arabia, the same questions could be used with the wording slightly changed. Often the better readers want to read the book themselves, and they are led into more extensive reading.

FICTION, ESSAYS, AND POETRY

Fiction, poetry, and essays can do much to vitalize and enrich geography. Geographical fiction stimulates the imagination and makes distant places and people take on a greater semblance of reality. They also are a means of extending children's interests, and are an aid in providing for individual interests. Such materials should be literature first, and have a definite appeal and value as literature. The geographic background—the locale, descriptions, ways of the people—should be true to the region and the people. George R. Stewart's *Storm* is an example of such fiction. It is the story of a cyclonic storm that had its beginning off the coast of Japan. He describes the resulting weather as the storm moves eastward over the Pacific, strikes the Pacific coast, and progresses across the United States. He pictures the relatively puny, but nevertheless prodigious, efforts of man to prepare for and to defend himself against the tremendous force of the storm.

Lois Lenski's *Boom Town Boy,* the story of the effects of the discovery of oil on a region and the people, is another illustration. Dhan Gopal Mukerji's stories of his native India—*Jungle Beasts and Men, Hari, the Jungle Lad, Kari, the Elephant*—are fascinating stories of life in India and the animals of the jungle.

Good geographical fiction

. . . fills the gaps in the pages of the textbook, make the inhabitants of other countries people, human beings like ourselves, instead of "natives," and gives richer concepts of their homes, their towns and cities, their landscapes, their recreation, their food, their work, and their play. . . . The best of the stories of other places are written from the point of view of the children whose homes and lives are duplicated, rather than from the point of view of American youngsters who visit a strange land and recount their experience there.[11]

Poetry, too, contributes to a greater appreciation of landscapes

---

[11] Marion Anderson, "Reading and Literature in the Area of Social Living," *The Sixth Annual Conference on Reading* (Pittsburgh, Pa., University of Pittsburgh Press, 1950), pp. 109, 111.

Geographic Reading Materials

and people. For instance, the following poem by Björnstjerne Bjornson, gives a vivid picture of Norway.[12]

> Norway, Norway,
> Rising in blue from the sea's gray and green,
> Island's around like fledgings tender,
> Fiord-tongues with slender
> Tapering tips in silence,
>
> Norway, Norway
> Houses and huts, not castles grand,
> Gentle or hard,
> Thee we guard, thee we guard,
> Thee, our future's fair land.

Uses of Recreatory Reading

A poem, a story, or an incident from a story may be used to introduce a unit. The teacher may read the poem, story, or incident to the class and use it as a basis for an informal discussion to arouse the interest of the class. The teacher should keep in mind that such materials are not meant for intensive study. They are primarily for enjoyment and appreciation, even though they are of value for providing additional details.

The teacher should not hesitate to read aloud to a class. Children can understand and appreciate poems, stories, and incidents that they could not, or would not, read for themselves. The teacher's voice, attitude, and comments bring out the latent beauty and drama that arouse the class.

Such recreatory materials should be available to the children in the library or in the classroom. An incidental reference to them by the teacher will cause some children to read them, or if he reads a chapter or dramatic incident, a child will often want to read more. The book should be left where a child can get it to read for pleasure during a free reading period.

In the use of such materials the teacher should realize that certain disadvantages much be considered. The children should un-

---

[12] Björnstjerne Bjornson, *Scandanavian Classics*, Vol. III (New York, The American-Scandanavian Foundation, 1915), p. 214.

derstand the differences between factual reference materials and fiction, in order that they will not confuse the impressions gained from stories with the basic facts and understandings secured from references. Also they should realize that even the best and most careful writer of fiction may not be accurate in all details. He depends to a certain extent on his imagination for vivid detail and he has his own ideas about people and countries which are bound to color his writing. Both the teacher and the pupils must be aware of these considerations.

However, the child, as he studies the geography of the world, needs to have such reading experiences as will reveal to him the interesting world in which he lives. He needs stories of family life in many lands as well as in the various regions of our own land. Perhaps, by wise use of both factual materials and literature, he may be freed of the false ideas of other peoples and countries that prejudice the thought and action of many adults. Through honest, interesting books, perhaps the child may come to know other lands and people, what they contribute to the world, what values they hold dear, and why they live and act as they do.

REFERENCES

ANDERSON, Marion A., "Reading and Literature In the Area of Social Living," *The Sixth Annual Conference on Reading* (Pittsburgh, Pa., University of Pittsburgh Press, 1950), pp. 107–116.

BOWLER, R. N., "The Factor of Place in Literature," *Journal of Geography*, Vol. 54 (November, 1955), pp. 309–402.

BRIGHAM, A. P., and DODGE, R. E., "Nineteenth Century Textbooks of Geography," *Teaching of Geography*, Thirty-second Yearbook, National Society for the Study of Education (Bloomington, Ill., Public School Publishing Co., 1933), Ch. I.

CALLOWAY, Katherine L., "Songs and Poems of Many Lands," *Journal of Geography*, Vol. 31 (November, 1932), pp. 330–342.

CHAMBERLAIN, J., "Literary Selections as an Aid in Teaching Geography," *Journal of Geography*, Vol. 15 (September, 1916), pp. 9–16.

EISEN, Edna, "Reading Materials," *Geographic Approaches to Social Education*, Nineteenth Yearbook (Washington, D.C., National Council for the Social Studies, 1948), Ch. X.

Geographic Reading Materials

GARLOCH, Lorene A. "Tools of Research," *Journal of Geography*, Vol. 46 (February, 1947), pp. 55–62.

HUS, Helen, "The Place of Recreatory and Related Readings in the Content Areas," *The Reading Teacher*, Vol. 8 (December, 1954), pp. 90–94.

JOHNSON, Hildegard B., "Geography In American Literature," *Education*, Vol. 77 (September, 1956), pp. 30–36.

KEINARD, M., "Using Music to Enrich Geography," *Journal of Geography*, Vol. 52 (May, 1953), pp. 189–191.

LEARY, Bernice, "Meeting the Needs of Children Through Literature," *The Seventh Annual Conference on Reading* (Pittsburgh, Pa., University of Pittsburgh Press, 1951), pp. 36–39.

McCUSKER, Laurette G., "Creative Teaching Through Fiction," *Education*, Vol. 77 (January, 1957), pp. 276–279.

MILLER, George J., and SLETTEN, Cora, "Source Materials," *Geographic Approaches to Social Education*, Nineteenth Yearbook (Washington, D.C., National Council for the Social Studies, 1948), Ch. XVII.

RENNER, M. P., "Geography in Poetry," *Journal of Geography*, Vol. 28 (October, 1929), pp. 292–298.

STIMSON, Catherine D. J., "The Use of Literature in Teaching Geography," *Education*, Vol. 77 (September, 1956), pp. 24–29.

WOFFORD, Azile, "Standards for Choosing Books About Other Countries," *Elementary English*, Vol. 24 (November, 1947), pp. 469–473.

9

Unit Planning and Functional Activities

A GEOGRAPHY UNIT is a meaningful body of subject matter that is so organized with appropriate learning activities as to lead to the mastery of a major geographic understanding. A major geographic understanding involves the ability of an individual to interpret or explain the relationships between man and the natural environment in a specific region, or in specific types of activities. To gain a major understanding involves the mastery of numerous concepts and the ability to see their interrelationships.

A concept is an idea. It may be *concrete* or *abstract*. A concrete concept is the idea of a thing which can be comprehended by the senses from immediate experience, such as a tree, stream, rain, house, and so forth. An abstract concept involves ideas of qualities or attributes; "states of being" rather than "being." There is also a difference in the complexity of geographic concepts. Ideas with reference to features of the landscape, for instance, may refer to concrete particulars, such as a hill, river, grass, and the like. Conceptions of states of action or activity are more complex and less concrete, such as plowing, building a house, irrigating a field, wind blowing, and so forth. These complex concepts are formed by re-

Unit Planning and Functional Activities

lating several simple ideas. Ideas of condition, states of being, are more general and formed of several particulars, for instance, the ideas involved in the terms *marine climate* and *mild rainy winter*. A concept is mastered only when a person can easily discuss or describe the concept and use it readily to express himself.

A regional major understanding is a generalization growing out of the concepts and relationships developed in a unit. No major understanding can be gained without the individual knowing the reasons for the many specific things which a people in a certain region do. Such reasons are not understood unless one sees clearly *what* the people are doing, and *what* helps to explain *why* they do it. In order that the pupils gain such an understanding, many carefully selected details must be presented and much concrete material used. The teacher must keep in mind that the major understanding is the goal to be reached. The mastery of this understanding cannot be given by the teacher, but is attained by the pupils through the guidance of the teacher. The teacher must select the necessary materials, suggest and direct the learning activities, and test for evidence of mastery. The pupils must be the active agents.

If the teacher keeps in mind the major goal, the major understanding to be gained, he can more easily exclude material that is merely interesting. He will include only the facts which are essential in gaining the major understanding. He has a criterion for the selection of the maps, pictures, and reference materials for the unit. He also has a criterion for the selection of learning activities, application exercises and tests.

As Edgar B. Wesley has said:[1]

> By focusing upon a significant outcome, the unit prevents a mere survey of facts, and by including the facts, it forestalls the acquisition of a generalization which may be merely a hollow verbalism. William James once observed that one's insight into a generalization extends no further than his command of the details on which it rests. The unit provides the necessary details.
>
> The factual content is not only important; it is indispensable. It

[1] Edgar B. Wesley, *Teaching Social Studies in the Elementary School* (Boston, D. C. Heath and Company, 1946), pp. 166–167.

constitutes the means, the road by which the pupil arrives at the desired goal. The facts never wear out; they can be used again and again in a variety of contexts. They are permanent stepping stones which lead to many places, and not drifting rafts which serve only once.

The activities in which pupils engage in their study of a unit are equal in importance to the factual content. Indeed, without them the content is inert and lifeless. By writing, constructing, reporting, debating, cooperating, discussing, reading, and organizing the pupil gains command of the content and uses it to reach understanding.

The essence of the unit is the understanding which is sought. Both the contents and the activities are contributory to this main purpose. The existence of new skills, new interests, new ideas, and new ways of reacting and behaving is evidence of the achievement of the purpose.

STEPS IN THE PREPARATION OF A UNIT

The Teacher's Preparation

The teacher's first step in the preparation of a unit is to examine the basic text for content, maps, pictures, and study questions bearing upon the region, topic, or problem. He will then know what basic materials the class has to work with. Next, he should examine other geographical materials on the region. A college geography text usually will provide a fairly broad background, with additional readings from other books, magazines, and newspapers. As he reads and makes notes, he should keep in mind the interests, needs, and abilities of his class. Oftentimes he will find in a college text, a travel book, a magazine article, or a newspaper item, interesting, thought stimulating, or illustrative material within the understanding of his pupils.

The teacher now should be ready to outline the content or subject matter of the unit. In his selection of content he must keep in mind the major geographic understanding that he wants to develop concerning the specific region. In general terms, this major geographic understanding is how the people of such a region have adjusted their work activities and ways of living to their natural environment. These characteristic adjustments serve to distinguish the particular region from others, that is, they give the region individuality.

Unit Planning and Functional Activities

After outlining the subject matter that he expects to use, the teacher should select the maps, pictures, films, references, and other instructional materials. Now he is prepared to write the unit. Writing the unit requires clear thinking and hard work. There are many different formats for the organization of a unit. However, the following format has been found suggestive and helpful to many teachers in their attempts to organize geographical materials more effectively for teaching purposes.

FORMAT FOR A GEOGRAPHY UNIT

I. Goals.
   A. The major geographic understanding to be gained.
   B. The geographic relationships to be discovered by the pupils. These relationships or minor understandings lead to the major understandings.
   C. The vocabulary and concepts needed.
   D. Map and picture reading, and other skills to be checked or developed.
   E. Other goals: attitudes, appreciations, and habits.
II. Steps in the Development of the unit.
   A. Introduction or motivation.
   B. Teacher-pupil planning.
   C. The assimilation or problem-solving step.
   D. The presentation step.
   E. The application step.
III. Testing.

Goals

The major understanding has already been explained. The teacher should state it at the beginning of his unit so that he may keep in mind definitely the main goal of the unit. The act of expressing this clarifies the teacher's thinking and assists him in securing balance. By balance is meant that the types of adjustments in a specific region receive attention in proportion to their relative importance. Unless the teacher is careful, minor but interesting or unusual adjustments may be given emphasis far beyond their real importance in a specific region. Of course, this first statement of the major understanding is for the *teacher only*.

An illustration of a major understanding is the following for a unit on Alaska:

Alaska is a vast, sparsely populated land. The population is unevenly distributed, chiefly concentrated along the Pacific Coast and coastal valleys. Mining and fishing are the outstanding types of work, while fur trading, farming, and lumbering are minor types. The United States maintains important air and weather bases in Alaska. Air transportation is commonly used. The people are courageous and resourceful. The people's work activities and ways of living are related to a natural environment with these outstanding characteristics: location in high latitudes distant from the United States and near the Soviet Union, a fiord Pacific Coast and a long coastline facing the Bering Sea and Arctic Ocean, abundance of salmon and halibut in adjacent waters, forests, fur-bearing animals, mineral resources, a cool rainy climate, a short growing season, and in the interior long severe winters and short warm summers.

The chief specific relationships which are needed in order to reach the major understanding should be stated by the teacher for his own guidance as the unit develops. For instance, some relationships needed in study of Alaska are: (1) Fishing is important in southern and southeastern Alaska because of the abundance of salmon in the streams from May to August, and also because of the abundance of halibut which are to be found in the waters off the coast. (2) Mining is important due to the deposits of gold, copper, coal, and other minerals. (3) Comparatively few people are engaged in farming because the summer season is too short for most plants to mature, and the soil is difficult to cultivate.

The concepts and vocabulary needed should be listed. For instance, in a study of Alaska the pupils would need to gain such concepts as these: fiord coast, hydraulic mining, and so forth. If the teacher fails to analyze the subject matter for the new terms and concepts, he may find the pupils running into unexpected difficulties. By listing them he can be prepared with pictures and explanations.

By stating the other goals—map and picture reading skills and the attitudes and appreciations,—the teacher has a guide in developing learning exercises and later for testing. Each unit should

Unit Planning and Functional Activities

contribute to the development of the ability to use such learning tools as maps, pictures, and reference materials effectively. For instance, examples of map and picture reading abilities are: (1) The recognition of such map symbols as fiord coast, glaciers, mountains, rivers, and so forth; (2) ability to recognize the locations of important cities such as Anchorage, Fairbanks, Juneau, Seward, and Nome; (3) the recognition in pictures of a fish wheel, a fish cannery, a mining dredge, a glacier, and so forth. In the case of appreciation: (1) An appreciation of the natural beauties of Alaska, and an understanding of how these may be an economic asset; (2) a realization and an appreciation of the problems the people face as a result of natural factors in developing Alaska.

STEPS IN THE DEVELOPMENT OF A UNIT

Introduction

The introduction of a unit is very important. The purposes of the introduction are: (1) to arouse the interest of the class; (2) to challenge the group, and (3) to stimulate the questioning attitude. In planning the introduction, the teacher should seek to accomplish all three of the above purposes. He wants to arouse the desire and the willingness of the class to think, and both to think about and to think through a definite problem or problems. The teacher's own problem is what materials to present and how to present them.

The teacher may use appropriate pictures, maps, graphs, statistics, current events, or a story as a means of introducing a unit. In previous chapters the use of each one of the above has been discussed and illustrated with specific examples. For instance, a unit on Alaska might be introduced with class discussion of a set of pictures showing the outstanding work activities. These should stimulate questions on the where, how, and why of these activities. Specimens of gold, copper, and furs, and models such as a sledge with dogs could initiate a class discussion. A current newspaper item of value and interest concerning life in Alaska could be read and discussed. Advertising materials sent out by railroads, steamship lines, and tourist agencies may be used. One class set to work to discover how accurate such material was in presenting the interesting sights and opportunities in Alaska. One teacher used the story of the purchase of Alaska and people's attitude at that time toward the purchase. The public's attitude was represented by such expressions as, "Seward's Ice Chest," "Seward's Folly," and "The Polar Bear Garden." After discussing the price paid for Alaska and these expressions, the class went on to discover how true or false they were, and if Alaska had been worth the price.

Teacher-pupil Planning

This takes place after the interest of the class has been enlisted and after the problem or problems have been set up. Then, planning together, the teacher and pupils decide on lines for attacking the problem, special topics, committee work, and other activities. They also suggest sources of information and materials that will be needed in solving the problem, and consider the possible means of presenting individual and committee findings to the group.

The teacher's responsibility is to guide the class as plans are discussed, to make suggestions, and finally to organize the class' plans. Many classes, after some experience under the guidance of a skillful teacher, can do a good job of organizing their work. The teacher should keep in mind two points: (1) that the pupils are to be guided by questions and exercises to find for themselves the answers to their problems, and to check their ideas by comparing the information secured from different sources; (2) that the various activities are to be worthwhile geographically, that is, each one should contribute something definite toward understanding the relationships between man's activities in the particular region and the conditions of the natural environment.

Assimilation or Problem-solving

After the problems have been set up and the method of attack planned, the class is ready for study. All members of the class understand that each one is responsible for the solution of the prob-

Unit Planning and Functional Activities 243

lem and also for special contributions according to his abilities and interests. The pupils now gather information through reading, studying maps and pictures, interviewing persons with special knowledge, and perhaps doing some field work.

During this period, the teacher is busy helping slow pupils, directing some to additional readings, watching the progress of committees, and at times having group or class discussions.

This assimilation period may take several days. The teacher is responsible for deciding when the class is ready to present and share their findings.

Presentation

The method of presentation will vary with the type of unit and the plans of the class. It should include a discussion of the minor problems or questions and a summary of the findings bearing on the solution of the main problem. It will include committee and individual reports. Each of these should be followed by class discussion and evaluation. The discussion gives other pupils an opportunity to add pertinent information, give opinions, and ask questions of the speaker. If any criticism is made, the teacher should insist that it be constructive. The speaker should also quiz the listeners about the information he has given or about the chart, map, or picture he has presented. Although the discussion should be mainly among the pupils, the teacher should not hesitate to take part to clear up points, make corrections, and add to the topic.

Application

The application step is important because it tests the pupil's ability to use or apply their learnings gained in the study of the unit to a new situation. Such application exercises should test the ability of the pupils to effectively use the information gained, that is, to think critically.

Such exercises are not easy to make, but they are necessary if both teacher and pupil are to achieve a real feeling of accomplishment. Some types of application exercises are:

1. Making comparisons and drawing inferences.
2. Recognizing in the local environment examples of things he has studied about, such as—signs of soil erosion, effects of weather and climate, and good or poor adjustments man has made to the natural environment.
3. Understanding people's problems in making workable connections with their natural environments and their inherited customs, attitudes, and so forth.
4. Explaining or interpreting the geography behind current events.
5. Explaining a quotation from a travel book.
6. Explaining why one would or would not like to live in the region.
7. Picking out geographic ideas and relationships in a story about a region.

Some specific illustrations of application exercises, drawn from a number of different units, are:

1. *Australia:* Explain, "Shearing time in October and November is the main harvest time in the sheep lands of Australia." Compare life on a sheep station in Australia with life on a ranch in the western United States.
2. Compare the means of transportation in _____ with those in your community. In what ways are they alike? In what ways are they different? Why?
3. If you lived in _____, how would your life be different from your present life? Why?
4. If you were appointed as a technical adviser to the farmers of _____, what should you know about the country and its people before you went there?
5. Write an advertisement that is for the purpose of attracting visitors (tourists) and also business men interested in investing money in the development of industry in a particular country or region.

Testing

Testing is an important step in developing a unit, consequently the construction of a good test requires careful study and planning. Good tests can do much to improve the quality of the teaching and

Unit Planning and Functional Activities

the effectiveness of the pupils' study habits if they fit the goals or aims of the geography unit.

The major, general aims for testing for geographic learnings, understandings, and skills are:

1. To test the pupils' basic geographic information.
2. To test the ability of the pupils' to use data effectively, that is, to apply the information and understandings gained.
3. To test the pupils' skills in (a) map reading and interpretation; (b) reading and interpretation of pictures, statistics, and graphs.
4. To test the pupils' visual imagery.
5. To test types of critical thinking.
6. To test the pupils' attitudes and appreciations.

Both objective and essay types of tests should be used. All of the above may be tested with carefully constructed objective tests. But the essay type should also be used in order to give the pupil practice in organizing and expressing his knowledge and understanding. In every unit test, the essay question should be included and count for one-fourth to one-third of the total value. Since beginning teachers and others often are unfamiliar with the variety of tests which can be constructed, examples of many of these are given in the following section.

TYPES OF OBJECTIVE TESTS

Completion

In making a completion test select relatively simple statements, but those which contain *truths* in subject matter. Make the statement, then strike out significant word or words. The words omitted should be the *only* ones that will fit the blank. Be careful that the meaning is clear and definite. Do not eliminate too many words in a sentence.

Examples:

1. _____ is the largest city in New England.
2. Glasgow is known for its building of _____.
3. In the sentence below fill in the blanks with the words or phrase

from the following list best suited to complete the statement correctly:

Minneapolis is located near ──────── which furnish ────────.

(a) waterfalls; (b) a river or canal; (c) mountains; (d) power; (e) means of transportation; (f) protection from winds; (g) manufacturing; (h) commerce; (i) agriculture; (j) rainfall.

One-word Answer

In the one-word answer type of question, select items of importance. One one answer is possible, and the question should be stated as definitely and as briefly as possible.

Examples:

1. Name the largest city in New England.
2. What is the name of the largest city in New England?

Multiple Choice

There are a number of ways of writing multiple choice questions, such as the following.

Examples:

1. Underline the name of the largest city of New England. (a) Providence; (b) Boston; (c) New Haven; (d) Worcester
2. Philadelphia is located on the ────────.
 (a) Piedmont Plateau
 (b) Coastal Plain
 (c) Interior Lowland
 (d) Allegheny Plateau

In making multiple choice questions, prepare a fact sheet containing a list of the statements to be used. Give the students four or more choices, one of which makes the statement true, and vary the placing of the correct answer.

Matching

The matching type is another test which may be stated in a variety of ways. In preparing a matching test, make a list of the statements or facts to be used. Separate the groups and arrange in

Unit Planning and Functional Activities

chance order, eliminating possibility of duplication in pairing. Ten to twenty items are sufficient.

Examples:

I. Match the product with the region in which it is produced.

Hardware _____	1. Texas and Oklahoma
Spring Wheat _____	2. Great Lakes region
Iron ore _____	3. Arizona and Montana
Copper _____	4. North and South Dakota
Petroleum _____	5. New England States.

II. Put in the parenthesis before each paragraph the number of the city whose growth the paragraph in part explains.

1. St. Paul 2. Duluth 3. Milwaukee 4. Minneapolis

( ) It is near the head of river navigation, by the Falls of St. Anthony, and is near a great wheat-producing region. It owes its development largely to the flour milling industry which these facts help to make profitable.

( ) Its location on the westernmost part of the Great Lakes, near the Minnesota iron-ore region and near a great wheat-producing region has helped it to grow. Lumber, ore, and grain are shipped from its docks to eastern lake ports.

III. Matching facts and explanation or reasons for the facts. Place the number of the fact given in Column I before the reason or explanation given in Column II.

I	II
1. In the southern Appalachian Highlands, the people are very backward. They raise their own crops, spin their own cloth, and make their own tools, in part, because	...... the fields must be flooded while the grain is growing.
2. In the corn belt most of the work is done by machinery. It is easy to use machinery.	...... the mountains are very steep
3. The homes in the southern states are not heated by furnaces as our homes are because	...... on such level land and fine soil.

4. Around the Great Lakes iron ore is mined by steam shovels because ...... as there are no roads, there are no markets. The region is shut-in by mountains.

5. Rice must be raised on level land because ...... the land is lower than the river, and when the floods occur the people move to the higher land.

6. The roads of the Rocky Mountains wind back and forth around the slopes because ...... their winters are not nearly as long as ours, nor nearly as cold.

7. The movie industry is very important in and near Los Angeles because ...... the mines are open-pit and the ore is fine.

8. It is sometimes necessary for the people living near the Mississippi to camp in tents on the levees because ...... California has a variety of scenery, much sunshine, and warm weather.

Miss Edith Parker, of the University of Chicago, first used the locational relationship. In the locational relationships, a set of human activities are given and opposite each one is stated the geographic conditions which make the human activity possible in a specific region. The children are to name the region in which that activity is carried on under the stated geographic conditions.

Each of the following relationships should suggest to you a city or region in Italy, or Italy as a whole. For example, number "1" applies to the Po plain. After the relationship, write the name of the city, region, or country which that relationship suggests.

1. Dairying—moist meadows near rivers, many streams from which water can be taken conveniently for irrigation. _____
2. Silk manufacturing—climate of nearby lands suited for mulberry trees; water power in nearby mountains. _____
3. Olives an important crop—warm, rather dry summers; mild, moist winters. _____
4. Large production of wine—long, warm summers; sunny slopes and lowlands; natural limestone caverns; local supplies of sulphur. _____

5. Rice an important crop—fertile plain; many streams supplying water for irrigation; long, warm summers. _____
6. Growth of a very great city in early times—a central position in a peninsula itself centrally located among Mediterranean lands; valley route leading into highlands; river crossing; group of low hills in midst of fertile plain. _____

The Problem

This is a difficult type to make, but is worthwhile because it tests ability to think as well as information. In making this type, prepare the problems with the correct answers, insert true facts with false facts, and arrange in chance order. The statements may include one true reason and the other statements may be true but not relevant. Many combinations are possible. The emphasis is on the selection of responses. The situation is complex and tests the quality of relational thinking that the pupil can perform. The statements must be clear and definite. Usually many choices should be given to reduce the amount of guessing, and the placing of the correct answer should be varied.

Examples:

1. Write in the parentheses the number of the correct or best answer.
   ( ) *Why is Chicago the greatest railroad center?*
   (1) Natural routes connecting the east and the west meet here.
   (2) It is located in Illinois on the Chicago river.
   (3) There are many rich people in Chicago.
   (4) Large meat packing plants are located in Chicago.
2. Cross out the wrong answer in the following statements that do not aid in answering the question.
   a. What factors have helped the British Isles become a great commercial region?
   (1) Climate of the British Isles.
   (2) Sparse population of the British Isles.
   (3) Regular coast line.
   (4) Extensive amount of coal, iron ore, and power.
   (5) Location of the British Isles.
   (6) The effect of the monsoon winds.
   (7) Large amount of irrigation.

3. Underline the right answer.
   a. New England is not an easy place to carry on farming. Why not?
      (1) The land is a great plain.
      (2) The soil is thin and stony.
      (3) The growing season lasts seven months.
   b. New England has a cooler climate than many other parts of the United States. Why?
      (1) It is very near the North Pole.
      (2) It is cooled by breezes from the ocean.
      (3) The winds which influence New England are land winds.
   c. Fishing is important along the New England Coast. Why?
      (1) There are many good harbors, and it is near one of the best feeding grounds.
      (2) Boston is a great fish market.
      (3) Boston is a railroad center.

Association

The association test may be used to test the student's ability to associate certain important geographical relationships with specific regions. It should be used chiefly in regional studies. For example, after a study of the five low latitude types of climates, a series of statements involving relationships and facts may be made. The student is required to attach the correct climatic type to each series of statements.

Examples:

Write the name of the correct climatic type in front of each statement.
1. Rainy Low Latitude; 2. Desert; 3. Wet and Dry; 4. Semi-arid
5. Mountain.
_____1. The forests are dark and depressing, crowded with creepers and plants of innumerable varieties, and rich in valuable woods and in sap products such as rubber.
_____2. The people's food is supplied chiefly from their flocks and herds of cows, goats, and camels.
_____3. The population is sparse, generally at a low stage of civilization, and lives along the rivers.

As many statements may be used as there is sufficient *worth-while* material. The series of units must be large in most cases, such as covering a continent or a nation as large as the United States.

Unit Planning and Functional Activities

Political units, if they are fairly good natural units, also, may be used. Care must be taken in stating the points so that they all are clear, definite, and apply to one type or region.

The following is a newspaper article that appeared in the *Pittsburgh Press:*

"DUST GALE HITS DAKOTA DURING SUB-ZERO WAVE"

"*Sioux Falls; S.D.*, March 9. (AP)—The phenomenon of a dust storm in sub-zero temperature was reported in Southeastern South Dakota today as the March lion continued to roar.

North winds of gale force kept the mercury at zero or below generally, and in addition swept the top soil from exposed places.

In Yankton and Sioux Falls a heavy film of dust was laid.

Below are two columns. Column I gives a fact found in the newspaper article. Column II gives the reasons for the facts. Place the number of the fact before its reason.

I	II
1. Such a dust storm could not happen in New England because	...... the mountains would shut off and break up the winds.
2. The wind could easily carry the soil in South Dakota because	...... they were land winds which are cold in winter.
3. The winds were cold winds because	...... the soil is fine, rich, and deep.
4. Temperatures of below zero are not unusual in South Dakota because	...... the soil is stony, thin, and rocky.
5. Such fierce wind storms could not take place in the Appalachian Highlands because	...... the land is far from the sea, and the winds are cold when they reach here after crossing the cold land.

Testing Imagery

One of the important objectives of geographic instruction is to build accurate images in the children's minds. Geographic thinking must be based on such imagery or it is likely to be vague and inaccurate. Visual imagery can be tested with descriptive paragraphs, pictures, and maps. Edith Parker, of the University of Chicago, developed a number of such tests.

Examples:

1. Answer each statement with "yes" or "no" in the following list, concerning the region about which the following paragraph is written.
    a. From May to December the southwest monsoon winds sweep in from the ocean. Slopes of the eastern Himalayas and the west coast of Ceylon are affected most by the rainfall. Over much of the eastern part of this country it is so hot in the hottest part of this season that the English residents move to higher and cooler regions.

   (1) The country is Great Britain. _____
   (2) The country is India. _____
   (3) The rainfall is heavy. _____
   (4) The rainfall is light. _____
   (5) It is the wet season. _____
   (6) It is the dry season. _____
   (7) Sheep are raised extensively. _____
   (8) Tea is grown. _____
   (9) The country is Australia. _____
   (10) Light weight clothing will be worn by the people. _____

Give the child a number of pictures, and a map on which letters are put to indicate places where the pictures were taken. The child is to match the picture and letters correctly.

2. Using a set of pictures:

I	II	III
Uncaptioned picture showing physical environment typical of Switzerland	Uncaptioned picture showing physical environment typical of Norway	Uncaptioned picture showing physical environment typical of Holland

Part A. Write in the parenthesis after I the number of the country in the following list in which you think picture I was taken; after II, the number of the country in which II was taken; and so on.

Unit Planning and Functional Activities

1. Egypt	3. Japan	5. Arabia	7. Central Russia
2. India	4. Switzerland	6. Norway	8. Holland

    I. ( ) II. ( ) III. ( )

Part B. Does any one of these pictures show a region described by the first group of words in the following list? If so, put the number of the picture in the parenthesis at the end of the group, and so on.
 1. A mountainous region near the sea. ( )
 2. A plateau region near the sea. ( )
 3. A low plain near the sea. ( )

Part C. In the column under I, check the activities which you think would be encouraged by the kind of region shown in picture I; and so on.

 Activities   I II III
Rearing dairy cattle
Using water power for manufacturing
Deep sea fishing
Transporting goods in
boats on rivers and canals

Part D. Put a check after the number of the picture showing the region which you would expect to support the densest population.
    I. ( ) II. ( ) III. ( )

Part E. Put a check after the number of each picture in which you think there are evidences of very scant rainfall.
    I. ( ) II. ( ) III. ( )

In using pictures in testing, care must be taken that the question can be answered from the pictures directly or by inference based on the items in the picture.

Map Test

1. On the map three states are numbered. Write the names of these states after their respective numbers on the blank lines below.
 I._____ II._____ III._____
2. Three cities are represented on the map by the symbol, •, and each is followed by a capital letter. Write the names of these cities after their respective letters on the blank lines below.
 X_____ Y_____ Z_____

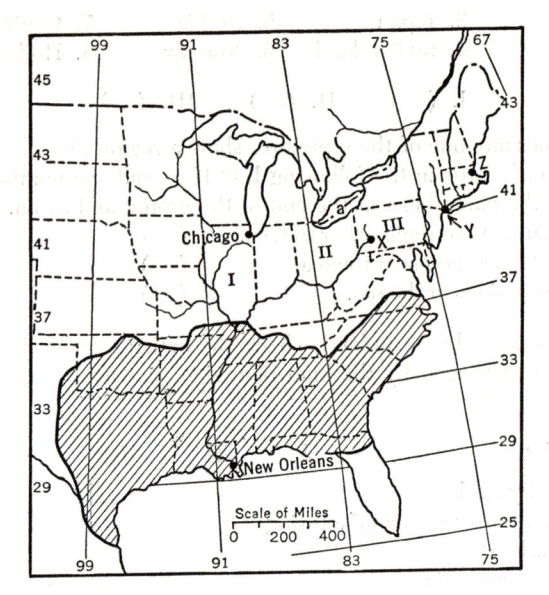

Fig. 23. An example of a map used for testing.

3. One of the Great Lakes is lettered *a*. Write the name of this lake on the line below.
    a. _____
4. If you flew in a direct course from Chicago to New Orleans about how far would you fly?
    a. _____ miles
5. Underline the word which tells the direction an airplane would travel in going in a direct course from Chicago to New Orleans.
    North, east, south, west, northeast, southeast, northwest, southwest
6. On the map a large area is lined. This lined area represents a region that produces a great amount of a particular product. Write the name of this product on the line below.
    a. _____

LEARNING AND APPLICATION ACTIVITIES

The terms *activities* and *expression work* to many teachers mean something that the children are doing with their hands. This is a

Unit Planning and Functional Activities

narrow definition that restricts the educational value of the terms. True, learning is achieved through activity on the part of the pupil, but the learning activity must be appropriate in kind and form with the abilities that are to be developed. In considering the use of learning activities the teacher of geography should ask himself these questions:

1. What are the learning activities appropriate to my class and to the unit being developed?
2. What activities are worthwhile considering the *time required,* the skills, habits, attitudes, and appreciations involved, and the knowledge gained?
3. Do these activities assist the pupils in mastering geographic understandings and skills, and to visualize the localities in the region or country they are studying?
4. Do these activities assist the pupils in understanding the people of the region or country, their problems, and their relations to us and the other peoples of the world?

Of course every activity will not meet all of the above criteria, but each should contribute to one or more of the above. Activities may grow out of teacher-pupil planning, special interests or experiences of an individual pupil or a committee, or, on the high school level, may develop through some community needs, problems, or interests such as a community survey or land-use mapping. A brief discussion of types of activities and expression work may be of value and of special help to the beginning teacher.

Reading Activities

Reading activities have been discussed in Chapter 7, but they may be summarized here, for many teachers do not think of reading as a type of activity.

1. Analytical or intensive reading is a distinct type of reading skill for which specific training is necessary.
2. Relative rapid reading of materials is for the purpose of quickly locating specific information.
3. Reading for pleasure or a general impression is extensive in character. In geography it involves the reading of books of travel, fiction,

essays, or poems. As appreciation is involved the directions or study questions must be carefully stated, such as, "This _____ is to be read for enjoyment. No questions will be asked, but we hope that you will share it with the class." "This _____ will help you to imagine yourself in the forests of Amazonia." "If you are interested in knowing more about the customs of the Eskimoes read *Northward Ho!*"

4. Reading to supplement the ideas or facts gained from the text or a class discussion is an activity to be encouraged.

5. Reading to visualize is a type that should be encouraged more by specific directions, such as: "Read the _____ paragraph or paragraphs and try to imagine what you would see if you were traveling from _____ to _____."

6. Oral reading is a different activity from silent reading and involves different skills. Good oral reading involves silent reading to select a passage and understand it. Oral reading is a legitimate activity both from the study and the expression standpoint. It can be introduced or directed by such directions as, "Find a passage in _____ describing a tropical forest and be prepared to read it to the class." "George has found a passage describing a sand storm in the desert. He wishes to read it to the class."

Interpreting charts, diagrams, and graphs is an important activity in the study of geography. It is an entirely different activity from reading word materials, but it is essential in the study of geography. This is also true of reading and interpreting maps and pictures. Such activities must be directed by the teacher until the pupils have acquired the skill and habit of reading these source materials.

Observing and Handling Materials

The observing and handling of models, specimens, souvenirs, and curios is a means of vitalizing geography. Such articles give concreteness to distant places and people. This examination may be for the purpose of securing information or for the imaginative or emotional appeal.

The viewing of actual or reconstructed scenes is also worthwhile in gaining geographic concepts. Geographical formations of interest and value in the locality may be visited. A model of an area is

Unit Planning and Functional Activities 257

also of value in giving children a better understanding and mental image of an area.

Listening Activities

Children need training in listening activities because so much information is received through radio and television. To become intelligent listeners is almost as necessary today as to be intelligent readers. Attentive listening during the formal presentation of materials such as individual or committee reports is a definite study activity. In some respects it resembles analytical reading, for the pupil should be selecting the important points from the materials being presented, and recalling associations, experience, or knowledge. It could be termed creative or dynamic listening, for the individual is going out to meet and appropriate the materials. It implies that as he listens he is re-creating the materials in his consciousness.

While listening during class and committee discussions the pupil follows the "give and take," informally attentive to the material and alert to make his contribution. His listening should be a stimulus to learning while it is also an actual procedure of learning.

Listening during personal interviews, such as during a consultation between teacher and pupil during a study period or an interview with a person from whom the pupil is seeking information, is another type of intelligent listening.

Oral Activities

Answering questions is a traditional activity of the pupil in the classroom. Such an activity serves, in part, as a test of the pupil's reading, observing, and thinking, but it is equally a phase of study. A pupil learns by formulating and giving an answer to a question.

Asking a question is no less valuable in study than answering one. Pupils should be encouraged to ask questions in order to formulate the problems they encounter. Of course this should not be carried to the extent of leaning upon another person. Worthwhile questions reveal both thinking and intellectual curiosity.

The taking part in an individual interview or conference is a conversation between pupil and teacher, or pupil and pupil. It may be formal or informal. In the formal type, the pupil is contributing to a conversation on a given topic as in a panel discussion. Its value lies in expression and the exchange of ideas.

Other kinds of oral activities are: conducting a meeting, giving a special report or floor talk, engaging in a debate, and taking part in a dramatization.

Writing Activities

There are innumerable writing activities. Some are rather simple learning activities such as: completing a statement, making a list, completing a list, and classifying items. Classifying items is a step beyond making a list. It involves a type of inductive thinking which is valuable in study.

Making an outline involves summarizing material and classifying it in logical order. Pupils should have training and much practice in outlining, as it is one of the valuable study activities.

Writing an advertisement or a slogan in connection with a geography unit is often worthwhile. It involves the terse expression of a thought in a striking phrase. In a sense it is both a means of learning and a test of learning. An example of a slogan is, "Alaska: America's last frontier." An advertisement might extol the scenic wonders of a place, its advantages for vacationers, or its economic opportunities. To write an accurate yet attractive advertisement requires knowledge of the area or region, as well as a command of English.

Writing letters or travel accounts describing an imaginery journey or experiences in a region is excellent creative activity for geography. It involves reorganizing the pupils' knowledge and the ability to visualize people and lands.

Similar types of creative writing activities are writing a dialogue for a geographic play or pageant, writing a newspaper account featuring a geographic incident such as a flood, writing a diary giving each day's events on an imaginary trip or life in the coun-

Unit Planning and Functional Activities

try or region being studied, writing a story using geographic material, and writing a critical review of a book or article which is on a geographic subject or contains geographic material.

Drawing Activities

The expression of ideas by means of drawing pictures is a legitimate form of study and application, for instance, drawing a picture of a scene or activity described in a paragraph. A student in a geography class represented geographic relationships by means of drawings. On the left hand side of the paper he drew and painted a picture of lumbering, then, on the right hand side, he drew and painted a scene representing the natural environment characteristic of where the activity took place. He made a series of these paintings representing the work activities and the natural environment of the Pacific Coast States.

Other activities involving drawing are making a diagram or chart, making a graph, drawing a sketch map, and recording information by means of map symbols on an outline map. All of the above should be for a definite purpose, such as, to illustrate a geographic concept, or to express geographic content in a clear and functional manner.

Manual Activities

These types of activity must be evaluated carefully if they are to have real learning value.

The construction of models and miniatures is of value if their construction is an application of facts learned. They involve research on the part of the makers, and give both the maker and the class a better image of the region or the activity. All parts should be constructed by the pupils.

A notebook can be of great value if it represents creative activity on the part of the student. It may take the form of a diary recording the events on an imaginery journey and illustrated with drawings, maps, and pictures. It may be prepared as a series of articles written by a traveller or newspaper reporter similar to such articles that appear in current newspapers and magazines. It may be a collection of newspaper articles and pictures relevant to the region or country being studied. However, for these to be of value the pupil should comment on each article or picture stating the relation of each to the unit, and pointing out its geographic significance.

Other manual activities are performing an experiment to illustrate some process such as soil erosion, making posters, collecting and mounting pictures, constructing sand table scenes, making a "movie," and making charts. Definite standards for all of these should be set up by the teacher and pupils working together. Such standards should include neatness, good or artistic arrangement, functional value, geographic value, and other points.

General Activities

Some general class or committee activities are maintaining a bulletin board, holding a geography exhibit, making a geographical survey, planning a project such as an assembly program, making a bibliography, and preparing geography games and drill work.

Not all the possible activities and expression work have been listed and discussed. The above constitutes a list of possible activities and possible assignments that may be of value to a teacher. In the chapter references may be found accounts of how teachers have developed units and used various activities.

Who should make teaching units? is a question frequently asked. Unit planning takes time and energy. The individual teacher can work out in detail only three or four during a year. But through such planning he will gain a mastery of his subject and a feeling of confidence that makes the effort worthwhile. He will be able to meet with assurance the unexpected questions, the problems, and the incidents which occur almost daily in every classroom. Teacher committees is another means. A committee of teachers can select

Unit Planning and Functional Activities

the content, then divide the work, one member making the list of references and other materials, another framing the objectives, and others preparing questions, exercises, and tests; and finally, after discussion and critical evaluation, put the unit into final shape. Of course each teacher will adapt the unit to his particular class and situation. Both the individual teacher and the committee can get much help through examining units in various professional magazines, such as the *Journal of Geography* and *Social Education*. Units should be filed for future reference and use. A unit once made in detail can always be adapted to another class. A committee making a unit should suggest a number of ways for introducing the unit, then the teacher has at hand a number of suggestions from which to select one suitable for the class and the particular situation.

One teacher, after experimenting with teaching units, expresses her reactions as follows:

To me, the Unit Method presents many features which stand in marked contrast to those in my former method of teaching. The outstanding features are: (1) More definite objectives. (2) Better subject matter. (3) Improved methods of working and learning. (4) A more desirable spirit. In my former method of teaching, I followed closely the content of the textbook, the pupils lacked interest, and the content studied did not relate to what they would really need in performing life's activities. By this method, what was to be learned was assigned from a text book, and the progress from day to day depended upon what occurred in the text. In the unit study, the pupils are given guidance which will train them in study habits and social relations. The unit method centers around interests in the everyday life of the children. It induces the teacher to be on the alert to discover new lines of investigation and arouse enthusiasm in the class. In our study of a unit, the work of the class was so developed that pupils were constantly confronted with interesting problems, and with real needs for information and skills which they did not possess. In their study, the members of the class used not only their textbooks but many textbooks, encyclopedias, maps, charts, and magazines. Each child became responsible for doing something of interest to himself, and of value to the entire group because of its relation to their total undertaking.

AN ILLUSTRATIVE UNIT: THE WESTERN STATES

Objectives:
1. A knowledge and appreciation of the interrelationships existing between man and the natural environment in the West.
2. A knowledge of geographic facts, concepts, and relationships in the Western States, which will enable the pupils to form their own opinion and express their ideas concerning the current problems of the people of the West, such as the problem of marketing their products, problems of irrigation, and others.
3. An understanding of the value of copper, lead, gold, silver, zinc, and other natural resources which are found in the West.
4. Ability to gather data and form conclusions regarding the wiser use of natural resources found in this section of states.
5. The ability to make worthwhile use of leisure time, by planning tours through the Western States; by reading books and current articles concerning the leading cities and industries; and by using information secured from radio and television.
6. A recognition and appreciation of the value of human labor required for mixed farming, grazing, mining, lumbering, salmon canning, fruit growing, and fruit canning.
7. Ability to appreciate the economic and social life of the Western States, and understand how they depend upon other regions.
8. A knowledge of suitable references and maps to be used in the study of the Western States.
9. Ability to interpret physical maps, maps showing where various crops and products are produced, and also graphs and charts.
10. A knowledge of the location of rivers, lakes, mountains, mining centers, railroad centers, seaports, and other important places in the Western States.

INTRODUCTION:

For the introduction of the Western States, I used pictures which were characteristic of the rocky and mountainous surface of this section of the United States. After looking at the pictures of the mountains and high cliffs, the children wanted to know how the people of these rough mountain slopes made a living. We chose for our problem: *How Do People Make a Living in These Rough Mountain Lands?* Then, the pupils suggested topics and questions that would help them to solve the problem. They suggested a study of maps to find the location, the topography, and facts concerning the climate. They listed on the blackboard what they thought were the leading industries of the western states.

Unit Planning and Functional Activities

Assimilation or Problem-solving

I. How Do People Make a Living in these Rough Mountain Lands?
   A. *Agriculture*
      1. Some farming land.
         a. Why is mixed farming done here?
         b. Trace these places on the map, think of them as farming lands.
            (1) Great Plains.
            (2) Valleys in the heart of the Rockies.
            (3) Valleys east of the Coast Range.
            Why are these places suitable for farming?
         c. Read about lava soils.
         d. Why do the Washington wheat fields yield so much?
         e. Explain the difference between the ripening of wheat in the western states and in the eastern states.
         f. What are the leading farm crops in this section?
      2. A serious hindrance to western farmers.
         a. How much rainfall is sufficient for crops?
         b. Examine the Rainfall map and find out the amount—
            on the Great Plains,
            in the Rocky Mountains and plateau areas, and in the valleys of the Pacific slope.
         c. Why is a large area of the western states so dry?
         d. Explain the reasons for the different temperatures.
      3. Irrigation and dry farming.
         a. Describe an irrigation system.
         b. All farmers can not afford to own an irrigation system, yet they have irrigation for their farms. Why is this possible?
         c. Make a list of crops grown on irrigated lands.
         d. What recent project will be of much help to the people here? (Collect material from papers and magazines.)
         e. What is dry farming? Why is it not as profitable as farming by irrigation?
         f. What crops are grown by dry farming?
      4. Truck farming, or garden truck.
         a. Where, in this group, is garden truck raised on a large scale? Why is this possible?
         b. Why is truck farming not as important as it is in the eastern section of the United States?

  c. Make a graph of the leading vegetables found in these states. (Material from the World Almanac.)

 B. *Mining*

  1. Why is mining done on a large scale in this section of the United States?
  2. List the kinds of minerals found here. Why?
  3. Name and locate sections or centers for each.
  4. Which is more important, gold or silver? Why?
  5. What is a smelter?
  6. Make a list of states which produce copper.
  7. List the states that have coal. Why have not all available coal beds been mined?
  8. Describe two ways for mining gold. What states lead in the output? Make a graph of the gold producing states.
  9. Of what use do the people of California make of the oil found there? Name other states which have oil wells.
  10. Los Angeles is the largest city in this whole group. What reasons can you find to account for this?

 C. *Grazing*

  1. Why are sheep adapted to the scanty pasture of the rough lands?
  2. What are the sheep fattened upon?
  3. Describe a sheep ranch; size of the flocks; care of the sheep; and sheep shearing.
  4. Where are cattle raised? Why?

 D. *Fruit growing*

  1. Why is this section favorable for fruit raising and fruit drying?
  2. List the principal fruits found in these states. Make two columns, keeping the citrus fruits separate.
  3. Name and locate centers for production and shipment.
  4. Where are raisin grapes grown? How are they prepared?
  5. Make a graph comparing the western states with the United States in fruit raising. (Material from appendix)

 E. *Lumbering*

  1. Examine the forest map. Why are there forests here? Compare with the physical map; the rainfall map; and the forest map.

Unit Planning and Functional Activities

   2. Why are there more uplands than lowlands in these states?
   3. Make a list of the states in this section which have extensive forest areas.
   4. List facts about the forests in the Rocky Mountains.
   5. What is meant by the timberline? Cause?
   6. Explain the work of a forester; describe a lumber camp; tell how the trees are felled and trimmed; and how the logs are taken to the mill.
   7. What part of the lumber of the United States comes from the West?
   8. Locate the great lumber markets. Why are they located where they are?

F. *Fishing*
   1. From the labels on salmon cans, find out where some of the canneries are located. Why are they located there?
   2. Read about the life habits of the salmon.
   3. How are the life habits of the salmon related to the time and methods of catching them?
   4. What are the ways of preparing the salmon for food?
   5. Compare fishing on the western coast with that of the eastern coast.

G. *Manufacturing*
   1. Summarize all the occupations you have found for people in the Western States.
   2. Indicate whether these industries would require many or few laborers.
   3. Why is manufacturing connected with nearly all of these occupations?
   4. What effect does the environment have upon the types of manufacturing done here?
   5. List some important manufactured products. State reasons for these.
   6. What different kinds of power are used in this section?
   7. Account for the difference in population between the North Central States and the Western States.
   8. Why have the Western States developed so rapidly?

H. *The moving picture industry*
   1. Why is the moving picture industry well adapted to Southern California?

2. What eastern state is closely connected with this industry?

I. *Accommodations for tourists*
  1. The tourist is an important industrial resource to this region. Account for the rapid growth of this industry.
  2. What are the attractive features of Yellowstone National Park?
  3. Why is the Grand Canyon famous?
  4. What is the cause of Great Salt Lake?
  5. Why is the Yosemite Valley an attractive place to visit?
  6. List three interesting facts about the big trees of California.
  7. Why has the National Government set aside Crater Lake National Park?
  8. Collect pictures and make a booklet on the scenery in the West.
  9. What recreations are offered tourists?
  10. List all the places you would like to visit if you were making a tour through the West.

J. *Write a paragraph in which you will summarize your material.*

The class carried out the above assignment in three weeks. During this time the pupils drew graphs, maps, made charts, and wrote reports on various topics in the assignment. In addition to the wall maps and those of our textbooks, we had two large maps (from railroad companies) which were helpful in locating many places, especially those noted for their scenery.

DISCUSSION OR EXPRESSION PERIOD
  A. Exhibition of maps, pictures, graphs, booklets, and other work done by the class in the work period.
  B. The presentation of special reports by individual members of the class.
  C. Class criticism of reports.
  D. A very interesting talk on California was given by a lady who had lived there. This gave the class many important facts about the West, and they appreciated it very much.
  E. Questions for discussion:
    1. Why do sheep rather than cattle graze for the most part on the mountain pasture?
    2. How is the airplane useful in protecting the great forests?

Unit Planning and Functional Activities

3. Why is one able to swim in Great Salt Lake without sinking?
4. Why is the land of the "West" called the land of "Great Differences?"
    a. Complete the following:
    The West has greater differences in (1) _____ of the land, (2) amount of _____ that falls each year, and (3) length of _____ than any other part of the United States.
5. Fill in the chart:
    a. The products of the Western mountains:

PLATEAU STATES

Grazing	Mining	Forestry	Agriculture

PACIFIC STATES

Grazing	Mining	Forestry	Agriculture

6. Summary of assignment questions and a comparison of the Plateau and Pacific States.

TESTING

I. *Association*
    A. Tell where you would see each of the things named below—in the states bordering the Atlantic coast, in the states bordering the Pacific coast, or in both groups of states. (Mark A, P, or B.)

( ) 1. Citrus-fruit groves.
( ) 2. Salmon canneries.
( ) 3. Cranberry bogs.
( ) 4. Fruit drying in the sun.
( ) 5. Oyster canneries.
( ) 6. Dairy farms.
( ) 7. Placer mining for gold.
( ) 8. Codfish drying in the sun.
( ) 9. Irrigated farms.
( ) 10. Ships from distant lands.
( ) 11. Turpentine pines.
( ) 12. The greatest forests in the country.

II. *Completion Test*
  A. Complete the following sentences.
    1. The leading sheep raising states are_____, _____, and _____.
    2. The five most important metals mined in the West are _____, _____, _____, _____, and _____.
    3. The leading copper-mining state is_____.
    4. The state that ranks first at the present in the production of silver is _____.
    5. The great copper mining center in Montana is _____.
    6. The great copper mining center in Utah is _____.
    7. The most important metal mined in the Coeur d' Alene district of Idaho is _____.
    8. The leading gold mining state is _____.
    9. The two leading oil producing states of the West are _____ and _____.
    10. The greatest lumber producing state is _____.
    11. The state that leads in the canning of fish is _____.
    12. Petroleum is used in California for _____ and _____.

III. *One Word Test*
  A. Write one answer only.
    1. What is the chief field crop in the Pacific group of states? _____.
    2. Name the most important place in our country for the catching of salmon. _____.
    3. Railroads which stretch across the continent are called _____.

Unit Planning and Functional Activities

    4. Name the seaport on San Francisco Bay. _____.
    5. What seaport is near the junction of the Willamette and Columbia rivers. _____.
    6. Name the largest seaport on Puget Sound. _____.
    7. What inland city has become a seaport? _____.
    8. Name the largest city in the Sacramento Valley. _____.
    9. What is the largest city in the San Joaquin Valley? _____.
    10. What railroad center is on San Francisco Bay? _____.

IV. *Multiple Choice*

    A. Underline the correct word.
        1. The principal forage crop of the Western States is oats, alfalfa, barley, corn.
        2. The most important money crop in the mixed farming lands is sugar beets, wheat, potatoes, fresh vegetables, fruit.
        3. Most of the fruit in the West is sold fresh, canned, dried.

V. *A Combination Test*

    A. This test is a combination of making choices and giving reasons. In each sentence you are to choose the correct word or phrase from those in parentheses, and then complete the sentence by giving reasons for the fact which it states.
        1. Much of the western part of the Great Plains is used for (dairying) (grazing) (mixed farming) because _____.
        2. There are many (mining) (manufacturing) (fishing) centers in the Rocky Mountains because _____.
        3. Many farmers in the Columbia Plateau raise (corn) (oats) (wheat) because _____.
        4. There are many (irrigation projects) (summer playgrounds) (national forests) in the Western plateaus because _____.

5. The Puget Sound Lowland and the Willamette Valley have many (steel mills) (lumber mills) (smelters) because _____
_____.

6. The valley lowlands of California are great (lumbering) (coal mining) (fruit growing) regions because _____
_____.

VI. *Problem*

A. Write in the parentheses the number of the correct or best answer.
   ( ) 1. Why has Denver become an important distributing center for food, clothing, and mining supplies for the many small mining communities in the mountains?
      a. Short distance from the foot of the Rocky Mountains.
      b. It stands near one of the best gateways to the Rocky Mountains and the Far West.
      c. Near the great mining region of Colorado.
      d. It is a natural railway center.
   ( ) 2. Why is Salt Lake City a flourishing railway and distributing center?
      a. Receives supplies from mining towns, and ships out products from the surrounding farms.
      b. An attractive city, lying close to high mountains on the east.
      c. Only a few miles from Great Salt Lake.
      d. The first railroad, the Union Pacific, was built by the way of Salt Lake City.
   ( ) 3. Why is San Francisco the chief city of the Pacific Coast?
      a. Chief trade center with Asia and the Pacific islands.
      b. San Francisco began its growth in the days of the "Gold Rush" to California.
      c. One of the most densely settled parts of California is around San Francisco Bay.
      d. Location and fine harbors.

Unit Planning and Functional Activities

VII. *Grouping Pictures*

A. Below is a list of pictures, and a list of the states in which the scenes are found. The number after each state tells how many of the pictures belong with that state. Under each state list the scenes found there.

LIST OF PICTURES

Natural bridges	Great Salt Lake
The Petrified Forest	The Golden Gate
Glacier National Park	Mount Rainier
Geysers	The Painted Desert
An active volcano	Cliff dwellings
Crater Lake	Mount Whitney
The Grand Canyon	The Big Trees

LIST OF STATES

1. Arizona (3)

_____

_____

2. California (4)

_____

_____

3. Colorado (1)

4. Montana (1)

5. Oregon (1)

6. Utah (2)

_____

7. Washington (1)

8. Wyoming (1)

REFERENCES

ABERNATHY, Irene, "Training in Democracy Through a Geographic Study of Switzerland," *Journal of Geography,* Vol. 39 (February, 1940), pp. 63–70.

ANDERSON, T. J., and KENNAMER, L., "Geography Posters: A Way to Review," *Journal of Geography,* Vol. 55 (November, 1956), pp. 388–399.

ANDERZHON, Mamie L., "Illustrations of Learning Experiences Which Lead to the Development of a Geographic Point of View," *Geographic Approaches to Social Education,* Nineteenth Yearbook (Washington, D.C., National Council for the Social Studies, 1948), Ch. XX.

BACON, H. Phillip, "How's Your Hawaiian? A Technique in Introducing a Unit," *Journal of Geography,* Vol. 52 (February, 1953), pp. 19–21.

BARROWS, H. H., "Critical Problems in Teaching Elementary Geography," *Journal of Geography*, Vol. 30 (December, 1931), pp. 353–364.

BARTON, Thomas F., "A Geographic Materials Strip," *Journal of Geography*, Vol. 54 (March, 1955), pp. 140–144.

BATEMAN, C. L., "The Magnetic Map," *Journal of Geography*, Vol. 54 (December, 1955), pp. 455–456.

BAXTER, Eugenia, and MONTGOMERY, Kathryne, "Creating Environments for Geographic Education," *Journal of Geography*, Vol. 55 (September, 1956), pp. 271–278.

BLANCHARD, W. O., "Find the Strategic Materials—A Puzzle in Economic Geography," *Business Education World*, Vol. 23 (November, 1942), p. 149.

BLOUCH, Adelaide, "A City Study in the Upper Elementary Grades," *Journal of Geography*, Vol. 47 (November, 1948), pp. 306–311.

BONHAM, John A., "A Successful Method of Teaching Geography at the Junior High School Level," *Journal of Geography*, Vol. 56 (January, 1957), pp. 22–26.

BURTON, C. B., "A Unit on Africa," *Journal of Geography*, Vol. 28 (December, 1929), pp. 373–378.

CASTE, E. Ray, and Beard, G. C., "The ABC's of the ABC Countries," *Journal of Geography*, Vol. 38 (March, 1939), pp. 112–114.

DEAN, L., "A Sixth Grade Travels in Lands Overseas," *Journal of Geography*, Vol. 52 (September, 1953), pp. 239–248.

EISEN, Edna, "Exhibits of Geography Work," *Journal of Geography*, Vol. 32 (March, 1933), pp. 108–114.

ELLER, Lulu, "Land Use in Southwestern Nebraska; A Unit for Grade 8," *Education*, Vol. 77 (September, 1956), pp. 52–53.

GALFORD, Mary, "Activities in Geography Classwork," *Journal of Geography*, Vol. 40 (February, 1941), pp. 64–66.

HANNA, Lavone A., POTTER, Gladys L., and HAGAMAN, Neva, *Unit Teaching in the Elementary School* (New York, Rinehart and Co., Inc., 1956).

HOFFMAN, Hazel W., "Iceland, a Fourth Grade Unit of Study," *Journal of Geography*, Vol. 56 (May, 1957), pp. 232–235.

JAMES, Mrs. Linnie, "Applied Geography," *Journal of Geography*, Vol. 39 (February, 1940), pp. 71–77.

JEWETT, D. F., "Geography Clubs," *Journal of Geography*, Vol. 34 (November, 1935), pp. 335–337.

LOGAN, Marguerite, "A Guide to the Organization of a Geographic Unit," *Journal of Geography*, Vol. 31 (October, 1932), pp. 269–278.

Unit Planning and Functional Activities 273

Lucas, W. C., "Making Geography Teaching Click," *Journal of Geography*, Vol. 38 (December, 1939), pp. 349–354.

Mattocks, Loretta, Pettigrew, Gwendolyn, and Sutherland, Jean, "Scholars Learn About Skippers," *Journal of Geography*, Vol. 55 (January, 1956), pp. 24–27.

Montgomery, Katheryne, "Greensburg Junior Geographers," *Journal of Geography*, Vol. 54 (May, 1955), pp. 252–254.

———, "Northwest Junior Geographers; Describes Club Projects," *Journal of Geography*, Vol. 54 (February, 1955), pp. 57–59.

Phillips, Mary V., "Unit I, For Course in Global Geography," *Journal of Geography*, Vol. 44 (November, 1945), pp. 324–332.

———, "Unit II, Climate and Weather," *Journal of Geography*, Vol. 45 (March, 1946), pp. 103–108.

———, "Unit III, Population, For Course in Global Geography," *Journal of Geography*, Vol. 45 (April, 1946), pp. 149–152.

———, "Unit IV, The Pacific and Its Islands," *Journal of Geography*, Vol. 45 (September, 1946), pp. 234–253.

———, "Unit V, Japan," *Journal of Geography*, Vol. 47 (January, 1948), pp. 18–23.

———, "Unit VI, The U.S.S.R.: Land of the Soviets," *Journal of Geography*, Vol. 47 (September, 1948), pp. 227–233.

Ray, J. B., "Dramatized Radio Program," *Journal of Geography*, Vol. 53 (October, 1954), pp. 307–309.

Riley, N. "A Glossary Game," *Journal of Geography*, Vol. 39 (December, 1940), pp. 365–366.

Svec, Melvina, "Time Clocks to Teach Time Belts," *Journal of Geography*, Vol. 52 (May, 1953), pp. 188–189.

Trussell, M. Edith, "The Opaque Projector as a Teaching Aid," *Journal of Geography*, Vol. 55 (December, 1956), pp. 425–429.

White, Helen M., "The Geographic Unit," *Journal of Geography*, Vol. 33 (November, 1934), pp. 304–308.

Tests and Testing

Brockmeyer, Irene, "Testing with Pictures," *Journal of Geography*, Vol. 50 (February, 1951), pp. 54–57.

Lancaster, Freda, "Measuring Results in Geography," *Journal of Geography*, Vol. 30 (November, 1931), pp. 342–344.

Lange, Stella, "A Geography Test," *Journal of Geography*, Vol. 34 (January, 1935), pp. 40–42.

Lichon, Elizabeth S., "Tests Which Provoke Interest," *Journal of Geography*, Vol. 42 (December, 1943), pp. 321–326.

MIKESELL, Ruth W., "Geographic Tests: A Tool for Guidance," *School Science and Mathematics*, Vol. 41 (June, 1941), pp. 517–520.

SCHERRER, Chas. F., "St. Louis Can Be Bombed," *Journal of Geography*, Vol. 42 (March, 1943), pp. 112–115.

SVEC, Melvina M., "A Method of Testing," *Journal of Geography*, Vol. 32 (October, 1933), pp. 295–297.

WELLS, Robert, "Objective Test in Geography," *Journal of Geography*, Vol. 42 (September, 1943), pp. 233–235.

10

A Geographic Readiness Program

THE VALUE OF A GEOGRAPHIC READINESS PROGRAM

A GEOGRAPHIC READINESS program is for the purpose of building a concrete basis for the formal geography which usually begins in the fourth grade. Such a program is necessary as:

1. A means of broadening and deepening the children's background. Many of the children have limited backgrounds. This is especially true of children in crowded districts of the city. Furthermore, they need to be made conscious of their immediate environment.

2. A means of giving experiences connected with their local environment which will provide materials for association and comparison with new ideas and vicarious experiences.

3. A preparation for informational type of reading. Much of the reading in the primary grades is pleasure reading, consisting of stories and poems. The children need to be prepared for the large amount of informational type of reading which is required in the middle and upper grades.

4. An aid in gaining concrete concepts and visual imagery which help the children to secure new ideas.

5. A means of increasing the children's vocabularies through direct experiences with their environment.

6. A means of guiding the children in investigating their natural environment and noting the simple adjustments that they and others are making.

Children are curious about the world and are interested in investigating it. They want to know—"What," "What for?" and "Why." They will investigate it, draw conclusions, and absorb current conceptions which frequently are unscientific or even mere superstition. Through a well-planned program, the teacher is able to guide their observations and experiments, and lead them to correct although simple generalizations. The teacher should remember that, "A child can see in any person, social group, or situation only what his personal experience brings him the power to see." It is during these early years that children are gathering the great mass of concrete, significant materials upon which they later build their imaginations and are able to see the world beyond their immediate environment. Thus, it is extremely important that in the primary grades the children learn to see and read the story of their own environment.

OBJECTIVES OF A GEOGRAPHIC READINESS PROGRAM

The major objectives of a Geographic Readiness Program are:

1. To lay the foundation for the scientific attitude through helping children to develop the habit of keen, independent, and correct observation, and the ability to give accurate expression of the results of such observation.

2. To assure children such contacts and experiences as will guide them to an intelligent, sympathetic appreciation of the environment in which they live.

3. To help children realize the dependence of man upon the various forms of life and forces of nature, and also the interdependence of man.

4. To develop in children desirable attitudes and ideals: (*a*) with reference to nature phenomena, stressing conservation of the useful and control of the injurious; and (*b*) with reference to health, and other problems of their environment.

5. To create in children an abiding interest in the wonders and

beauty of nature, and a companionship with life and world surroundings which may bring enjoyment and employment for leisure hours.

6. To aid the children in understanding how the forces of nature and science may be used for human welfare.

7. To develop in children the ability and habit of reading with understanding and satisfaction the literature dealing with the subject.

8. To develop in children an understanding and a realization that they have a personal responsibility to their social group for making their local environment better.

A PROGRAM FOR THE FIRST GRADE

Most of the work in the first grade should be based on observation and personal experience. From their observations and discussion, the teacher and class together should develop simple reading lessons as soon as the children have the ability. The topics discussed in the following pages are not completed at any one time, but are continued at intervals throughout the year. The learnings are cumulative.

Direction

The concept of direction is of slow growth and must be developed through a series of carefully planned lessons combined with frequent use. The teacher and the class should discuss the need for knowing the directions when travelling, and for other purposes. Direction should be taught in relation to sun position through observation and discussion. The teacher should ask the class such questions as: Where is the sun early in the morning? Where is it at noon? Where is it in the late afternoon? He should tell the children the names of the directions and have them point each time. They should discuss what they do in the morning—getting up, having breakfast, going to school. When the sun is high in the south it is noontime—they have lunch, perhaps play. Then, in the afternoon, when the sun is in the west, what do they do? In this way, direction, sun position, time, and their activities are associated.

At another time, the teacher and the class should talk about the sun and what it does for us. The teacher and class should develop a short story about the directions and the sun.

Later, have the children observe the direction each one's home faces. If possible, build a model of the school area on a large sand table or on the floor. Put in the school, streets, roads, and as many of the children's homes as possible. Then, use the model by having the children tell how they come to school, how they go home, and how they go to visit other children. In giving these directions, they should use the terms *north, east, south* and *west*.

Weather Observations

Weather observations and discussion should be carried on throughout the year. This activity is for the purpose of noting the relationships between weather conditions and the children's activities. It also serves to enlarge the children's vocabularies. Make a large calendar, at least 36 to 48 inches long and 24 to 36 inches wide, with a sheet of paper for each month. Each sheet is divided by weeks and days as is the usual calendar. The observation and recording of the weather conditions should be recorded at the *same time* each day, preferably as soon after nine o'clock as possible. The children discuss and decide on the symbols to be used.

Record on the calendar such items as the following:

1. Sky: sunshiny, cloudy, or rainy. A bright orange disk may indicate a sunshiny day; for rain, perhaps an open umbrella or the drawing of clouds and raindrops; a cloudy day, a half-open umbrella.
2. Temperature: use descriptive terms such as *hot, warm, cool, cold,* and *mild.*
3. Wind: breezy, windy, very windy, or calm. Bring in direction *from* which wind is blowing. "West wind is blowing from the west." Help them *gradually* to associate wind direction and weather conditions. For instance, after several weeks or months of such weather association, someone in the class may observe that a north wind

usually brings cooler weather, or perhaps in their locality someone may notice that rainy weather follows an east wind.
4. Rain: much rain, showers, drizzle, and so forth.

At the end of each month the class and the teacher, working together, should write a brief story summarizing the weather for the month—so many sunshiny days, so many cloudy days, so many rainy days. The class may want to include some outstanding event, such as someone's birthday or a special visit.

This calendar and monthly summary should be saved and carried with the class into the second grade to be used as a basis for a comparison with the weather record they will make in the second grade.

Stories and poems concerning wind, rain, clouds, and the sun should be used throughout the year. Most first grade readers contain many such stories, or the children can make their own.

Seasonal Changes and Sun Position

The lessons on the seasonal changes should be carried on at intervals throughout the year. The following observations and discussions are suggested:

To observe the changing position of the sun during the seasons, if the school room faces east, west, or south, select a point or place where the sunlight strikes a desk, the floor, or the wall at a certain time during the day, for instance, at 9:30 A.M. Note and mark the place early in September. Discuss this in connection with direction and sun position. The teacher and children watch how this spot moves from week to week, or at longer intervals, marking it each time with the date observed. This sun spot will change until December 22, then, it will begin a return journey. Thus, through their own observation and with the discussion directed by the teacher, the children learn that the changing position of the sun is related to seasonal changes and length of day.

The seasonal landscape and other topics related to the changing seasons furnish materials for observations and discussions. Observe and discuss the appearance of the autumn landscape, noting the changing color of the leaves, fall flowers, fruit, and so forth. If possible take a field trip, or at least a walk around the schoolyard, to observe trees, leaves, and flowers. All of the work on seasons should be related to the weather discussions. Use these observations and discussions as a basis for making experience stories for reading and for art work.

The children should learn the names of several local trees and learn to recognize them by their leaves, bark, and shape. Select one tree for special study and observation throughout the year.

Watch for birds and, if possible, select several for study and recognition. What birds selected depends on the interest of the class and the locality. The class may become interested in bird migration as they note the disappearance of birds. Discuss and read stories of some animals and how they prepare for winter.

The effect of fall and the coming of winter on man's activities should not be neglected. Note how the shorter and cooler days affect the children's activities—games, clothing, and so forth.

During the winter months, the winter landscape should be observed and discussed; the appearance of the trees and other vegetation. Other subjects for observation and discussion are, the birds in winter, feeding the birds, and the changes in some animals. If a snow comes, there should be a study of snowflakes—their size and shape, what snow is, the value of snow, the melting of snow. In late winter note the appearance of tiny leaf buds on trees and some bushes.

The influence of winter weather on the children's activities is an important topic. The change to winter weather affects their clothing, often changes their plans, and sometimes affects their health. Much valuable health instruction may be introduced—the value of wearing coats and hats, taking off coats and sweaters in the house, habits of cold prevention, and the care of nose and throat.

During March, April, and May, the rapidly changing spring landscape should be observed and discussed—the coloring of the young leaves as the trees and shrubs leaf out, the swelling of the flower

A Geographic Readiness Program

buds and how they fairly burst out, and the effects of spring showers. Note the changing temperature conditions and relate these to sun position and the length of day. Watch for the return and the activities of the birds in the spring. Discuss how the children's various activities change in the spring.

At the end of the school year, encourage and stimulate the children to continue their observations and related activities during the summer months. The calendar should be reviewed, and the class' monthly summaries discussed, before it is turned over to the second grade teacher. Also, the teacher and children should review and check their gains in vocabulary and other learnings. Such an evaluation gives both teacher and pupils a feeling of accomplishment.

Special Activities

The following special activities for each season may be suggested. During the fall months:

1. Collection of leaves, drawing and making prints of leaves, and mounting of leaves.
2. Sketching the tree selected for special study.
3. Developing experience reading charts.
4. Collection, packaging, and labeling of seeds.

During the winter months the following activities may be carried out:

1. An excursion in late November or December to observe the landscape.
2. Feeding the birds by making a feeding tray and keeping it filled.
3. Collecting pictures of local birds and animals, and making a booklet.
4. Collecting snowflakes on a piece of dark cloth, and examining them under a hand magnifying glass. Packing a cup full of snow, melting it and noting the amount of water.
5. Collection of advertisements and pictures illustrating changes in our activities during the winter.
6. Experiments to show that air is all about us—clapping erasures over a radiator and noting the movement of the dust, fanning

ourselves, opening a window and noting the movement of the air, and making toy windmills.

Some spring activities are the following:

1. An excursion to study the spring landscape, especially the signs of spring.
2. Keeping a bird calendar, and watching the birds build nests. Hanging out pieces of string, rags, and so forth, for the birds.
3. Watching for the first spring wild flowers. Gathering wild flowers, and drawing and coloring them. Making a flower chart.
4. Arranging flowers for schoolroom decoration. Keeping cut flowers supplied with water.
5. Transplanting a violet. Taking care of the plant, and drawing the leaves and flower.
6. Transplanting dandelions. Observing the cycle—bud, blossom, fruit. Observe their night habits. Cut out dandelions and paint them.
7. Making a school or home garden.
8. Gathering sprays from trees and watching the development of the buds.
9. An excursion to visit the tree studied in the fall. On the same excursion note new plants, especially baby trees.
10. Planting a tree with the Arbor Day Program.
11. Making sketches to illustrate March winds and April showers.
12. Studying pictures to show the characteristics of the four seasons, or drawing pictures to show these characteristics.

Keeping the daily weather calendar and the monthly summary should be continued throughout the school year in order that the class will have it for comparison with their second grade calendar.

A PROGRAM FOR THE SECOND GRADE

The main topics for the second grade are the same as in the first grade. The second grade teacher should be familiar with the first grade work so that she can build on that foundation. The principle of *cumulative* learning is too frequently neglected in our teaching. In the second grade, simple problems may be introduced, such as —How do insects survive the winter? How do different plants prepare for winter? What foods do birds eat? Can they find this food in the winter? Why do some animals change their coats in winter? As in the first grade, most of the work should be based on direct observations by the children and the actual handling of materials. The work should be informal, with the children encouraged to do the talking.

Direction

Review the cardinal directions in relation to sun position. Find new situations, in connection with field trips or other experiences, in which the children need to use direction. In conversation lessons, when they tell about their summer trips, they need to tell in what direction they went from their home. They should learn northeast, northwest, southeast, and southwest, in addition to the cardinal directions, north, east, south, and west, which they learned in the first grade.

The Sun and Sun Position

In the study of the sun and its seasonal path, a shadow stick may be used. To make a shadow stick, take an eighteen-inch-square board and in the center drive a nail about 2 inches long. Place the board in a window where the sun shines on it as much as possible during the day, or fasten it firmly on top of a post in the schoolyard where the sun will shine on it all day. Now begin observing the shadow of the nail, noting its length and the direction it is pointing, and mark the length at certain dates a month apart. September 20th or 21st is a good day to begin recording the length and position of the shadow. Both direction and length will change as autumn advances and winter comes. The greatest length will be observed at December 21st or 22nd, after which date the shadow will shorten. The best time to observe the shadow is as near noon as possible. If this is not practical, select some specific time during the day and make each monthly observation at the same time. In all cases, the children should do the marking, discuss the changes, and ask most of the questions.

Such a study of shadows may arouse many questions and much

real thinking. Have the children observe shadows in pictures, and have them draw pictures of shadows as they appear at different times of the day and at different seasons. Read and discuss stories and poems about shadows. Make experience reading lessons on shadows. As these activities proceed, some of the children should begin to realize that we can tell direction and approximate time by shadows.

The sun and its importance to life should be discussed, basing the work on the first grade learning, but extending the children's knowledge of the sun.

Weather Observations

A weather record should be kept throughout the year in a form that the children can carry on into the third grade. It may be kept on a large calendar as in the first grade, however, the children may wish to change the symbols. The same items should be recorded as in the first grade.

At the end of each month, the class should write a story of the weather and compare it with the summary from their first grade observations. They should discuss the common characteristics and any differences. By making these comparisons based on their own observations, they will be learning to gather data, compare data, and draw inferences. In other words, they are thinking scientifically basing their thinking on what they observe, record, and discover for themselves. The calendars and summaries should be kept and carried on into the third grade.

Along with the weather recordings, there should be frequent discussion of how the weather is affecting the children's and their family's activities. Often the weather makes news, such as an unusually heavy rain or snow, floods, and storms which also may be discussed.

Wind

Although wind and wind direction are recorded, there should be some lessons or a short unit on the wind. Such a unit would grow

A Geographic Readiness Program

out of the weather observations and the children's questions. Children often ask such questions as:

> Why can't we see the wind?
> How can we tell from which way the wind is coming?
> What makes the wind hot or cold?
> How does the wind help us?

The unit should include discussions of the wind and how man has used the force of the wind. Experiments with pin wheels, paper gliders, the drying of wet clothes in the wind, and other activities illustrate the work of the wind. Both teacher and pupils should collect for class use, songs, poems, and stories about the wind. March or April is a good time to initiate such a unit.

Seasonal Changes

Continue the seasonal observations begun in the first grade. Study the landscape during each season, noting the appearance of the sky, the clouds, and the general atmospheric conditions, as well as the characteristics of the trees, flowers, and other features. In their stories and other written work, help the children to think of and use vivid descriptive terms.

Use stories and reports, for instance, ask each of the children to find a story or a poem in which you can tell what the season is. When the pupil is ready to report, he is to tell the class the title of the poem, or story, what the season is, how he can tell the season, and where in the sky the sun would be. The pupils may also make up their own stories and make a chart illustrating seasonal games and activities.

Birds and Animals

Add to the list of birds recognized in the first grade. Discuss such topics as: What do the birds eat, How birds help us, How birds should be fed in winter, How the birds build nests—the materials used, where they are placed, and the care of young birds. In the spring, note the return of the birds. Some classes may wish to keep a bird calendar. If possible, the class should watch birds building their nest. If one is being built near the schoolhouse all may watch it. Otherwise, encourage pupils to note where nests are being built, and to make such observations as they can without alarming the birds. They may hang out pieces of string, rags, and other material for the birds to use.

Encourage the observation of young birds to note the feeding and general care given by the mother, and the efforts of the young birds learning to fly. Have the pupils listen to calls and songs of birds, and have them attempt to imitate these songs and calls.

In the second grade, the work on animals can be centered around pets—kinds of pets, care of pets, and other topics. Explain what is meant by the terms *wild animal* and *domestic animal*. In this connection discuss the value of domestic animals.

Plants and Trees

In the study of trees and plants, these points should be emphasized: (1) How plants grow from seeds; (2) The importance of the roots; (3) The conservation of wild flowers. Some activities that may be used are:

1. Collecting of seeds in the fall.
2. Discussion of how the seeds of wild plants get distributed.
3. Planting bulbs.
4. During the winter, the study of one evergreen tree or conifer.
5. In the spring emphasize wild flowers. Transplant a violet plant and a dandelion and bring into the schoolroom to observe the bud, the formation of the flower, and the seed. The conservation of wild flowers should be stressed. Many are disappearing because of the people's carelessness in picking them. Sometimes people pull up the flower by the roots. The children should be taught to enjoy the flowers without destroying them. They should be taught which flowers can be picked or transplanted without doing any harm, and which flowers cannot be picked or moved.

Forms of Water and the Work of Water

In this unit discuss uses of water—how people, animals, and plants need water. To show that plants need water and sun, plant corn or beans in three pots. Keep the pots in a warm sunny win-

A Geographic Readiness Program

dow and water the seeds a little every day. When the plants appear, put pot No. 1 in a warm dark place and water it a little every day. Keep pots No. 2 and 3 in a warm, sunny window. Water pot No. 2 a little every day, but do not water No. 3. Have the children observe and record what happens to the plants in each pot.

Boil water in the classroom and note its disappearance into the air in the form of steam or water vapor. Freeze water so that the children may watch the formation of ice crystals. Freeze a bottle of water with the cork in it, noting how water expands when it freezes which may break the bottle. If this is studied during the winter, find examples of how water freezing breaks up rocks, concrete sidewalks, and kills plants. Explain how the freezing of the moisture in plants breaks the cells and kills the plant. Some plants draw much of their sap into underground parts, the roots, out of the exposed part and thus survive the winter. When a frost comes, have the children observe it and note the tiny crystals which become water as they melt.

Develop the concept of evaporation with experiments. Use three pans of water of the same size. Place one in the sun, one in the shade, and another on a radiator or stove. Have the children note the relative rate that the water disappears in each one. Observe the loss of water in flower pots, and in the drying up of paste or ink.

At another time, develop the concept of condensation. Observe steam on cold windows and drops of water condensing on the outside of a glass of ice water. Connect the term *condensation* with how rain, dew, and frost occur, and the formation of snow and ice.

If possible, study a small stream in the locality. From observation and discussion learn the meaning of the source of a stream, the channel, the banks, and the current. Note how the stream carries silt, sand, and other materials, and how it cuts into its banks.

Understanding Other People

A beginning should be made to develop an understanding of other people in our own community, in our nation, and the world.

This topic may come up quite naturally from children's personal experiences with people of other lands, such as foreign children in their own school, letters, stories, news items, and so forth. Endeavor to develop the realization that children of other lands are much like American children. Their pets, toys, and games, are similar, and they need the same essentials of life—food, clothing, and homes. If their food, clothing, and homes differ, explain the reasons for these differences.

Some additional activities that may be possible during the year are:

1. Excursions during each season to observe the landscape. In the spring there should be two excursions—one when spring is just starting, and one when spring is at its height.
2. Making sketches after each trip. Save sketches and make comparison of colors used.
3. Observation of sky colors.
4. Writing summaries of weather conditions. Making a sketch or poster illustrating the weather conditions prevalent during each month.
5. Melting of ice in the sun. Observation of the melting of ice and snow in the sun, and in a shady place.
6. Trips to see spring wild flowers. Drawing and coloring three wild flowers. Arranging wild flowers which may be gathered for schoolroom decoration. Transplanting violets and other wild flowers.
7. Observation of garden flowers. Sketching the whole plant.
8. Watching insects which visit flowers. Looking for the "golden dust" carried from flower to flower by insects and wind. Listening to a simple story of pollination. Making charts to show flower visitors.
9. Bringing sprays of buds into the schoolroom. Forcing buds. Observation of opening buds on trees. Taking a walk to note colors in the young leaves. Sketching and coloring young leaves. Planting a tree.
10. Setting up experiments to show what seeds need to grow. Watching these experiments. Ordering penny seed packets. Planting seeds in eggshells, window boxes, and in the home garden. Cultivating and watering plants. Keeping a record in sketches of plant development.

A Geographic Readiness Program

11. Reports on activities of animals which the children may see in parks or in the country.
12. Making a collection of animal picture books for the schoolroom.
13. An excursion to see a turtle in its own home, and observation of a land turtle in the schoolroom. Feeding the turtle. Keeping a record of the number seen.
14. Making and keeping a bird chart. Putting out strings, rags, feathers, and other materials to help the birds build their nests. Observing birds build their nest. Locating nests. Observing how different birds bathe. Decorating the schoolroom with bird pictures. Imitating calls and songs of birds. Bird games.
15. Watching butterflies and moths emerge from cocoons and chrysalides. Special observation of one moth and one butterfly.
16. Making a chart showing changes in the shape of the moon throughout a month.
17. Illustrating what the sun does for us.
18. Telling time with a shadow stick and sun dial.

A PROGRAM FOR THE THIRD GRADE

The geography readiness program in the third grade is built on the first and second grade programs. The teacher should check the students' background, and plan to strengthen any weaknesses found. Observation should continue, but text and references may be used to fill in, extend, and check the children's personal observations and experiences.

The major objectives for the third grade geographic readiness program are:

1. To give the children certain fundamental geographic experiences which will give meaning:
    a. to the words of the printed page in the textbooks which they will use later;
    b. to the map symbols that they will meet.
2. To give the children some knowledge of the geography of their own town and the surrounding area.
3. To give the children a feeling of the relationship between man and his home—the earth—and how man is dependent on the earth as the basic source for food, clothing, and shelter.
4. To introduce the map to children, and to begin to teach them the language of maps.

Direction

Review direction, because even in the third grade many children do not know how to find direction. There are many situations, with use of the shadow stick and the development of their first map, in which they will need to know and use direction. Also, they should use direction in connection with their weather observations; wind direction; direction from which a storm comes; and direction from which the rain is coming.

Sun Position

Review what the class has learned about shadows: direction in which shadows point in the morning, at noon, and in the afternoon; length of shadow in relation to the position of the sun in September, in December, in March, in May, or June. Note the relation of length of day to sun position and length of noonday shadow. Have them observe their own shadow at different times of the day and at different seasons. Observe shadows in pictures and try to determine the approximate time of day from the position and length of the shadows.

Start a sun chart in September, recording each month on the same date the following data:

Date	Time and direction of rising	Time of setting	Length of day	Noon shadow	Position of noon sun
For example: September	5:27 A.M. North of east	6:31 P.M. North of west	13 hr. & 4 min.	Length of ———	Getting lower in southern sky

The time of sunrise and sunset may be found in an almanac or in most daily newspapers. The approximate direction may be found through observation. The teacher should help the children determine the length of day. The length of the midday shadow and the position of the sun at midday should be recorded from personal observation.

Telling Time

This topic should start with a review of the class' previous work on sun position and shadows. Robert L. Stevenson's poem, "My Shadow," may be read. To aid in developing the idea of telling time from the sun, ask such questions as: "When is your shadow very, very tall? When does he get 'so little that there is none of him at all?' Let us watch our funny shadows 'shoot up taller like an India-rubber ball.'" Help them to see how people once-upon-a-time depended upon the sun to tell the time of day. Other methods of telling time may be suggested by children in the class. Thus, the child may be stimulated to observe more closely, and some may make shadow sticks or sun dials at home. Helen Crew's "The Sun Dial," and other poems may be used. In their readers and reference books, the children may find stories and descriptions of various means man has used to tell time, for instance, the water clock of Egypt, and the hourglass.

Weather and the Seasons

The third grade should continue observing and recording their weather observations. This year, they could use a Weather Rose (see Fig. 24) in which to record their observations, recording the daily temperature, sky condition, and precipitation in an arm of the rose which shows the wind direction for the day.

The schoolroom should have a large thermometer outside a window, or some other convenient place outside. Have a committee read the temperature at nine o'clock each day, and discuss temperature, wind direction, condition of the sky, and so forth. The children will soon observe that on most rainy days (east of the Rocky Mountains) the winds are from the east, northeast, or southeast, whereas on clear days, the winds are usually from the west, northwest, or southwest. Thus they learn to associate wind direction with types of weather. However, local conditions vary, and also the effect of the prevailing winds may vary with the seasons. Only by means of careful observations and with records will they

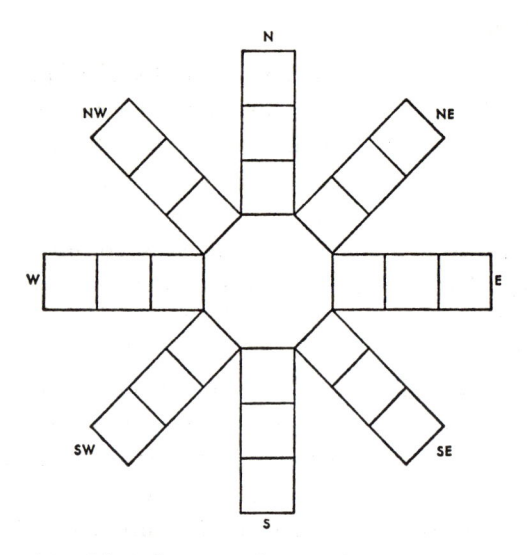

Fig. 24. A diagram of a weather rose form.

be able to make generalizations concerning the local relationships between wind direction and weather conditions.

In order to identify and describe the force of the wind, the following terms should be taught.

Calm—no wind
Light wind—leaves move
Moderate wind—branches move
Brisk wind—branches sway and dust blows up
High wind—trees sway, and twigs and limbs are blown to ground

At the end of each month, a longer and more specific summary than those of the first and second grades should be made. The pupils should compare their summaries for each month with their summaries of the two previous years. Now they are ready to summarize the general characteristics of each one of the months.

Also, from their three year's records, they should now be able to summarize the characteristics of each of the seasons. By the end

A Geographic Readiness Program

of the third grade, the children should have acquired the following understandings:

1. An understanding of the characteristic weather of each of the four seasons.
2. An understanding of how we measure temperature with a thermometer.
3. A beginning understanding of the relation between wind direction and weather conditions.
4. An understanding of the relation between seasonal sun position and length of day.
5. A beginning understanding that sun position and temperature are related.

In discussions, more emphasis should be placed on the effects of weather on the activities of the community, for instance, the drugstore sells more ice cream and cold drinks in hot weather. Ask such questions as: "When is the coal or the fuel oil dealer busiest? What is the effect of weather on streets, highways, and buildings? What are some of the preparations for winter weather made by the community?"

In grades one and two the emphasis is on the child's own activities, and the family's. Now, he should be aware of the community, and its activities as related to weather conditions and other elements of the natural environment.

The Work of the Wind

Sometime in the third grade, the wind and its work should be discussed based on the knowledge gained in the second grade. Such a unit may grow out of the weather record at an unusually windy period, or when some event connected with a storm has occurred. Review, through questions and discussion, the children's background and go on from there. In listing the work of the wind, no doubt, the children may repeat many points that they mentioned in the second grade, but also add many new ones, for instance, a boy may mention the effect of a tail wind or head wind on an airplane's rate of flying; kites and gliders may be mentioned; or how winds carry volcanic dust or radioactive dust from atomic explosions long distances. In this unit, the central idea to be stressed is the relation of the wind to man's activities, both good and bad effects of the wind, its value to life, and how man has learned to use its power. There are many songs, poems, and stories which may be used effectively. The manual expression work which can be done to illustrate the unit is both attractive and worthwhile —making and flying kites and gliders, making drawings and paper cuttings of a child carrying an umbrella blown wrongside out and many others which the children will suggest, and collecting pictures and current events concerning winds and storms.

The Work of Water

This unit is an extension of the work on water and its forms that was developed in the second grade. Review the children's background to discover how much they recall and to lay a basis for the additional work.

By means of field trips, help the children secure from their immediate environment mental pictures of creeks and rivers, lakes, islands, flood plains, deltas, alluvial fans, slopes, divides, gullies, valleys, and other water and land forms resulting from the action of water. A visit to a roadside stream or gully after a rain will provide the opportunity for many of these forms to be observed, and on some schoolyards the work of water may be seen.

Point out some of the responses man makes to both land and water forms in your own locality in building roads, railroads, and homes. Look for signs of soil erosion on the playground, along the side of a road, or in a nearby field. To show the children the causes of soil erosion, get two boxes, and in one put dry soil and in the other a piece of sod. Tilt the boxes and pour water on each of them. When the soil is dry, let the children take turns blowing over the two boxes. The children may observe what causes erosion (wind and rain); what roots do to prevent erosion (hold soil); and why erosion is bad for our land.

Other activities include collecting pictures, and making booklets or posters of man's activities in using streams. From their second

A Geographic Readiness Program

grade work, they should realize the necessity of water for plants and animals, but if they don't, repeat some experiments.

Review evaporation and condensation if the class has had these concepts developed in the second grade. If these are new to them, carry out the experiments suggested in the second grade program.

The class should gain an understanding of how rain, snow, sleet, hail, and even dew and frost provide the earth with water. Also, they should have gained a beginning understanding of what becomes of rain from a story of a drop of water to illustrate the *water cycle*.

The following outline is for a study based on observing a stream in the locality. Even if this has been done in the second grade, new pupils will benefit and the others will take pride in displaying their knowledge.

HOW WE MAY STUDY A STREAM

1. The beginning or source of the stream.
2. Its channel and banks. Does it flow swiftly or slowly? Learn through observation the meaning of *upstream* and *downstream.*
3. The work of the stream.
   a. Cutting its channel.
      (1) How it cuts a channel.
      (2) Where and when it cuts most rapidly.
   b. Carrying its load.
      (1) What it carries.
      (2) How it is able to carry soil, sand, gravel and rock.
      (3) What it does with its load. (The formations such as sand bars, deltas, flood plains, and so forth found on the trip.)
      (4) Why the stream drops this material; which kind of material is dropped first; reasons.
4. The way man uses streams.

This last topic should include a discussion of the enormous amounts of water now being used in homes and for industries. The proper use or conservation of water is a serious problem in many areas today. It is no longer a problem only of the semiarid West but also of the humid East. Modern industries use enormous quantities of water. A study of a local industry may illustrate this problem. Of course, it is also a health problem.

This unit is not only of immediate importance to the child's development but the concrete images and the understandings gained form a foundation for associations when the children study rivers and land forms in various parts of the world. On the field trips, the teacher should lead the children to see the responses which man makes to these various land and water forms. In going out of doors to see geography, the teacher must look for two things: (1) *The condition of the environment;* (2) *The behavior of plants, animals, and humans in response to those conditions.* Every locality shows some examples of decided response to one or more of these forms. For instance: a farm where only the part of the land that is in the valley is cultivated, a highway following the windings of a stream, and a city built in a valley or at the junction of two rivers.

Before the work is finished, the observations and discussions should be summarized. At the beginning of the work, the teacher should *make an outline* of the material which he wants to cover, and at the close, *check up* to see to what extent she has carried out her plans. The class should have some objective in putting their information into an organized whole. This may be in the form of a story, as "The Story of a Drop of Water." The teacher should plan such trips carefully—what she is going to show the children and the questions she is going to ask in order to make important points and indicate causal factors. She should not be content to point out one island, delta, or sandbar, but as many of all types that happen to be in the stream, until the children are able to find them without her help. Usually after the first one or two are found, competition develops among the children as to who can first spy another. In each case, the reason for the formation of that particular form should be sought. Sometimes it is the presence of a stick, a stone, or a log which slows up the current, again, at the mouth of a tributary stream, a delta or bar forms because the current of the tributary stream has been checked on entering the larger stream.

A Geographic Readiness Program

On return to the classroom, probably in the class discussion the next day, the outline may be worked out so that the class will have what they learned on the trip in a form for future reference. Pictures of similar formations in rivers and streams should be brought to class, and the children should try to discover in the pictures the various formations they saw on their trip. This is a good test and review. A booklet or poster illustrating land and water forms, and one illustrating man's use of water and streams are attractive expression activities.

Rocks and Soils

Another unit suitable for the third grade is one on rocks and soil. The formation of soil, kinds of soil, how plants grow in different kinds of soil, as well as soil erosion, are important facts and ideas with which the children should become acquainted. The following outline is suggestive for such a unit:

THE ADVENTURES OF SOME GRAINS OF DUST

1. How are grains of dust formed?
   a. How rocks are broken up. (Friction, water, ice, plants, and so forth.)
   b. How experiments show the breaking up of rocks.
   c. Find illustrations in the locality of the breaking up of rocks to form soil. (Even in a city, examples can be seen, such as sidewalks, pavements, and so forth.)
   d. How plants decay and form soil.
2. What rocks and soil may we collect? (Encourage the children to collect rocks and samples of soils, and learn to identify them.)
3. How are the grains of dust transported from place to place?
   a. How the wind carries dust and sand.
   b. How the rain and the streams carry silt and sand.
   c. How plants, animals, and man help to transport soil.
4. How do we use the grains of dust?
   a. How the soil feeds the plants.
   b. How we make bricks and tile from clay.
   c. How we make glass from sand.
   d. How we make pottery and china.

The subject matter discussed in the above units is sufficient to give suggestions to the teacher. He may select from these units or add others which are more appropriate to the locality. The methods of treatment are merely suggestive. After a teacher gains a little self-confidence and practice, many ideas will come to him for introducing and developing a topic. He will also acquire skill in seizing upon the experiences and interests of the children and capitalizing them. There are a few points upon which he should check himself. He should be sure that the information which he is giving the children or leading them to discover is worthwhile and accurate. By being worthwhile is meant that the knowledge or experience has both immediate and deferred value in the child's development. The information should be accurate from the geographical point of view, uncolored by prejudice and superstition. He should endeavor to make sure that the real interest of the children has been aroused, and that the work appears to be reasonable and worthwhile to them. He can do this if he carefully studies and analyzes the contacts and interests of the children, and then uses these as leads in introducing ideas to start the children thinking along certain desired lines.

Two questions will help him in determining what is important in the home region. Does it concern the lives of the people? Does it have fundamental geographic significance? In connection with the latter question, he must remember that in every locality there are two important geographic factors, namely: The geographical variables—weather and seasons, and the geographical constants—land forms and water bodies. These geographic factors in their various relationships affect the ways of living of the people. The study of these units which are common to all localities gives the children a conception of the vital connection between their lives and natural forces, and is probably the most important of all the work in geography. It does not comprise, however, all of the work. A study of the home region is of value because it is a study of the response of man to his environment, and at the same time it is a

A Geographic Readiness Program

means of giving the children a basis for clear conceptions of other lands.

Development of the First Map

In the third grade, the first map is developed with the children. A detailed discussion of this activity is given in Chapter 3.

A Geographical Study of the Home Community

During the latter part of the third grade, a geographical study of the home community may grow out of the field trips and other activities of the year. Such a study is a pulling together of the many observations and learnings accumulated during the three years of primary work. It is based on the children's field trips and their personal experiences. The aim is to develop an awareness of how the people of the community have adjusted to the local environment.

The first step is a discussion and listing of the natural features of the local landscape. These features should include the kind of surface (level, hilly, rolling, or mountainous), the soils and rocks, the seasonal weather, natural resources if there are any, streams, and rivers. Then, the cultural features are discussed and listed—streets, roads, highways, buildings, dams, bridges, irrigation works, fields, crops, occupations, and the various means of transportation.

The third step is to relate the cultural and physical features. How is the street pattern, the railroad route, or the highway route related to the topography? If it is a hilly region, even the way the houses are built may show the effect of the topography. Stairs may be used to reach some streets. In other places, drainage may be necessary because the surface is low or so level that water does not drain off. The direction from which wind and rain come may be noted by the effects of weathering on the houses, or the closing in of one side of a porch.

The use of the local streams, the source of the water supply, the kinds and use of any local natural resources, and the location of parks are other topics to be studied as affecting the ways of living in the community. In a rural community, note how the fields are laid out, the kind of crops, the pastures, the woodlands, and often the location of the home and the barns are related to the natural conditions.

As the class, through field trips, discussions, and interviews gathers information, committees and individual pupils should write brief reports. These reports, together with photographs taken by the children, may be put in a little book, telling the story of how the people are using their natural environment.

The Rotation of the Earth

Whether this unit is taught depends on the maturity of the group. Most third graders are interested in the topic. During the year, no doubt, they have discussed the sun in connection with their weather observations. Sometimes a child brings up the question as to what would happen if the sun should shine all of the time, or if the sun should not come up some morning. In this conversation, some of the benefits of the sun and how our lives are regulated by the fact that we have day and night should be brought out. Robert L. Stevenson's poems, "Night and Day" and "The Sun's Travels," are helpful in illustrating the effect of day and night upon the children's lives. The effect of having day and night upon plants and animals should be noted. The work of the previous years will be of value here. Before discussion is finished, it is probable that someone in the class will raise the question why the sun comes up and goes down. Various reasons will be given, and also suggestions as to the size and shape of the earth. After the children have expressed their views, the teacher should bring out the idea of the earth as a great ball or sphere, and what it would look like if we were a long way off and could look at it as we do the sun. The poem, "The Ball Itself," which is to be found in Andrews, *Seven Little Sisters*,[1] may be used effectively in this connection. The

[1] Jane Andrews, *Seven Little Sisters Who Live on the Round Ball that Floats in the Air* (Boston, Ginn and Company, 1924).

children often want to learn parts or all of the poem. At this time, the globe as a picture or symbol of the earth may be introduced. All of the children are familiar with photographs, and perhaps even with models, so they can grasp the idea that the earth is so large that for convenience we make a small model of it which we call "the globe." The children will ask many questions which the teacher should endeavor to explain to the best of his ability. The full concept of the globe, however, is one of slow growth, and just a beginning is made in the third grade, especially in the first few lessons.

There are many simple ways of showing how the rotation of the earth gives us day and night. That method which is most convenient for the teacher should be used. One of the simplest and safest methods is to darken the room and use an electric light bulb or a flashlight for the sun. Rotate the globe slowly so the children may see how part of the globe is in the light while the other section is in darkness. If a pin or a thumbtack with a bright colored head is stuck into the globe so that the children can watch it as it goes out of the light and comes back in with the rotation of the globe, the idea may be clearer. Do the experiment slowly, several times so that all of the children will grasp the idea, at least to some extent. If they want it repeated, do so. Repetition, as long as there is interest, is valuable. Be very careful, however, to have the globe in the proper position, rotating from west to east and the north pole pointing north. If each teacher is careful to keep all relations correct, even though they are not mentioned or even apparently noticed by the children, there will not be so many wrong ideas to correct in the upper grades.

GOALS OF THE PRIMARY PROGRAM

As a result of three years of planned cumulative learnings, the children should have acquired certain skills, attitudes, and habits, as well as considerable knowledge of their environment.

Skills

The children's ability to observe and report accurately what they see in their environment, and in their own way to interpret it, should have been developed. Their ability to express their ideas fluently and accurately in oral and written expression should have increased. In this respect, the majority of the children should be able to discuss a previously developed topic for several minutes before the class. They should be able to enter into a group discussion, to express an opinion and uphold it, and to ask and answer questions of other members of the class. By now they should have the ability to select and organize materials in short outlines. They should have considerable skill in the collecting and organizing of materials which illustrate a given unit. They should have some skill in representing their ideas by means of various activities, such as making posters, sketches, exhibits, simple maps, and other types of constructive work.

They should have acquired the ability to use direction in space to orient themselves. They should have the ability to read and use symbols to represent features of the landscape as they read or make simple maps. They should understand that the globe is a representation of the earth.

They should have acquired the ability to recognize simple direct relationships between man's activities and the natural environment, and how man may change his environment to fit his needs in certain instances.

Attitudes

The children should have acquired certain definite attitudes toward their environment. They should have begun to realize that many of their own activities, and those of their families and of the community, are affected by the weather and other conditions of the natural environment. They should have begun to understand that our natural resources should not be wasted by carelessness. Their appreciation and understanding of nature should have increased greatly.

Habits

There are a few habits which should have been formed during this year. Some desirable ones are: Endeavoring to trace life responses back to geographic conditions, consulting books and other written material for information, and endeavoring to express their ideas through other means than speech. These are habits which are of value in life, aside from their direct value in the study of geography. They function not only in the present but in the future.

REFERENCES

BARTON, Thomas F., "Geographic Instruction in the Primary Grades," *Geographic Approaches to Social Education*, Nineteenth Yearbook (Washington, D.C., National Council for the Social Studies, 1948), Ch. 18.

―――, "Primary Geography," *Journal of Geography*, Vol. 39 (September, 1940), pp. 243–246.

―――, "Teaching Soil in the Lower Grades," *Journal of Geography*, Vol. 45 (November, 1946), pp. 309–317.

―――, "The Penguin and the Ostrich," *Journal of Geography*, Vol. 38 (May, 1939), pp. 188–191.

COLLAMORE, Edna, "Organizing a Pre-geography Vocabulary," *Journal of Geography*, Vol. 32 (December, 1933), pp. 372–376.

GREGG, F. M., "Important Principles in Teaching Primary-Grade Geography," *Elementary School Journal*, Vol. 41 (May, 1941), pp. 665–670.

GUNDERSON, A. G., "Geographic Materials Contained in Readers for the First Three Grades," *Elementary School Journal*, Vol. 33 (April, 1933), pp. 608–615.

HAHN, H. H., "The Teaching of Home Geography," *Journal of Geography*, Vol. 38 (January, 1939), pp. 1–8.

HILEMAN, Mary L., "Adios for Mexico: A Social Studies Unit for the Third Grade," *Journal of Geography*, Vol. 38 (December, 1939), pp. 359–363.

―――, "A Visit to Reindeer Land," *Journal of Geography*, Vol. 37 (October, 1938), pp. 278–283.

KELLEY, Jean Summers, "A Study of Direction in the Second Grade," *Journal of Geography*, Vol. 50 (November, 1951), pp. 317–321.

MASON, Carol Y., and RUTZ, Winefred, "A Hopi Indian Project," *Journal of Geography*, Vol. 38 (February, 1939), pp. 75–81.

MEIGHEN, M., and BARTH, E., "Geographic Materials in Third Grade Readers," *Elementary English Review*, Vol. 15 (December, 1938), pp. 299–301.

MITCHELL, Lorena, "Geography Tests for Grade One," *Journal of Geography*, Vol. 55 (October, 1956), pp. 354–358.

――――, "Keeping a Weather Chart: A First Grade Activity," *Journal of Geography*, Vol. 54 (January, 1955), pp. 17–19.

MITCHELL, Mary A., "How and When Does 'Activity' Contribute to Social Education," *Journal of Geography*, Vol. 46 (December, 1947), pp. 352–357.

MORAN, Grace, "Pre-geography Learnings Resulting from Community Life Studies," *Journal of Geography*, Vol. 34 (May, 1935), pp. 196–201.

PACE, Ethel, "Construction Activity Follows First Grade Geography Trip," *Journal of Geography*, Vol. 52 (April, 1953), pp. 144–146.

――――, "Some Tests for First Grade Geography," *Journal of Geography*, Vol. 53 (January, 1954), pp. 11–14.

PALMER, Laurence, "Right Outside Your Window," *NEA Journal*, Vol. 41 (November, 1952), pp. 484–485.

PRICE, Ethel, "Nine-year-olds Study Community Health," *Social Education*, Vol. 11 (February, 1947), pp. 68–70.

ROBERTSON, Dolyne, "The Globe as a Geography Tool," *Journal of Geography*, Vol. 55 (January, 1956), pp. 35–37.

SCHELCHTY, Pauline, "Source Unit for Third Grade Community Geography," *Journal of Geography*, Vol. 52 (November, 1953), pp. 339–347.

――――, "Using an Encyclopedia for Third Grade Geography," *Journal of Geography*, Vol. 51 (November, 1952), pp. 322–324.

TRAIL, R. W., "Maps in the Primary Grades," *Journal of Geography*, Vol. 51 (September, 1952), pp. 238–244.

VOUGH, M., "Adventures in Geography in Second Grade," *Journal of Geography*, Vol. 49 (January, 1950), pp. 26–29.

WALL, Edith, "A Thunder Shower," *Journal of Geography*, Vol. 38 (May, 1939), pp. 191–192.

WHEELER, Lois, "Experiences in Teaching Third Grade Geography," *Journal of Geography*, Vol. 51 (October, 1952), pp. 281–282.

11

The Teaching of Weather and Climate

OF ALL THE FEATURES of our natural environment, the weather draws our attention and affects our living and actions more frequently than any other one factor. In most of the United States, the question "What is the weather today?" is one of the first questions asked or in the minds of people as they arise. They listen to the morning weather reports on radio and television, or consult the weather map and the forecast in the daily papers. The daily weather reports and forecasts enter into the plans and operations of most people's daily activities, as well as of most business activities throughout the country. A business trip, a vacation, transportation by air, land, and sea, crop yields, production of livestock, construction activities of all types, and military operations are all dependent upon weather conditions.

Weather forecasting has become an important public service as people realize more and more the value of knowing ahead of time the probable weather conditions. The following quotation gives an idea of the extensive use of weather reports:[1]

[1] F. W. Reichilderfer, "The Weather Bureau—How It Serves You on Land and Sea, and in the Air," U.S. Department of Commerce Bulletin (Washington, D.C., U.S. Government Printing Office, 1946), pp. 80–84.

Railroads, express trucking lines, and river and ocean freighters make almost continuous use of weather forecasts in protecting the shipments they carry. . . . With notices of an approaching cold wave, utilities that provide heat and light make preparations for increased demands. Fuel gas and electric plants boost their output. . . . Concrete construction work is stopped. . . . Iron ore piled up for vessel shipment is stored in the holds of ships, if possible, to prevent the wet ore from freezing so hard that it cannot be worked. . . . Merchants curtail advertisements for warm weather goods and direct attention to cold weather articles.

Rain forecasts are used by contractors in concrete construction and roofing repairs. City departments estimate the number of trucks needed for street cleaning and sprinkling; railroad companies guard against bridge and roadbed washouts; and irrigation companies control the output of water in accordance with the forecasts of rainfall. . . . Advance information of temperature and moisture conditions assist in blast furnace operations to determine quality of output. [Such weather information is also of importance] in the manufacture of articles where changes in temperature, moisture, or weather elements affect the quality of the product. This is the case at certain stages in the manufacture of brick, cement, lime, oils, paper, photographic supplies, varnish, and other chemical products, as well as in the production of many foodstuffs such as pastries, chocolate candies, cereals, and macaroni.

The above examples are only a few of the almost innumerable ways in which weather and climate affect man's activities. The average person readily admits that to the farmer, the fisherman, the herdsman, the pioneer, the explorer, and to the aviator, "the weather has always been a silent partner, a partner with whom they cannot argue, but whose ways they may learn and profit by." But they do not realize that today all of us cannot ignore the effects of weather conditions if we are to utilize modern technology most efficiently. In fact we need more and better weather information. As a result, thousands of businesses subscribe to private commercial weather forecasting companies to secure specialized weather information which the United States Weather Bureau cannot supply because it lacks sufficient personnel and facilities. Yet it does an enormous and remarkable job with limited personnel and facilities.

The importance of weather and climatic conditions in modern

The Teaching of Weather and Climate

civilization makes essential more knowledge and understanding of weather and climate by all of us. For this reason, the study of weather should begin in the primary grades and be continued throughout the grades and high school. Such study is not only of practical value but is also a delightful hobby. As has been said,

> To step out into the weather is to be liberated from the man-made. The atmosphere is tameless, free, and full of peril, like the ocean. It is greater than all the oceans. It is the medium of the future. So the weather-lover, although thinking that his pleasure was self-indulgence, has been pursuing a very practical interest all the while, in spite of himself.[2]

The knowledge and understanding of weather comes from cumulative learnings and the application of the knowledge gained from year to year. The concepts of weather and climate are complex and must be built up gradually.

WEATHER AND CLIMATE IN THE PRIMARY GRADES

In Chapter 10, weather has been discussed as developed in the first, second, and third grades. If such studies are carried through the primary grades, the following concepts and understandings should have been gained by the end of each grade.

First Grade

The children should have acquired the following concepts and understandings:

Concepts—(1) Rain; (2) Temperature; (3) Wind, as air in motion; (4) The forms of water—dew, frost, rain, snow, ice, steam; (5) Direction; (6) Air is all about us; (7) A beginning concept of the position of the sun in the sky in the morning, at midday, and in the late afternoon.

Understandings—(1) We need shelter to protect us from the weather; (2) We fit our work and play to the daily weather and

---

[2] T. Morris Longstreth, *Knowing the Weather* (New York, The Macmillan Co. 1945), pp. 126–127.

the seasons; (3) The weather changes almost daily; (4) The weather helps us to decide what to wear if we are to be comfortable; (5) Air is a necessity for plants, animals, and man. (6) Wind has force, and man can make use of it (7) The changing seasons cause changes in the landscape—trees, flowers, and the appearance of certain birds and animals; (8) The sun at midday is always in the southern sky in our country, and in the summer the midday sun is higher in the sky than it is in the winter.

Second Grade

The weather studies started in the first grade are continued, but deepened and made more exact. The concepts which are developed further are: weather, temperature, moisture in its various forms, the seasons and their characteristics, sun position at the various seasons, air, wind, and wind direction.

The understandings that are extended and developed more specifically are: (1) An understanding of the probable weather of each month and its relation to man's activities; (2) A broader understanding that man fits his activities to the daily and seasonal weather conditions; (3) A broader and more exact understanding of the importance of air and wind.

Third Grade

By the time the children reach the third grade they should have a good foundation for their weather studies. By the end of the third grade the following concepts should have been acquired: (1) How we can read temperature by means of a thermometer; (2) A more accurate concept of wind direction, such as a northeast wind as well as north, east, south, and west winds; (3) Rotation of the earth; (4) Evaporation; (5) Condensation; (6) All forms of water; (7) Thunderstorm, a drizzle, and other types of rain storms.

The understandings that should have been gained are: (1) A beginning understanding of the relation between wind direction and weather conditions; (2) A beginning understanding of the relation between sun position and length of day; (3) A beginning under-

The Teaching of Weather and Climate

standing that sun position and temperature are related; (4) A beginning understanding of the rotation of the earth and how rotation causes day and night; (5) An understanding of the characteristics of the seasons in their locality; (6) An understanding of how rain, snow, sleet, hail, and even dew provide the earth with water; (7) A beginning understanding of the water cycle; (8) A *beginning* realization that most of the weather is due to the condition of the air itself. For instance, if the air moves, it is windy; if the air is warm the day is warm; and so forth. Also, that the condition of the air is due in part to the sun, so that the sun really makes the weather; (9) A fuller realization of the numerous relationships between man's activities and well-being and weather.

WEATHER AND CLIMATE IN THE INTERMEDIATE GRADES

Fourth Grade

In most schools, the geography or social studies units are selected from type regions which illustrate peoples' ways of living in various parts of the world. Some of these type regions are:

1. Living in the Congo or in Amazonia (a hot rainy region)
2. Living in the Nile Valley and in the Sahara (a hot dry land)
3. The Mediterranean Lands (lands with hot dry summers and cool rainy winters)
4. A Mountain Land—Switzerland
5. A Lowland by the Sea (Holland)
6. A Highland by the Sea (Norway)
7. Arctic Lands
8. From North to South in Australia
9. Antarctic—A Land of Ice and Snow

In some schools, unfortunately, only a few of these units are developed. In others, where the importance of geography is recognized, all of the above or similar units are taught. The main idea or major understanding to be gained from such a series of units is: Where one lives on the earth affects the ways in which one lives. The location of a place in relation to the equator is an important factor in determining the kind of weather and climate the place has. Weather and climate affect the vegetation, the animal life, and people's ways of living.

In the fourth grade only a beginning understanding of this big idea is gained, but it is of vital importance that the foundation is laid at this stage in the child's development. In order that the children are not confused, and that the idea is developed logically, the series of units should begin in one of the equatorial regions, move northward to the Arctic, and then southward into the southern hemisphere. Children are very logical oftentimes, to the dismay of adults. A logical order appeals to them. The order suggested for the units develops the major idea cumulatively.

In the study of these regions, the weather concepts and understandings gained in the primary grades are used for comparison with the weather of the new regions. In this way the new concepts and understandings are more easily acquired. Also, a beginning concept of climate is gradually developed. The study of local weather is continued and a concept of the local climate is developed.

As each region is developed, the weather and climatic conditions of the new region should be constantly compared or contrasted with the local weather and climate. For instance, in developing a unit on "Living in the Congo," the weather there may be compared to the hot rainy midsummers of most parts of the United States east of the Great Plains. The text may state that, "every day in the year is like summer. Heavy clothes are not needed. Trees, grass, and flowers grow all through the year. Rains come almost every day. The Congo is a rainy land with no winters." But these few words are insufficient to give the children the real feel of the climate. The teacher must guide them in imagining from their own experiences what it is like to live where day after day, all the year, the weather is hot and drippy with moisture, as is a July day before, during, and following a midsummer thunderstorm. How did they feel? How did they dress? What did they do? How do grass, trees, and flowers respond to such weather day after day? Merely

The Teaching of Weather and Climate

reading the few words in the text will not make the land, the weather, and the effects of the weather real to the children. They must be guided in applying their own experiences, extending their imaginations, and expressing their ideas as to the weather conditions and the resulting effects on the people.

In areas such as California and the dry western states, the children's weather experiences also can be used. But they must be reminded of how things grow when irrigated, and then imagine how the landscape in their locality would blossom out if there were rain almost every day along with the heat.

When "A Mountain Land—Switzerland" is studied, a new idea is introduced, that altitude or height above the sea also affects weather and climate. Children in the mountain states should have the idea from their own experiences, but in many sections of the United States this new concept will need to be carefully developed. In some instances, the vacation or travel experiences of individual children may be utilized to give reality to the textbook description.

As each region is developed, the teacher should ask himself such questions as: "How can I make use of the children's knowledge and understanding of our local weather to make the weather conditions of this new region real to them? How can I guide them to think how the people's ways of living in this land are affected by the daily and seasonal weather? How are their homes, food, clothing, means of transportation, kinds of work, the way the work is done, their sports, and games affected by the weather and other conditions in each region?" The teacher must plan definite activities to give the children the experiences to make the regions and peoples real to them.

Activities. Every textbook suggests some activities, but the following are especially helpful in aiding the children to grasp the main ideas.

1. The position of the sun at midday in each region should be compared with its position at the home locality in September, December, and June. For instance, in the Congo region the children will learn that

the sun is almost directly overhead all the year, in contrast to its changing position at their home. Also, they will learn that the high or vertical sun position is one reason why the weather is hot all the year.

2. Frequent comparison of the length of day at different times of the year in each region should be made with the length of day in the home region, and the resulting effects. For instance, in the equatorial regions the day is 12 hours long throughout the year, in contrast to our long summer days and short winter days; on the other hand, in Norway and the Arctic regions the summer days are even longer than ours, and the winter days are shorter.

In both of the above activities the class is making use of their own weather records.

3. From their textbooks and in stories of the people, find words, sentences, and paragraphs which describe the weather and climate, and how people are fitting their ways of living to the weather and climatic conditions.

4. Collect pictures which show evidence of climate in each region. Save these for discussion, comparison, and review as new regions are taken up.

5. List and explain new terms you have learned which have to do with weather and climate.

6. Make a list of the occupations and other activities people in the region may be doing when we are having winter, spring, summer, and autumn. Explain why their activities are like ours, or are different.

7. Make a list and discuss the products that we receive from the region because the weather and climate are different.

8. Watch the newspapers for news items concerning the weather and its effects in the various regions, for instance, such an item as this, "113 degree heat stops North African railroad. A heat wave in North Africa recently caused railroad tracks to twist, stopping traffic on the Tunis-Carthage line."

The children should continue the study of the local weather and keep weather records. The following activities should be carried on in this study:

1. Keep a daily weather record, recording temperature, amount of rainfall and other types of precipitation by measurement, wind direction, and sky conditions, including cloud forms.

2. Use a weather vane to tell wind direction.

3. Measure amount of rainfall by means of a straight-sided can placed out in the open.

The Teaching of Weather and Climate

4. Watch the newspapers for local weather forecasts, and listen to radio and television weather reports. Note the reports of temperature and precipitation, and compare with the class records.

5. Learn to recognize cumulus, cirrus, stratus, and nimbus clouds, and discuss the significance of these four cloud types.

6. Collect pictures of the cloud types.

Concepts. By the end of the fourth grade the class should have a fairly clear idea of the meaning of the following concepts, and be able to use them:

1. Cloud forms—cirrus, nimbus, stratus, and cumulus.
2. Inches of rainfall.
3. Wind has force.
4. Length of day varies with distance north and south of the equator.
5. The noon sun is high in the sky near the equator.
6. As one goes farther and farther north or south of the equator, the noon sun is lower and lower in the sky.
7. The landscape changes as one travels either north or south from the equator.

Understandings. The class should have acquired the following understandings and appreciations:

1. An understanding that the landscape changes as one travels either north or south from the equator due to changing climatic conditions.
2. A beginning understanding that location of a place on the earth determines the climate that it has. Be able to associate location on the earth with sun position, length of day, seasons, and seasonal characteristics.
3. An understanding that man must adjust his ways of living to the climate of his home land.
4. A beginning understanding that there is a variety of climates on the earth.
5. A beginning understanding that altitude causes differences in temperatures and consequently that people in mountainous regions must fit their ways of living to the mountain climates.
6. An understanding that the sun really makes the weather, but that other factors such as mountains and nearness to large bodies of water also affect the weather of a place.
7. An understanding of the weather significance of the cloud types.

Fifth Grade

Generally in the fifth grade units on the United States and Canada are taught. In connection with the development of these units, the teacher should provide opportunities for the class to apply weather knowledge already acquired, and to broaden their concepts and understandings of weather and climatic conditions. Constant comparisons should be made of local weather and climatic conditions of the various regions of the United States as the regions are taught. If Canada and other areas are studied, such comparisons should be continued. More detailed observations and records should be made of weather and climate in their own locality.

In the United States there is a large variety of climates, but for general purposes the country may be divided into six types which roughly approximate the usual regional divisions as used in most textbooks. In the fifth grade, these climatic types are not given technical names but are designated by the names commonly used for the section. As a rule, the United States is divided into the following sections for regional study:

The Northeastern States
The South
The North Central States or the Middle West
The Mountain and Plateau States
The Northwest
California

Some textbooks sub-divide these sections, but in general the above areas are used. For a study of Canada the following divisions are usually made:

Eastern or Marine Canada
The Prairie Provinces
The Pacific Coast
Northern Canada—Forest and Tundra

In the study of each section, the seasonal characteristics of the weather and climate should be discussed, explained, and the ef-

The Teaching of Weather and Climate

fects upon crops and man's various activities emphasized. In each region, there are characteristic storms which are of importance because they affect people, for instance, the tornado in the South and Middle West, the hurricane in the Southeast, and the blizzards and hailstorms in the Middle West and sometimes in the Northeast.

In the fifth grade, the children should learn to read the average annual rainfall or precipitation map and the length of growing season or the frost-free season map. They should learn to compare these maps with crop distribution, and discover the relation between certain crops and the amount of precipitation and the length of the growing season or the frost-free season. Some books use length of growing season, which is the average time between the last killing frost in the spring and the first killing frost in the fall. Others use the frost-free season, which is the average time between the last spring frost and the first frost in autumn. The latter, of course, is a shorter period.

The term *latitude* must be introduced and explained. Latitude means distance from the equator. It is important because it makes a difference in sun position, in the length of the seasons, and in the length of day and night, and these conditions make a difference in the way people live, work, and play. The east-west lines, or parallels, on the globe and map show us the distance from the equator or how to read the latitude. Parallels also show direction straight east or west on the map or globe. After teaching latitude, the teacher should note opportunities for using it in connection with the discussion on growing season and crops, length of day in northern and southern United States and Canada, and also in locating places.

In the fifth grade, the effect of the prevailing westerly winds on the climate of the Pacific coastal regions of the United States, Canada, and southeastern Alaska north of 40° north latitude should be explained and illustrated with diagrams. In the winter and spring, the westerly winds bring warm moisture-laden air from the Pacific Ocean to the land. The result is mild winters, and as the air moves up the mountains it is cooled and rain falls. Have the class study the rainfall map and note where the heaviest rainfall is. Compare the rainfall map with a map showing the location of the mountains. In summer and fall the ocean is cooler than the land, and the winds off the Pacific seem cool, giving the coastal regions a rather cool summer.

The prevailing winds in North America north of 40° latitude are the westerlies, and they influence the weather and climate clear across the continent. If the class lives in a place north of 40° latitude, they should have discovered from their weather observations that the prevailing or most common winds are from the west, northwest, or southwest. Also, in the fifth grade, the children should be introduced to ocean currents and their influence on climate. For instance, the cold Labrador Current affects the weather and climate of Labrador, Newfoundland, the Maritime Provinces of Canada, and New England. Along our southeast coast the warm Gulf Stream affects the climate. When the winds come off the Atlantic and the warm waters of the Gulf Stream they bring rain and heat in summer, and the coastal region is warmer in winter than the interior.

The textbooks, as a rule, give very brief and general descriptions of the climate of the various regions. The teacher should expand the brief descriptions and also help the children to gain a better idea by applying their knowledge of the local weather and climatic conditions.

Activities. Most textbooks give very few activities or exercises on climatic conditions and its effects on man's ways of living in the United States and Canada. Many more are needed, and the following are suggested.

For each region the following activities should be given at the appropriate point in the study.

1. Note the distance of the region from the equator. By recalling fourth grade learnings, and by comparison with their own location, have the class suggest some possible results of the location of the area, such as sun position, length of day in winter and summer, and seasonal weather. These class suggestions are later checked from the textbook

The Teaching of Weather and Climate

and other sources. The World Almanac gives the time of sunrise and sunset for each month at Boston, New York, Washington, D.C., and Charleston, S.C. These serve for the states in the same latitudes across the United States. New England, New York State, Michigan, Wisconsin, North and South Dakota, Washington, and Oregon have approximately the same time of sunrise and sunset as Boston. For the local time, the local paper may be consulted.

2. The precipitation map should be studied to find the annual average rainfall. If possible, the seasonal distribution of the rainfall should be found. The teacher can find this information for 100 cities of the United States in the World Almanac. From these, he can easily determine the seasonal precipitation for any section of the United States. The seasonal distribution of precipitation is almost as important as the total amount.

3. The growing season or frost-free season map, whichever is given, should be studied and discussed. As farm operations and crops are discussed, the effects of the length of growing season or frost free season are discussed.

4. If a region has certain characteristic storms, such as hurricanes, tornadoes, hailstorms, ice storms, and so forth, the type of storm should be explained and its effects noted, and also how people have tried to guard against the storm damages. These storms are facts of the natural environment which man must face and prepare for. In 1957, Oklahoma and Texas had an unusual number of tornadoes. Some did little damage, but three destroyed two towns and a section of a city causing the loss of forty or more lives, hundreds of millions in property damage, and injuring hundreds of people. The heavy rains caused floods which added to the havoc. Yet in no year is that area entirely free of tornadoes.

5. People are likely to think that weather and climate have little effect on cities. Cities in the northern United States must allow for snow removal in their budgets. Public utilities, railroad companies, and highway crews in the northern half of the United States must take into consideration snow and ice, and in the South they must consider hurricanes, heavy rain storms, and floods. The children should be made aware of these conditions, and how man tries to protect himself and his property.

6. Watch newspapers for items concerning weather, storms, and floods in various parts of the United States and Canada. These clippings should be filed for use later, as each region comes up for study. On television and radio, daily weather conditions in many sections are

given each day. The children should be encouraged to listen and report, and also compare with local conditions.

7. Collect and exhibit pictures which show weather and climatic conditions in the various regions of the United States and Canada.

8. Arrange a set of pictures to show how crops change from north to south in the United States. Explain why the crops vary.

9. Learn to make and read simple rainfall graphs. Such graphs show average monthly precipitation in inches of a station by means of vertical columns.

10. From their textbooks and in stories about the different regions of the United States, list words, sentences, and paragraphs which describe the weather and climate and how people are affected by them.

The study of the local weather should be continued. The following activities are worthwhile:

1. Continue the class' daily weather record. Write to the United States Weather Bureau, Washington 25, D.C. for a sample copy of a weather map. Study the symbols used by the Weather Bureau. Then, the class should decide on the symbols suitable for the class record. The Beaufort Scale for reading wind velocity is given in the encyclopedia.

2. Observe and record types of storms characteristic of the home locality.

3. Keep a record of frosts, the time of occurrence in fall and again in spring, in order to discover the length of the frost-free season in the local region. Note damage caused by frost in the fall and in the spring.

4. Note frost damage at different elevations.

5. Make a dictionary of weather and climatic terms.

Concepts. The children should understand and be able to explain and use the following terms; *climate, frost, frost-free, season, frost damage, frost* or *air drainage, growing season, thunderstorm, tornado, hurricane, hailstorm, blizzard, humidity, evaporation, condensation, average annual rainfall, seasonal rainfall, average temperature, ocean current,* and *westerly wind.*

Understandings. The children should have acquired the following understandings:

1. How frost damages plants.
2. How man can protect some plants and crops from frost damage.

The Teaching of Weather and Climate

3. Why fruit trees planted on hillsides often escape frost damage in spring because the cold air drains downslope into the valley.

4. Why the length of growing season varies in different sections of the United States.

5. That there is a variety of climates in the United States.

6. That each type of climate has its characteristic seasonal weather.

7. That the different sections of the United States have certain characteristic types of storms.

8. How different types of rainfall act on the soil causing more or less soil erosion.

9. How crops vary because climatic conditions differ in the various sections of the United States.

10. How differences in latitude affect climate.

11. How the location of a place in reference to water bodies and land bodies affects both temperature and rainfall.

Some of these ideas have been introduced in the fourth grade, for instance, *altitude*, but the teacher should check the pupil's understanding of them and, if necessary, introduce the term again.

Sixth and Seventh Grade

In most schools, the sixth and seventh grade is the time when the child extends his interests to countries and areas of the world beyond the United States. Because weather and climate are important factors in the life and work of the people of any region, the development of an understanding and an appreciation of the climatic conditions of any region being studied is of outstanding importance. Not all countries or regions can be, or should be, studied during these two years. What is studied will be determined by a number of factors, such as, the children's and teacher's interests, the current importance of certain countries or areas, the local course of study, and perhaps the textbook which is used. However, those countries or areas selected for study should be thoroughly developed on the level of the children's understanding. The level of ability and understanding differs from year to year with different classes. One year a teacher may have a class of unusual ability, and the next year's class may not be average in ability. It is best to teach fewer countries or areas, but to teach those so well that the children will remember the important facts, ideas, and principles developed.

To teach well is to make the landscape and people live for the class. The facts about the life of the people and the characteristics of their land should be carefully selected, dramatized, and explained, then, the people and the country will be real to the children and will be remembered. The climatic characteristics of a region affects strongly the landscape and the ways of living of the people, consequently the climate and its effects should be, in a sense, dramatized as well as clearly explained. As Roderick Peattie says:[3]

> Climate may be made statistical only or a student may seemingly experience the freshness of the sea breeze on a sunny day on the Portuguese coast or the continual and depressing cloudiness of the Falkland Islands....
>
> Jungles are lands where green light filters through the trees. Those forests are alive with insects, one hears the cries of birds or the chattering of monkeys. But on the jungle path man feels lonely and almost as if he had no right to enter the forest vastness. The air is saturated with moisture. Every movement means perspiration, sweat. When it rains the water seems not so much to fall as to be squeezed from the air about you. The rain is breath-taking and for a long time the trees and undergrowth are dripping.

The teacher should use the children's knowledge and understandings of the weather and climates of the United States in the study of the new countries or areas. For instance, when studying any one of the Mediterranean countries of Europe, such as Italy or Greece, compare the seasonal weather and climate, the appearance of the landscape, and how the people have adjusted to the climatic conditions with climatic conditions and ways of living in California. In the study of the British Isles, Norway, and other northwestern European countries, the influence of the westerly winds and the warm North Atlantic Drift should be explained. The westerly winds from off the relatively warm waters of the North

---

[3] Roderick Peattie, *The Teaching of Geography* (New York, Appleton-Century-Crofts, Inc., 1950), pp. 11–12.

The Teaching of Weather and Climate

Atlantic give the British Isles and much of northwestern Europe a milder winter than one would expect from the latitude of those countries.

In the study of India and other southeastern Asiatic countries, the monsoons must be introduced because life in these countries depends upon the summer or wet monsoon. The term *monsoon* means seasonal winds. In summer the wet monsoon blows from off the warm oceans and brings rain. In winter the dry monsoon blows from the great land mass of Asia and brings cool dry weather. In some years, the summer southwesterly winds from the ocean come late or fail to come, and there is drought, crops fail and millions starve. Irrigation helps, but water to fill the wells, rivers, and reservoirs depends upon the summer monsoon. It is not enough just to tell the children or have them read the brief discussion in their textbooks. The effects of the monsoon on the landscape, on the activities of the people, and on the people themselves should be dramatized by means of vivid descriptions, stories, and newspaper accounts.

If the Soviet Union is studied, the teacher should emphasize its vast size, its location in high latitudes almost entirely north of 40° north latitude and extending to 70° north latitude, and its southern mountain rim cutting off the country from any warm waters. These factors influence the climatic conditions of the Soviet Union. The Soviet Union and its peoples cannot be understood unless one understands the significance of its location and its climatic conditions.

In studying any of the countries in the southern hemisphere, such as Australia, countries of South America, and South Africa, the teacher must explain the several seasons. The class may have some knowledge and understanding from their fourth grade work, but this will be meager. After two years without using the knowledge, most of the class probably have forgotten that the seasons are reversed in the southern hemisphere and that the noonday sun is in the northern sky. As units on the countries in the southern hemisphere are developed, the teacher should give the class exercises and activities which require an application of the facts concerning the reversal of seasons. The following may be suggestive:

1. Why are sheep sheared in Australia in October and November?
2. When is wheat harvested in Australia? (Chile, Argentina, South Africa)
3. Why does Christmas come in the summer in Australia? (Chile, Argentina, South Africa)
4. Fresh fruits such as grapes and peaches from Africa and Chile come to the New York market in March. Why?
5. If you lived in Argentina and wanted a bright sunny living room, in what direction should it face? Why?

Activities. Many activities are needed to aid the pupils in acquiring and applying the concepts and understandings concerning climatic conditions and their effects. The following activities are suggested in connection with the study of the various countries:

1. Collect newspaper items concerning weather and climate in the various countries studied. After discussing them, file for future reference.
2. Collect pictures illustrating weather and climate in the various countries.
3. Make posters or pictures illustrating climatic landscapes in the various countries.
4. Make a picture dictionary of all the weather and climatic terms that the class has acquired.
5. Learn to make and read a climatic graph on which both average monthly temperatures and rainfall are shown.
6. Find passages in stories, poems, and reference books descriptive of weather and climate in the countries, and also passages descriptive of specific seasons, such as June in England and summer in India or the coming of the rains.
7. Make maps of countries, such as India, to show the seasonal rainfall pattern.

Activities in connection with the study of local weather and climate should be continued. Some of these activities are:

1. Make a simple mercury barometer.
2. Keep a daily weather record. Record barometer reading, wind

The Teaching of Weather and Climate

direction, estimated wind velocity, cloud types, temperature, and the form and amount of precipitation.

3. Weigh a football or basketball before and after putting air into it to prove that air has weight.

4. Measure the air pressure in an automobile tire with a pressure gauge.

5. Find or recall other illustrations which show that air has weight.

6. Observe the circulation of air in a room, and note the movement of the warm air and the cold air.

7. Continue the study of clouds and learn their names. Note their relation to weather conditions.

8. Compare the class weather record with the daily United States weather map and the weather reports in the daily newspapers.

9. Make weather predictions for the coming day, using all available instruments and weather signs. Compare class predictions with predictions in the newspapers.

10. Discuss the advantages of weather predictions.

Concepts. By the end of the seventh grade the pupils should have acquired adequate functional concepts of the following terms: *climate, marine climate, continental climate, monsoon, latitude* and its relation to climate, *westerly wind belt, trade winds, ocean currents, barometer,* and *longitude.*

Longitude should be introduced in the sixth grade, and together with latitude used for locational purposes. Meridians should also be explained.

Understandings. During the sixth grade and seventh grade, the pupils should have acquired the following understandings and appreciations:

1. An understanding of how the location of a region in relation to a large water body and wind direction affect its climate. For instance, Northwest Europe facing on the North Atlantic Ocean with its warm North Atlantic Drift and the westerly winds coming off the ocean has milder winters and cooler summers than it would have otherwise.

2. An understanding of how the location of a region in relation to a large land body, such as a continent, affects the region's climate, for instance, India's location in relation to Asia.

3. An understanding of how the crops are, in part, determined by climatic conditions.

4. An understanding of how man is attempting to modify plants by plant breeding so that certain crops may be grown in regions with shorter growing seasons or with less precipitation.

5. An understanding of how and why man very early developed irrigation in certain regions in Asia and North Africa.

6. An understanding of air pressure and its relation to winds.

7. An understanding of monsoons and how monsoons affect people's ways of living in India and southeastern Asia.

8. An understanding of how distance east and west on the earth is measured by longitude.

9. An understanding of how the earth revolves in its orbit around the sun and the relation of this movement to the seasons.

WEATHER AND CLIMATE IN THE EIGHTH GRADE AND SENIOR HIGH SCHOOL

During the five years—eighth grade through senior high school—students should have the opportunity of acquiring a knowledge and an understanding of three basic world patterns. These three world patterns are: (1) the world climatic pattern; (2) the world pattern of industry and trade; and (3) the world political pattern. These three should be developed as a "world frame of reference" during the five years of high school. They are needed because today man must think in global terms. Man is living and working in a world environment, and his knowledge of the world must be organized in the form of world patterns which he can use constantly in his thinking.

World Climatic Pattern

The world climatic pattern is basic because the other world patterns are so closely related to it. For instance, the world vegetation pattern, the world soil pattern, and world distribution of population are directly or indirectly related to the distribution of world climates.

As has been said,

Three great patterns dominate the earth and are of tremendous importance to man—the pattern of climate, the pattern of vegetation, and the pattern of soils. When the three patterns are laid one upon another, their boundaries coincide to a remarkable degree because climate is the fundamental dynamic force shaping the other two. The relationships between these three patterns have been the object of considerable scientific study. . . . A fourth pattern laid upon the three is that of human culture, or civilization. Though modern man has some freedom to vary this pattern because of his control of other forces, he too cannot go beyond certain limits set fundamentally by climate.[4]

Furthermore, the world climatic pattern reveals one way in which the world functions as a physical unit. The arrangement or pattern of world climatic regions is not the result of mere chance. As the student gains a knowledge of the climatic regions of the world, he becomes aware of their orderly arrangement and acquires an initial understanding of their location and characteristics and how man has adjusted to the various climates.

The units for such a course should be:

1. Introduction: Man's Natural or Physical Environment—Climate the Most Important Element in Our Natural Environment
2. The Tropical Rain Forest
3. The Tropical Wet and Dry, or The Savanna
4. The Tropical Steppes and Deserts
5. The Mediterranean Climate
6. The Humid Subtropical Lands
7. The Marine Climatic Regions
8. The Humid Continental Lands
9. The Middle Latitude Steppes and Deserts
10. The Taiga or Northern Forest Climate
11. The Polar Region

In each unit the themes developed are: (1) the location of the specific climatic type; (2) its characteristics and, as far as possible, the reasons for the climate and its characteristics; and (3) how man has adjusted to the regional climatic conditions. In developing and giving meaning to the world climatic pattern, the distribution of people on the earth is studied, certain relationships between

[4] David I. Blumenstock and C. Warren Thornthwaite, "Climate and the World Pattern," *Climate and Man,* Yearbook of the Department of Agriculture (Washington, D.C., U.S. Government Printing Office, 1941), p. 98.

population density and the physical environment are noted, and how man has fitted his ways of living to the climate and other natural conditions in each area is explained. Maps of the distribution of land and water forms, the ocean currents, distribution of precipitation, world wind belts, and other world patterns are used. As man's ways of living and the characteristics of these climates are studied, the interrelations of the various world patterns are noted. Thus, through use, these world patterns become a part of the students' mental equipment.

Such a geography course has been given many different names in the school curriculum. Some of the titles are Global Geography, and Man and World Climates.

Economic Geography

The study of patterns of world industry and trade is given in many high schools under one of these titles: Economic Geography, Business Geography, or Commercial Geography. It is another world pattern of functional value if properly taught, with due emphasis on the natural factors involved as well as the cultural factors in world trade and industry.

In the development of units in economic geography, one of the natural factors often neglected is climate and its effect on production.

Climate limits the choice of crops and therefore the local production of food; and climate determines the site for the cultivation of those other foodstuffs and raw materials of industry which modern life demands; this climatic control of production and requirements is one of the bases of the world's trade. Climate controls the direction as well as the existence of trade routes.[5]

Everyone readily understands how the success of agriculture depends on weather and climate, because each species or variety of plants grows best within certain temperatures and precipitation limits. Humidity, sunshine, and winds also affect the success or failure of crops.

[5] A. M. Miller, *Climatology* (New York, E. P. Dutton and Co. Inc., 1953), p. 1.

Almost everyone has had some personal experiences with the effects of weather and climate on transportation. The means and the cost of transportation, whether by highway, railway, waterway, or by air, feel the effects of weather and climate.

Such reports as the following illustrate the effects of weather and climate. In 1955–56, the unusually severe winter caused widespread trouble. France lost half of its wheat crop and entire olive groves were ruined; in Great Britain industrial production was slowed down due to power shortages; and in Italy field after field of vegetables were killed resulting in high prices. In country after country, coal and fuel were scarce and transportation was so snarled on rivers, railroads, and highways that traffic was weeks in getting back to normal. You may wonder how climate affects the mining industry and manufacturing. The development of large deposits or iron and other minerals in the northern regions of Canada was delayed until man was able to overcome the hazards of the long winters and extremely low temperatures facing the workers. All equipment, housing, food, and fuel supplies had to be able to withstand the effects of temperatures far below zero and other climatic conditions. In other regions, such as the tropical deserts where vast oil deposits were found and, recently, other valuable minerals, the problems of very high temperatures, sand storms, and the other effects of an arid climate had to be solved.

As has already been mentioned, hundreds of manufacturing processes are affected directly by temperature and humidity. In recent decades, man with his intelligence, science, technology, and business organization has acquired the ability to avoid or partly overcome these effects of climate. But he has not overcome them without high cost and sacrifices. Costs, labor, and other factors enter into the final price of the product, and make such operations, especially in mining and manufacturing, hazardous and constantly in danger of failure. Oftentimes, neither the teacher nor the textbook discusses the above factors in connection with the study of mining, transportation, or manufacturing. In economic geography the pupils should be applying the knowledge and understandings which they have gained in previous courses.

Political Geography

Students need an understanding of the world political pattern today, because governments are taking such an active part in industry, trade, and transportation. The kind of government a nation has affects its economic life. In a political geography course, the geographic foundations of a nation should be studied and the effects of the natural environment—size, location, climate, mineral resources, and so forth—upon the development of the nation, as well as the people, the distribution of the people, of industry, and other cultural patterns, and finally, how the nation fits into the world political pattern.

As a result of the development of these three world patterns in the junior and senior high school, the students should have acquired an understanding of the modern world, and a realization that our orientation and outlook must be world wide, that today "our world" includes the whole earth and its peoples. They must have an awareness that the whole earth is now one, indivisible, if man and his culture are to survive.

REFERENCES

ANDERZHON, Mamie L., "Keeping a Daily Record of the Temperature," *Journal of Geography,* Vol. 44 (November, 1945), pp. 333–335.

———, "Observing the Position of the Sun through Systematic Recording of Shadows," *Journal of Geography,* Vol. 44 (December, 1945), pp. 355–357.

BRATTON, Sam T., "'Day' and 'Night' in Polar Areas," *Journal of Geography,* Vol. 38 (December, 1939), pp. 369–370.

BROWN, Andrew H., "Men Against the Hurricane," *National Geographic,* Vol. 98 (October, 1950), pp. 537–560.

Climate and Man, Yearbook of the Department of Agriculture (Washington, D.C., U.S. Government Printing Office, 1941).

FINCH, V. C., and TREWARTHA, Glen T., *Elements of Geography,* 4th ed. (New York, McGraw-Hill Co., 1957).

GLASSEY, F. P., "Finland-Helsingfors, A Contrast in Light and Shade," *National Geographic*, Vol. 47 (1925), pp. 597–612.
GREENLEAF, Peter, "Elementary Meteorology in High School," *Journal of Geography*, Vol. 44 (November, 1945), pp. 336–367.
HARRISON, Lucia C., *"Daylight, Twilight, Darkness, and Time"* (Chicago, Silver Burdette & Co., 1935).
HEINTZELMAN, Oliver H., and SMITH, R. M., *World Regional Geography* (Englewood Cliffs, N.J., Prentice-Hall, Inc., 1955).
KARNES, L. B., "Sunrise, Sunset, and Length of Day," *Journal of Geography*, Vol. 45 (January, 1946), pp. 10–13.
KEMLER, J. H., "Tracing the Footsteps of Autumn," *Journal of Geography*, Vol. 41 (September, 1942), pp. 234–237.
KENDREW, W. G., *Climates of the Continents*, 4th ed. (New York, Oxford University Press, 1953).
LONGSTRETH, T. Morris, *Knowing the Weather* (New York, The Macmillan Company, 1943).
MAYALL, R. M., "The Sun-dial, An Instrument of Education," *Journal of Geography*, Vol. 41 (May, 1942), pp. 169–178.
NEUBERGER, H. H., and STEPHENS, F. B., *Weather and Man* (Englewood Cliffs, N.J., Prentice-Hall, Inc., 1948).
PEATTIE, Roderick, *The Teaching of Geography* (New York, Appleton-Century-Crofts, Inc., 1950), Ch. 5 and 6.
PHILLIPS, Mary Viola, "Climate and Weather: For a Course in Global Geography," *Journal of Geography*, Vol. 45 (March, 1946), pp. 103–108.
RANKIN, Mary I., "A Device for Teaching the Sun, Shadows, and Seasons," *Journal of Geography*, Vol. 38 (October, 1939), pp. 276–278.
RAY, J. Bernard, "A Project Study of Climate," *Journal of Geography*, Vol. 56 (May, 1957), pp. 236–238.
SAGENDORF, R., "Odd Notes About the Weather," *The New York Times* (November 14, 1954), Section 6, p. 12.
STEVENS, G., and BELL, R., "Construction, Operation of a Low Cost, Scientifically Sound Weather Station for the Fifth and Sixth Grades," *Journal of Geography*, Vol. 52 (November, 1953), pp. 324–330.
STEWART, George, *The Storm.* (New York, Random House, Inc., 1941).
SVEC, M. Melvina, "Factors that Influence Climate Developed by Use of the Deductive Method," *Journal of Geography*, Vol. 45 (January, 1946), pp. 14–22.
TANNEHILL, Ivan R., *Weather Around the World* (Princeton, N.J., Princeton University Press, 1943).

THRALLS, Zoe A., *The World Around Us* (New York, Harcourt, Brace & Co., 1956).

———, *The World: Its Lands and Peoples* (New York, Harcourt, Brace and Co., 1948).

———, "World Patterns in High School Geography," *Journal of Geography*, Vol. 49 (January, 1950), pp. 22–25.

Weather is the Nation's Business, U.S. Document, C. 30.2 q W. 37/6.

WHITE, Langdon, and RENNER, George T., *College Geography* (New York, Appleton-Century-Crofts, Inc., 1957).

Index

Activities:
  application (functional), 254–271
  drawing, 259
  general classroom, 260–261
  listening, 257
  manual, 259–260
  observing, 256–257
  oral, 257–258
  reading, 255–256
  in weather and climate study, 311–312, 316–318, 322–323
  writing, 258–259
Adler, B., 20n
Agricultural Statistics, 131
Agriculture, value of geographic knowledge to, 7–9
Altitude, 41
American Geographical Society, 8, 187, 228
America's Strategy in World Politics (Spykman), 12n
Anderson, Marion, 214, 229n, 232n
Anderzhon, Mamie L., 27, 61n, 141
Andrews, Jane, 300
Anecdotes, use in motivating interest in reading, 199–201
Animals, observing of, 286
Antarctic Circle, 38, 39, 70
Application activities, 254–271
"Approach to Map Study, An" (Dudley), 25n
Arctic Circle, 38, 39, 70
"Armchair Exploration" (Stefansson), 222n
Art of Thinking, The (Dimnet), 164n
Asa, Jessie, 68, 69n
Assignment, reading in geography, 207–213

Association tests, 250–251
Audio-Visual Guide, 72n
Audio-Visual Materials and Methods in the Social Studies, National Council for the Social Studies, 149n
Australian Geographer, 228

Badeau, J. S., 13
Baker, Emily V., 68
Bar graph, 116–118
Baxter, Eugenia, 210
Bechdolt, Jack, 227n
Beebe, William, 230
Birds, observing of, 280–282, 285–286
Bjornson, Björnstjerne, 233
Blind, map use by the, 68
Blouch, Adelaide, 149
Blumenstock, David I., 325n
Boom Town Boy (Lenski), 232
Bowman, Isaiah, 5, 6, 20n, 22n
Brockmeyer, Irene, 94
Broken-bar graph, 116
Bulletin of American Geographic Society, 20n
Burgess, Alvin V., 65
Business, geography and, 7–9, 20–22, 112–113
Business Geography course, 326–328
Byrd, Richard E., 229

Canadian Geographical Journal, The, 228
Carpenter, Helen M., 219n

332   Index

Census Atlas Maps of Latin America, 228
Charts, map symbol, 26
"Child Looks Upon the Map, The" (Anderzhon), 27n
Christian Science Monitor, The, 186, 188
Circle graph, 119
Citizenship, geographic knowledge and, 10–12
Clayton's World Weather Records, 227
Climate, 142, 166, 324–326
   see also Weather and climate, teaching of
Climate and Man, Department of Agriculture Yearbook, 325n
"Climate and the World Pattern" (Blumenstock), 325n
Climatic Summary of the United States, 227
Climatology (Miller), 326n
College Geography (White and Renner), 152n
Colorful Geography Teaching (Walch, ed.), 177n
Commerce Weekly, The, 227
Commercial geography, 326–328
Commodity Yearbook, The, 132
Community study, 143–144, 145, 299–300
Completion tests, 245–246
Comprehension, landscape study an aid to, 142–143
Compton's Pictured Encyclopedia, 227
Cordell, Christobel M., 177
Cox, Catherine, 65
Crew, Helen, 291
Current events, 161–188
   mapping of, 67
   to motivate interest in reading, 197–198
   selection of, for study, 168
   sources of information, 186–188
   techniques of using, 169–177
   value as geographic educational tool, 162–168
   world news broadcast illustrated, 177–186

Davis, L. C., 141
Daylight, Twilight, Darkness and Time (Harrison), 48n
De Hutorowicz, H., 20n
"Diagnosing Children's Ability to Use Maps" (Baker), 68n
Dictionaries, 203, 228
Dictionary of Geography, A, 228
Dimnet, Ernest, 164
Direction, concept of, 70, 277–278, 283, 290
   teaching of, 28, 31–32, 33, 34–35, 37
Distribution maps, 40–47, 63–64, 166
Dohrs, F. E., 229n
Drawing activities, 259
Dudley, Elizabeth, 25

Earth's rotation, observing of, 300–301
East and West of Suez (Badeau), 13n
Economic geography, 326–328
Edge of the Jungle (Beebe), 230
Education, 195n, 212n
Educational Method, 141n
Eighth grade:
   weather and climate teaching in, 324–328
   see also Junior high school
Eiselen, Elizabeth, 228n
Eisen, Edna, 142, 145
Elkins, Annice, 211, 212n
Encyclopedias, 227
"Environments for Geographic Education" (Baxter and Montgomery), 210n
Equator, 37–39, 48, 70
Essays, geographic, 232
Exploration, spirit of, 141
Expression work, 254
   see also Activities

Fiction, geographic, 232
"Field Activities in the Middle Grades" (Blouch), 149n
Field trips:
   illustrative plans for, 154–158
   landscape analyzing, 151–153

Index

Field trips (*cont.*)
  organizing, 146–151
  see also Landscape study
"Field Work in Geography" (Davis), 141n
"Field Work in Junior and Senior High School" (Eisen), 142n, 145n
Fifth grade:
  field trip illustration, 155–158
  globe-use in, 71
  map-reading program, 40–51, 63–64
  weather and climate teaching in, 314–319
  see also Intermediate grades
Films:
  to motivate interest in reading, 197
  use as geography tool, 95–101
  see also Pictures
First grade:
  geographic readiness program, 277–282
  map activities, 31–32
  weather and climate teaching in, 307–308
  see also Primary grades
Focus, 228
Forbes, Rosita, 229n
Forecasting, weather, 305–307
Foreign Affairs, 14n
Foreign Agriculture, 227
Foreign Commerce Yearbook, The, 131
Foreign Crops and Markets, 227
Foster, Alice, 117
Fourth grade, 275
  field trip illustration, 154–155
  globe-use in, 69–70
  map-reading program, 35–40
  weather and climate teaching in, 309–313
  see also Intermediate grades

Geographical Dictionary, Webster's, 228
Geographical Magazine, The, 228
Geographical Review, The, 228
Geographic Approaches to Social Education, National Council for the Social Studies, *notes on* 54, 117, 144
Geographic education:
  current events as aid to, 161–188
  curricular enrichment through, 13–15
  functional activities, 254–271
  intellectual development and, 9
  reading as tool, 190–219
  travel enriched by, 15
  unit planning, 236–254
  value of, 7–15
"Geographic Field Work in Community Study for Junior High Level" (Anderzhon), 141n
Geographic News Bulletin, 228
Geographic readiness program:
  first grade, 277–282
  objectives of, 276–277, 289
  second grade, 282–289
  third grade, 289–301
  understanding of other people, 287–288
  value of, 275–276
  see also Geographic education
Geography, *passim*
  dynamic aspect, 5–6
  graphs as tool of, 112–113
  landscape as laboratory, 140
  nature of, 1–6, 76
  statistics as tool of, 112–113
  teacher of, 15–16
"Geography: A Group of People in a Place" (Smith), 195n
Geography in the Elementary School (Thralls and Reeder), 15n
Geography in Relation to the Social Sciences (Bowman), *notes on* 5, 20, 76
Geological Survey, United States, 61
Global geography, 326
Globes, 51, 58
  development of geography unit and, 63–69
  distinctive value of, 72
  graded use of, 69–73
  introduction of, 35, 37
Government, geography and, 7–9, 12, 14, 20–22, 113
Government journals, 227
Graphs, 112–139

Index

Graphs (cont.)
  assimilation stage of unit and, 127–128
  construction of, 120–121, 130–131
  illustrative lesson in, 132–138
  motivation value, 123–127
  objectives of instruction in, 113–114
  reading of, 121–123, 190–193
  testing value, 128–130
  types of, 114–120
Gray, William S., 193–194
Great Circle routes, 61, 72
Growing season maps, 44, 45
Guidance, in reading in geography, 207–213
Guide sheets, 211–212
  for field trip, 148–149

Hahn, H. H., 192
Hahn-Lackey geography scale, 192
Harrer, Henrich, 229
Harrison, Lucia C., 53n
High school:
  globe use, 71
  motivating reading in, 60–63
  weather and climate teaching in, 324–328
  see also Geographic education
"High School Class Surveys Its Town, A" (Stowell), 62n
Hile, Martha Jane, 89
History, geographic knowledge and, 13–14
Hoffman, G. W., and V., 227n
"Home Community, The" (Jensen), 144n
Home selection, value of geographic knowledge to, 9
Horn, Ernest, 114, 194n
"How of Map Use, The" (Miller), 72n
"How to Use the Textbook" (Upton), 199n
Hubbard, Henry D., 112

Idea Line, 213
Imagery tests, 251–253
In the South Seas (Stevenson), 229

Index, teaching use of, 214–216
India, Mukerji's stories of, 232
Industrial Reference Service, The, 228
Industry, geography and, 7–9, 20–22
Intermediate grades:
  map-reading program, 35–55
  weather and climate teaching in, 309–324
  see also Fourth, Fifth, Sixth, and Seventh grades
"Interpreting Maps and Globes" (Kohn and others), 30n, 49n
Iso, meaning of term, 58

James, Linnie B., 123n
Jefferson, Thomas, 188
Jensen, J. Granville, 144, 145, 146n
Jessop, Grace, 68
Journal of Geography, The, 228, 261; notes on 25, 27, 49, 62, 65, 68, 69, 77, 89, 90, 95, 123, 141, 142, 145, 149, 167, 192, 199, 204, 208, 210
Junior Britannica, The, 227
Junior high school:
  globe-use in, 71
  map-reading program, 55–60
  see also Seventh and Eighth grades
Junior and Senior Scholastic, 186

Key:
  as legend, 34, 121, 190
  use in index, 214, 215
Knowing the Weather (Longstreth), 307n
Kohn, Clyde F. (and others), 30n

"Ladder of Organization Skills" (Snedaker), 216
Landscape:
  cultural, 151–152
  as geography laboratory, 140
  importance of skill in reading, 190–193
  values of study of, 140–146
  see also Field trips
Latitude, 48, 53–54, 315

Index

Lawrence, T. E., 230, 231
Learning activities, 254–271
"Learning to Read in the Social Studies" (Anderson), 214n
Legend, 34
Lenski, Lois, 232
Lesseps, de, Ferdinand, 14
Lindbergh, Anne, 229
Line graph, 118–119
Listening activities, 257
Little America (Byrd), 229
Location, meaning of, 5
Locational geography, 49–50
Logan, Mary, 192n, 194
Longitude, 53, 323
Longstreth, T. Morris, 307n
Loya, Julia M., 95
Lyman, R. L., 191

McGirr, Mabel, 96n, 98
McKee, Paul, 207
Magazines, geographic, 228
"Making a Pace Map" (Bacon), 49n
Malayan Journal of Tropical Geography, 228
Man and World Climates course, 326
Manual activities, 259–260
"Map for Diagnostic Purposes, A" (Jessop), 68n
Map-making:
 in high school, 61–62
 introductory, 33–35, 50, 298
Map-readiness activities, 31–35
 see also Geographic-readiness program
Map-reading, 22–23
 basic principles, 25–28
 current events as aid to, 166
 in high school, 60–63
 importance of, 72–73
 intermediate-grade program, 35–55
 interpretive ideas, 29–30
 junior high school program, 55–60
 landscape study as aid to, 145
 objectives of, 23–25
 in primary grades, 31–35
 skill in, 30, 68, 190–193
 for slow learners, 68–69
 symbols used, 28–30
 tests in, 68
Maps, 19–73
 for the blind, 68
 distortion in, 59–62
 functions of, 22–23
 kinds of, 51, 55, 60–61
 large-scale, 52–53
 making of, *see* Map-making
 meaning of term, 19
 primitive, 20
 range of uses, 20–22
 reading of, *see* Map-reading
 seasonal, 315
 in textbooks, 225–226
 use in developing geographic units, 63–69
"Maps" (Whittemore), 54n
"Maps the Blind Can See" (Sherman), 68n
Maps of Primitive Peoples (Adler), 20n
"Maps and Slow Learners" (Asa), 69n
"Maps and Their Role in World Development," *United Nations Review*, 21n
Map tests, 253–254
Marcus Aurelius, 165
Matching tests, 246–249
"Meaning and Measurement of Longitude, The" (Harrison), 53n
Meridians, 53, 323
Methods of Instruction in the Social Sciences (Horn), 114n
Middlebrook, Pearl, 9
Miller, A. M., 326n
Miller, William S., 72
Mind at Work, The (Lyman), 191n
Minneapolis Star, The, 186
Montgomery, Katherine, 210
Monthly Weather Review, 227
Moore, W. G., 228n
Mukerji, Dhan Gopal, 232
Multiple choice tests, 246
"Mystery Country, The" (James), 123n

National Geographic Magazine, The, 228

National Geographic Society, 187
Newhouse, Lucille A., 95
New Kensington (Pa.) High School, 176
Newsweek, 186
New Zealand Geographer, The 228
North to the Orient (Anne Lindbergh), 229
Nystrom, A. J., and Co., 26n

Observing activities, 256–257
One-word answer tests, 246
Oral activities, 257–258
Orbis, 132
Organization skills, usefulness in reading, 216–218
Outline maps, 54
Outside Readings in Geography, 229

Parallels of latitude, 48, 53–54
Parker, Edith, 191, 248, 252
Peattie, Donald C., 19
Peattie, Roderick, 320
Petterson, D. R., 229n
Phillips, Mary V., 176
Physical-political maps, 40, 41, 43–45, 63, 166
Pictography, 114–115
"Picture Library and Its Use, A" (Riley), 90n
Pictures, 41, 76–111, 190–193
  criteria for selection and evaluation of, 79–84
  films and slides, 95–101
  as geography tools, 76–77
  illustrative units, 90–92, 101–108
  to motivate interest in reading, 197
  techniques in use of, 83–84, 85–88
  test use, 93–95, 99–100, 108
  textbook, 225–226
  in unit study, 84–93
Picture Study lessons, example of, 98–101
"Place of Geography in American Culture, The" (Middlebrook), 9n
Plain Dealer, Cleveland, 186
Plants, observing of, 280–282, 286
Poetry, geographic, 232–233

Polar projection map, 60–61
Poles, 37, 70
Political geography, 328
Population maps, 41–43
Precipitation map, 47
Primary grades:
  geographic readiness program, 301–303
  globe-use in, 69–70
  map-reading in, 31–35
  weather and climate teaching in, 307–309
  see also First, Second, *and* Third grades
Prime meridian, 53
Problem tests, 249–250
"Problems of Reading Geography, The" (Elkins), 212n
Progress reports, 210–211
Propaganda, map-use in, 62

Questions, use in motivating interest in reading, 198–199

Radio, 177, 187
Rand McNally Co., 26n
Readers, geography, 226–227
Reader's Digest, 19n, 222n
Readiness, geographic, program for, *see* Geographic readiness program
Reading, 167, 190–195
  activities in, 255–256
  basic skills, 195–196, 213–219
  guidance by teacher, 207–213
  motivating interest in, 197–202
  organization skills, 216–218
  rate of, 218–219
  recreatory, 233–234
  as tool, 190–219
  value of varied, 222–223
  vocabulary building, 202–207
"Reading as an Aid in Learning" (Gray), 194n
Reading in the Elementary School, National Society for the Study of Education, 194n, 207n

Index

"Reading and Literature in the Area of Social Living" (Anderson), 232n
Reading materials, 222–234, 238
　geography readers, 226–227
　imaginative, 232–233
　for reference, 227–229
　scientific reports, 229–231
　textbooks, 223–226
　travel books, 229–231
Reading Teacher, The, 203n
"Reading in the Various Fields of the Curriculum" (Snedaker and Horn), 194n
Reeder, Edwin, 15n
Reference reading materials, 227–229
Reichilderfer, F. W., 305n
"Relation of Reading to Development in Language Arts, The" (Strickland), 203n
Renau, Ernst, 14
Riley, Norma, 90
Rocks, observing of, 297–299
"Romance of Maps, The" (D. C. Peattie), 19n
Rotation, 70, 300–301

Scale, 34, 39, 48–49
Scarfe, Neville V., 77
Schauer, Virginia, 204, 208n, 213
Seasonal changes, 279–282, 285, 292–293
Seasons, 48
Second grade:
　geographic readiness program, 282–289
　map-readiness program, 32–33
　weather and climate teaching in, 308
Seven Little Sisters (Andrews), 300
Seven Years in Tibet (Harrer), 229
Seventh grade:
　weather and climate teaching in, 319–324
　see also Junior high school
Shadows, 32, 70
Sherman, John C., 68
Siegfried, André, 14n
Sixth Annual Conference on Reading (Pittsburgh), 214n, 232n

Sixth grade, 198
　globe-use in, 71
　map-reading program, 51–55
　map use, 64
　weather and climate teaching in, 319–324
　see also Intermediate grades
Sketch maps, 54, 62, 66–67
Skills in the Social Studies, National Council for the Social Studies, 30n
Slides, as geographic tools, 95–101
Smith, J. Russell, 195
Snedaker, Mabel, 194n, 216
Social attitudes, 167
Social Education, 261
Soils, observing of, 297–299
Sommers, L. M., 229n
Splendor of the Earth: etc. (Anderson), 229
Spykman, Nicholas, 12
Star and Times, Kansas City, 186
Statesman's Yearbook, The, 131
Statistical Abstract, United States, 127, 131
Statistics, 112–139
　in assimilation stage of unit, 127–128
　as geographic tool, 132
　illustrative lesson in use of, 132–138
　importance of skill in reading, 190–193
　learning to read tables of, 121–123
　motivation value, 123–127
　objectives of instruction in, 113–114
　sources of, 131–132
　testing value, 128–130
Steel industry, value of geographic knowledge to, 7
Stefansson, Vilhjalmur, 222
Steps in Map Reading (Anderzhon), 61n
Stevenson, R. L., 229, 291, 300
Stewart, George R., 232
Storm (Stewart), 232
Stowell, Margaret, 62n
Stream, study of, 295–297
Strickland, Ruth, 203

"Suez, The: International Roadway" (Siegfried), 14n
Sun position, 279–281, 283–284, 290–291
Symbols:
  graph, 114, 121
  index, 214
  map, 25–30, 36
  weather, 278
Tariff, geographic knowledge and, 8
Teachers, 15–16
"Teaching Africa by Regional Map Making" (Cox), 65n
"Teaching Children to Read the Textbook" (Schauer), 204n, 208n
"Teaching of Geography, The" (Parker), 191n
Teaching of Geography, The, (Peattie), 320n
Teaching of Reading: A Second Report, The, National Society for the Study of Education, 191n, 194n
Teaching Social Studies in the Elementary School (Wesley), 237n
"Techniques of the Reading Tool, etc." (Logan), 192n
Television, 177, 187
"Ten Commandments, etc." (McGirr), 96–98
"Testing Geographical Interest by a Visual Method" (Scarfe), 77n
Tests, 245–254
Textbooks, 39, 223–226, 316
"Theme of Modern Geography, The" (Thralls), 4n
Third grade:
  geographic readiness program, 289–301
  map-readiness program, 33–35
  weather and climate teaching in, 308–309
  see also Primary grades
Thornthwaite, C. Warren, 325n
Thralls, Zoe A., 15n
Time, telling of, 291
Time magazine, 186
Times, New York, 186
Topographic map, 60–61
Topography, 166

Travel books, 229–231
Travel experience, geographic enrichment of, 15
Trees, observing of, 280–282, 286
Trend graph, 118–119
Tropics, 37–38, 39, 70

Ungashick, Jane, 167n
United Nations Review, 21n
Unit planning, 236–254
  application exercises, 244
  current events use in, 169–186
  format, 239
  goals, 239–241
  graph and statistics use in, 123–138
  illustration of, 262–271
  map and globe use in, 63–69
  picture use in, 84–109
  steps in, 241–245
  teacher's preparation, 238–239
  testing, 244–254
Upton, Loula, 199
"Use of Current Events in Geography Teaching" (Ungashick), 167n
"Use of Maps in Developing Geographic Personalities, The" (Burgess), 65n
"Use of Photographic Material in the Teaching of Geography, The" (Hile), 89n
"Use of Statistics in Geographic Education" (Foster), 117n
"Use of Visual Aids in the Classroom, The" (Loya and Newhouse), 95n

Visualization, 141–142
Vocabulary building, 202–207

Walch, J. Weston, 177n
Water, observing of, 286–287, 294–297
"Weather Bureau, The" (Reichilderfer), 305n
Weather and climate, teaching of, 305–328
  in eighth grade through senior high school, 324–328

Index

Weather and climate (*cont.*)
  forecasting and, 305–307
  in intermediate grades, 309–324
  in primary grades, 307–309
Weather and Man (Newberger and Stephens), 58n
Weather maps, 56–58, 59
Weather observation, 278–279, 284, 292–293
Weather reports, 305–307
Weather rose form, 291
Webster's Geographical Dictionary, 228
Wesley, Edgar B., 237

White, C. Langdon, 228n
Whittemore, Katheryne T., 54
"Why Failures in the Study of Geography" (Hahn), 192n
Wind, observing of, 284–285, 293–294
Work sheets, 211–212
World Almanac, 131
World Book, The, 227
"World News Round-up" (Cordell), 177n
World pattern maps, 55, 58
Writing activities, 258–259